CHRIST AND CULTURE

Christ and Culture

H. Richard Niebuhr

HARPER TORCHBOOKS
Harper & Row, Publishers
New York, Cambridge, Philadelphia, San Francisco
London, Mexico City, São Paulo, Sydney

To Reinie

ISBN: 0-06-130003-9

First Harper paperback edition published 1975.

89 90   40 39

CONTENTS

6. Christ the Transformer of Culture

7. A "Concluding Unscientific Postscript"

Index

FOREWORD

The present volume makes available in print and in expanded form the series of lectures which Professor H. Richard Niebuhr gave at Austin Presbyterian Theological Seminary in January, 1949, on the Alumni Foundation. This lectureship was inaugurated in 1945. Since that time the Seminary has had the privilege of presenting to its students and alumni at the time of the midwinter convocations the reflections of leading Christian thinkers on important issues and, in part, of stimulating the publication of these reflections for the benefit of a wider audience.

The men and their subjects have been:

1945—Ernest Trice Thompson, *Christian Bases of World Order*
1946—Josef Lukl Hromadka, *The Church at the Crossroads*
1947—Paul Scherer, *The Plight of Freedom*
1948—D. Elton Trueblood, *Alternative to Futility*
1949—H. Richard Niebuhr, *Christ and Culture*
1950—Paul Minear, *The Kingdom and the Power*
1951—G. Ernest Wright, *God Who Acts*

Dr. Niebuhr makes a distinguished contribution in this clear and incisive study in Christian Ethics.

DAVID L. STITT,
President.

Austin Presbyterian Theological Seminary,
Austin, Texas

ACKNOWLEDGMENTS

The following essay on the double wrestle of the church with its Lord and with the cultural society with which it lives in symbiosis represents part of the result of many years of study, reflection and teaching. The immediate occasion for the organization and written composition of the material was offered by the invitation of Austin Presbyterian Theological Seminary to deliver and to publish a series of lectures on the subject. Back of the efforts to condense my observations and reflections into five lectures and then again to refine and elaborate them in the revision lie many other attempts at comprehension and organization of the complex data. Directly antecedent to the Austin lectures were courses in the history and the types of Christian ethics which I offered to students of the Divinity School of Yale University.

When a work has been so long in preparation the debts accumulated by the author are so many and so great that public acknowledgment is embarrassing since it must reveal his lack of adequate gratitude as well as of adequate ability to appropriate the gifts that have been offered him. There are reflections in this book which I regard as the fruits of my own effort to understand but which, nevertheless, are in reality ideas which I have appropriated from others. Some of my former students, should they read these pages, will be able to say at this or that point, "This is a fact or an interpretation to which I called my teacher's attention," but they will look in vain for the footnote in which due credit is given. Fellow students who have written on related subjects will be in the same situation. Yet there is more pleasure than embarrassment in acknowledging this unspecified indebtedness to members of that wide community in which all know that none possesses anything that he has not received and that as we have freely received so we may freely give.

I am most conscious of my debt to that theologian and historian who was occupied throughout his life by the problem of church and culture—Ernst Troeltsch. The present book in one sense undertakes to do no more than to supplement and in part to correct his work on *The Social Teachings of the Christian Churches.* Troeltsch has taught me to respect the multiformity and individuality of men and movements in Christian history, to be loath to force this rich variety into prefashioned, conceptual molds, and yet to seek *logos* in *mythos,* reason in history, essence in existence. He has helped me to accept and to profit by the acceptance of the relativity not only of historical objects but, more, of the historical subject, the observer and interpreter. If I think of my essay as an effort to correct Troeltsch's analyses of the encounters of church and world it is mostly because I try to understand this historical relativism in the light of theological and theo-centric relativism. I believe that it is an aberration of faith as well as of reason to absolutize the finite but that all this relative history of finite men and movements is under the governance of the absolute God. Isaiah 10, I Corinthians 12 and Augustine's *City of God* indicate the context in which the relativities of history make sense. In the analysis of the five main types which I have substituted for Troeltsch's three, I have received the greatest help from Professor Etienne Gilson's *Reason and Revelation in the Middle Ages,* as well as fruitful suggestions from C. J. Jung's *Psychological Types.*

Many colleagues, relatives, and friends have helped me with counsel, criticism, and encouragement in the course of the effort to give my reflections the unity and precision which written communication demands in the measure that the complexity of the data and the ability of the worker permit. I record my special thanks to my colleagues, Professors Paul Schubert and Raymond Morris, to my sister and brother, Professors Hulda and Reinhold Niebuhr, to Mr. Dudley Zuver of Harper & Brothers, at whose suggestion the last chapter was added, to my daughter and to Mrs. Dorothy Ansley who assisted with the typescript, to Professor Edwin Penick, who gave most careful attention to proof sheets and supplied the index, and to my wife. I recollect with gratitude the kindly reception given me at Austin by President Stitt and his colleagues and the part they played in helping me to bring this work to its present, tentative conclusion.

New Haven, Connecticut   H. RICHARD NIEBUHR

CHAPTER 1

The Enduring Problem

I. THE PROBLEM

A many-sided debate about the relations of Christianity and civilization is being carried on in our time. Historians and theologians, statesmen and churchmen, Catholics and Protestants, Christians and anti-Christians participate in it. It is carried on publicly by opposing parties and privately in the conflicts of conscience. Sometimes it is concentrated on special issues, such as those of the place of Christian faith in general education or of Christian ethics in economic life. Sometimes it deals with broad questions of the church's responsibility for social order or of the need for a new separation of Christ's followers from the world.

The debate is as confused as it is many-sided. When it seems that the issue has been clearly defined as lying between the exponents of a Christian civilization and the non-Christian defenders of a wholly secularized society, new perplexities arise as devoted believers seem to make common cause with secularists, calling, for instance, for the elimination of religion from public education, or for the Christian support of apparently anti-Christian political movements. So many voices are heard, so many confident but diverse assertions about the Christian answer to the social problem are being made, so many issues are raised, that bewilderment and uncertainty beset many Christians.

In this situation it is helpful to remember that the question of Christianity and civilization is by no means a new one; that Christian perplexity in this area has been perennial, and that the problem has been an enduring one through all the Christian centuries. It is helpful also to recall that the repeated struggles of Christians with this problem have yielded no single Christian answer, but only a series of typical answers which together, for faith, represent phases of the strategy of the militant church in the world. That strategy, however, being in the mind of the Captain rather than of any lieutenants, is not under the control of the latter. Christ's answer to the problem of human culture is one thing, Christian answers are another; yet his followers are assured that he uses their various works in accomplishing his own. It is the purpose of the following chapters to set forth typical Christian answers to the problem of Christ and culture and so to contribute to the mutual understanding of variant and often conflicting Christian groups. The belief which lies back of this effort, however, is the conviction that Christ as living Lord is answering the question in the totality of history and life in a fashion which transcends the wisdom of all his interpreters yet employs their partial insights and their necessary conflicts.

The enduring problem evidently arose in the days of Jesus Christ's humanity when he who "was a Jew and . . . remained a Jew till his last breath"[1] confronted Jewish culture with a hard challenge. Rabbi Klausner has described in modern terms how the problem of Jesus and culture must have appeared to the Pharisees and Sadducees, and has defended their repudiation of the Nazarene on the ground that he imperiled Jewish civiliza-

---

[1] Klausner, Joseph, *Jesus of Nazareth*, p. 368.

tion. Though Jesus was a product of that culture, so that there is not a word of ethical or religious counsel in the gospels which cannot be paralleled in Jewish writings, says Klausner, yet he endangered it by abstracting religion and ethics from the rest of social life, and by looking for the establishment by divine power only of a "kingdom not of this world." "Judaism, however, is not only religion and it is not only ethics: it is the sumtotal of all the needs of the nation, placed on a religious basis. . . . Judaism is a national life, a life which the national religion and human ethical principles embrace without engulfing. Jesus came and thrust aside all the requirements of the national life. . . . In their stead he set up nothing but an ethico-religious system bound up with his conception of the Godhead."[2] Had he undertaken to reform the religious and national culture, eliminating what was archaic in ceremonial and civil law, he might have been a great boon to his society; but instead of reforming culture he ignored it. "He did not come to enlarge his nation's knowledge, art and culture, but to abolish even such culture as it possessed, bound up with religion." For civil justice he substituted the command to nonresistance, which must result in the loss of all social order; the social regulation and protection of family life he replaced with the prohibition of all divorce, and with praise of those who "made themselves eunuchs for the kingdom of heaven's sake"; instead of manifesting interest in labor, in economic and political achievement, he recommended the unanxious, toilless life exemplified by birds and lilies; he ignored even the requirements of ordinary distributive justice when he said, "Man, who has made me a judge or divider over you?" Hence, Klausner concludes, "Jesus ignored everything concerned with material civilization: in this sense he does not belong to civilization."[3] Therefore his people rejected him; and

[2] *Ibid.*, p. 390.
[3] *Ibid.*, pp. 373-375.

"two thousand years of non-Jewish Christianity have proved
that the Jewish people did not err."[4]

Not all the Jews of his day rejected Jesus in the name of their
culture, and two thousand years of non-Jewish Christianity and
non-Christian Judaism may be appealed to in validation of
many other propositions than that Jesus imperils culture; but
it is evident that those two millennia have been full of wres-
tlings with just this problem. Not only Jews but also Greeks and
Romans, medievalists and moderns, Westerners and Orientals
have rejected Christ because they saw in him a threat to their
culture.

The story of Graeco-Roman civilization's attack on the gospel
forms one of the dramatic chapters in every history of Western
culture and of the church, though it is told too often in terms
of political persecution only. Popular animosity based on social
piety, literary polemics, philosophical objection, priestly resistance, and doubtless economic defensiveness all played a
part in the rejection of Christ, for the problem he raised was
broadly cultural and not merely political. Indeed, the state was
slower to take up arms against him and his disciples than were
other institutions and groups.[5] In modern times open conflict
has again arisen, not only as spokesmen of nationalistic and
communistic societies but also as ardent champions of humanistic and democratic civilizations have discerned in Christ a
foe of cultural interests.

The historical and social situations in which such rejections

[4] *Ibid.*, p. 391.

[5] "Christianity's battle with the inner faith of the pagan masses, with the
convictions of the leading spirits, was incomparably more difficult than was its
wrestle with the power of the Roman state; the victory of the new faith was in
consequence a far greater achievement than earlier times with their depreciation
of paganism have assumed." Geffcken, Johannes, *Der Ausgang des Griechisch-
Roemischen Heidentums*, 1920, p. 1. For other accounts of the conflict see *Cambridge Ancient History*, Vol. XII, 1939, and Cochrane, C. N., *Christianity and
Classical Culture*, 1940.

of Jesus Christ have taken place have been extremely various;
the personal and group motivations of opponents have been of
many sorts; the philosophical and scientific beliefs which have
been arrayed against Christian convictions have often been more
sharply opposed to each other than to the convictions themselves. Yet in so far as the relation of Jesus Christ to culture is
concerned considerable unanimity may be found among these
disparate critics. Ancient spiritualists and modern materialists,
pious Romans who charge Christianity with atheism, and nineteenth century atheists who condemn its theistic faith, national-
ists and humanists, all seem to be offended by the same elements
in the gospel and employ similar arguments in defending their
culture against it.

Prominent among these recurrent arguments is the contention that, as Gibbon states the Roman case, Christians are
"animated by a contempt for present existence and by confidence in immortality."[6] This two-edged faith has baffled and
angered glorifiers of modern civilization as well as defenders of
Rome, radical revolutionaries as well as conservers of the old
order, believers in continuing progress and desponding antici-
pators of the decline of culture. It is not an attitude which can
be ascribed to defective discipleship while the Master is excul-
pated, since his statements about anxiety for food and drink,
about the unimportance of treasures on earth, and about fear
of those who can take away life as well as his rejection in life
and death of temporal power, make him the evident source of
his followers' convictions. Neither is it an attitude that can be
dismissed as characteristic of some Christians only, such as those
who believe in an early end of the world, or ultraspiritualists.
It is connected with various views of history and with various

6 *The Decline and Fall of the Roman Empire*, Modern Library ed., Vol. I,
p. 402.

ideas about the relations of spirit and matter. It is a baffling attitude, because it mates what seems like contempt for present existence with great concern for existing men, because it is not frightened by the prospect of doom on all man's works, because it is not despairing but confident. Christianity seems to threaten culture at this point not because it prophesies that of all human achievements not one stone will be left on another but because Christ enables men to regard this disaster with a certain equanimity, directs their hopes toward another world, and so seems to deprive them of motivation to engage in the ceaseless labor of conserving a massive but insecure social heritage. Therefore a Celsus moves from attack on Christianity to an appeal to believers to stop endangering a threatened empire by their withdrawal from the public tasks of defense and reconstruction. The same Christian attitude, however, arouses Marx and Lenin to hostility because believers do not care enough about temporal existence to engage in all-out struggle for the destruction of an old order and the building of a new one. They can account for it only by supposing that Christian faith is a religious opiate used by the fortunate to stupefy the people, who should be well aware that there is no life beyond culture.

Another common argument raised against Christ by his cultural antagonists of various times and persuasions is that he induces men to rely on the grace of God instead of summoning them to human achievement. What would have happened to the Romans, asks Celsus in effect, if they had followed the command to trust in God alone? Would they not have been left like the Jews, without a patch of ground to call their own, and would they not have been hunted down as criminals, like the Christians?[7] Modern philosophers of culture, such as Nikolai

[7] Origen, *Contra Celsus*, VIII, lxix (*Ante-Nicene Fathers*, Vol. IV, p. 666).

Hartmann, find in this God-reliance of faith an ultimate antinomy to the ethics of culture with its necessary concentration on human effort.[8] Marxists, believing that men make history, regard trust in the grace of God a sleeping pill as potent as the hope of heaven. Democratic and humanistic reformers of society accuse Christians of "quietism," while popular wisdom expresses its tolerant unbelief in grace by saying that God helps those who help themselves and that one must trust in Him but keep one's powder dry.

A third count in the recurring cultural indictments of Christ and his church is that they are intolerant, though this charge is not as general as are the former accusations. It does not occur in the Communists' complaint, for it is not the objection which one intolerant belief raises against another but rather the disapproval with which unbelief meets conviction. Ancient Roman civilization, says Gibbon, was bound to reject Christianity just because Rome was tolerant. This culture, with its great diversity of customs and religions, could exist only if reverence and assent were granted to the many confused traditions and ceremonies of its constituent nations. Hence it was to be "expected that they would unite with indignation against any sect of people which should separate itself from the communion of mankind and claiming the exclusive possession of divine knowledge, should disdain every form of worship except its own as impious and idolatrous."[9] Toward Jews, who held the same convictions as Christians about the gods and idols, Romans could be somewhat tolerant, because they were a separate nation with ancient traditions, and because they were content for the most part to live withdrawn from the social life. Christians, however, were members of Roman society, and in the midst of that society

[8] Hartmann, Nikolai, *Ethics*, 1932, Vol. III, pp. 266 ff.
[9] *Op. cit.*, Vol. I, p. 446.

explicitly and implicitly expressed their scorn for the religions of the people. Hence they appeared to be traitors who dissolved the sacred ties of custom and education, violated the religious institutions of their country, and presumptuously despised what their fathers had believed true and reverenced as sacred.[10] We need to add that Roman tolerance, like modern democratic tolerance, had its limits just because it was carried out as a social policy for the sake of maintaining unity. Whatever religion man followed, homage to Caesar was eventually required.[11] But Christ and Christians threatened the unity of the culture at both points with their radical monotheism, a faith in the one God that was very different from the pagan universalism which sought to unify many deities and many cults under one earthly or heavenly monarch. The political problem such monotheism presents to the exponents of a national or imperial culture has been largely obscured in modern times, but became quite evident in the anti-Christian and especially anti-Jewish attacks of German national socialism.[12] Divinity, it seems, must not only hedge kings but also other symbols of political power, and monotheism deprives them of their sacred aura. The Christ who will not worship Satan to gain the world's kingdoms is followed by Christians who will worship only Christ in unity with the Lord whom he serves. And this is intolerable to all defenders of society who are content that many gods should be worshipped if only Democracy or America or Germany or the Empire receives its due, religious homage. The antagonism of modern, tolerant culture to Christ is of course often disguised because it does not call its religious practices

[10] *Ibid.*, p. 448.

[11] *Cambridge Ancient History*, Vol. XII, pp. 409 ff.; 356 ff.; Cochrane, C. N., *op. cit.*, pp. 115 ff.

[12] Cf. Barth, Karl, *The Church and the Political Problem of Our Day*, 1939; Hayes, Carlton J. H., *Essays in Nationalism*, 1933.

religious, reserving that term for certain specified rites connected with officially recognized sacred institutions; and also because it regards what it calls religion as one of many interests which can be placed alongside economics, art, science, politics, and techniques. Hence the objection it voices to Christian monotheism appears in such injunctions only as that religion should be kept out of politics and business, or that Christian faith must learn to get along with other religions. What is often meant is that not only the claims of religious groups but all consideration of the claims of Christ and God should be banished from the spheres where other gods, called values, reign. The implied charge against Christian faith is like the ancient one: it imperils society by its attack on its religious life; it deprives social institutions of their cultic, sacred character; by its refusal to condone the pious superstitions of tolerant polytheism it threatens social unity. The charge lies not only against Christian organizations which use coercive means against what they define as false religions, but against the faith itself.

Other points are frequently made in the attacks on Christ and Christianity by those who see in them the foes of culture. The forgiveness that Christ practices and teaches is said to be irreconcilable with the demands of justice or the free man's sense of moral responsibility. The injunctions of the Sermon on the Mount concerning anger and resistance to evil, oaths and marriage, anxiety and property, are found incompatible with the duties of life in society. Christian exaltation of the lowly offends aristocrats and Nietzscheans in one way, champions of the proletariat in another. The unavailability of Christ's wisdom to the wise and prudent, its attainability by the simple and by babes, bewilder the philosophical leaders of culture or excite their scorn.

Though these attacks on Christ and Christian faith underscore and bring into the open—often in bizarre forms—the nature of the issue, it is not defense against them that constitutes the Christian problem. Not only pagans who have rejected Christ but believers who have accepted him find it difficult to combine his claims upon them with those of their societies. Struggle and appeasement, victory and reconciliation appear not only in the open where parties calling themselves Christian and anti-Christian meet; more frequently the debate about Christ and culture is carried on among Christians and in the hidden depths of the individual conscience, not as the struggle and accommodation of belief with unbelief, but as the wrestling and the reconciliation of faith with faith. The Christ and culture issue was present in Paul's struggle with the Judaizers and the Hellenizers of the gospel, but also in his effort to translate it into the forms of Greek language and thought. It appears in the early struggles of the church with the empire, with the religions and philosophies of the Mediterranean world, in its rejections and acceptances of prevailing mores, moral principles, metaphysical ideas, and forms of social organization. The Constantinian settlement, the formulation of the great creeds, the rise of the papacy, the monastic movement, Augustinian Platonism, and Thomistic Aristotelianism, the Reformation and the Renaissance, the Revival and the Enlightenment, liberalism and the Social Gospel—these represent a few of the many chapters in the history of the enduring problem. It appears in many forms as well as in all ages; as the problem of reason and revelation, of religion and science, of natural and divine law, of state and church, of nonresistance and coercion. It has come to view in such specific studies as those of the relations of Protestantism and capitalism, of Pietism and nationalism, of Puritanism and democracy, of Catholicism and Romanism or Anglicanism, of Christianity and progress.

It is not essentially the problem of Christianity and civilization; for Christianity, whether defined as church, creed, ethics, or movement of thought, itself moves between the poles of Christ and culture. The relation of these two authorities constitutes its problem. When Christianity deals with the question of reason and revelation, what is ultimately in question is the relation of the revelation in Christ to the reason which prevails in culture. When it makes the effort to distinguish, contrast, or combine rational ethics with its knowledge of the will of God, it deals with the understanding of right and wrong developed in the culture and with good and evil as illuminated by Christ.

When the problem of loyalty to church or state is raised, Christ and cultural society stand in the background as the true objects of devotion. Hence, before we undertake to outline and to illustrate the main ways in which Christians have dealt with their enduring problem, it is desirable that we seek to state what we mean by these two terms—Christ and culture. In doing this we shall need to exercise care lest we prejudge the issue by so defining one term or the other or both that only one of the Christian answers to be described will appear legitimate.

II. Toward a Definition of Christ

A Christian is ordinarily defined as "one who believes in Jesus Christ" or as "a follower of Jesus Christ." He might more adequately be described as one who counts himself as belonging to that community of men for whom Jesus Christ—his life, words, deeds, and destiny—is of supreme importance as the key to the understanding of themselves and their world, the main source of the knowledge of God and man, good and evil, the constant companion of the conscience, and the expected deliverer from evil. So great, however, is the variety of personal and communal "belief in Jesus Christ," so manifold the interpretation of his essential nature, that the question must arise whether the Christ of Christianity is indeed one Lord. For some Christians and parts of the Christian community Jesus Christ is a great teacher and lawgiver who in what he said of God and the moral law so persuades the mind and will that there is henceforth no escape from him. Christianity is for them a new law and a new religion proclaimed by Jesus. In part it seems to be the cause which they have chosen; in part it is a cause which has chosen them, by wresting consent from their minds. For others Jesus Christ is not so much a teacher and re-vealer of truths and laws as in himself, in incarnation, death, resurrection, and living presence the revelation of God. Jesus Christ, by being what he was, by suffering what he did, by being defeated in crucifixion, and by returning victoriously from death, makes evident the being and nature of God, exercises the claim of God on human faith, and thus raises to a new life the men he encounters. For still others Christianity is primarily neither new teaching nor new life but a new community, the Holy Catholic Church; hence the work of Christ which occupies the center of their attention is his founding of this new society which mediates his grace through word and sacrament.

There are many other views of what it means to "believe in Jesus Christ." Yet this variety in Christianity cannot obscure the fundamental unity which is supplied by the fact that the Jesus Christ to whom men are related in such different ways is a definite character and person whose teachings, actions, and sufferings are of one piece. The fact remains that the Christ who exercises authority over Christians or whom Christians accept as authority is the Jesus Christ of the New Testament; and that this is a person with definite teachings, a definite char-acter, and a definite fate. Important as are the once debated question whether Jesus ever "really" lived, and the still moot problem of the trustworthiness of New Testament records as factual descriptions of actual events, these are not the questions of primary significance. For the Jesus Christ of the New Testament is in our actual history, in history as we remember and live it, as it shapes our present faith and action. And this Jesus Christ is a definite person, one and the same whether he appears as man of flesh and blood or as risen Lord. He can never be confused with a Socrates, a Plato or an Aristotle, a Gautama, a Confucius, or a Mohammed, or even with an Amos or Isaiah. Interpreted by a monk, he may take on monastic characteristics; delineated by a socialist, he may show the features of a radical reformer; portrayed by a Hoffman, he may appear as a mild gentleman. But there always remain the original portraits with which all later pictures may be compared and by which all caricatures may be corrected. And in these original portraits he is recognizably one and the same. Whatever roles he plays in the varieties of Christian experience, it is the same Christ who exercises these various offices. The founder of the church is the same Christ who gives the new law; the teacher of truths about God is the same Christ who is in himself the revelation of the truth. The sacramentalist cannot escape the fact that the one who gives his body and blood is also the giver of the new commandments; the sectarian cannot avoid meeting in the ethical authority the forgiver of sins. Those who no longer know a "Christ after the flesh" still know the risen Lord as the same one whose deeds were described by those who "from the beginning were eye-witnesses and ministers of the word." However great the variations among Christians in experiencing and describing the authority Jesus Christ has over them, they have this in common: that Jesus Christ is their authority, and that the one who exercises these various kinds of authority is the same Christ.

As soon, of course, as we undertake to define the essence of the Jesus Christ who is one and the same, or to say what it is that gives him his various kinds of authority, we enter into the continuous debate of the Christian community. We encounter two difficulties in particular. The first is the impossibility of stating adequately by means of concepts and propositions a principle which presents itself in the form of a person. The second is the impossibility of saying anything about this person which is not also relative to the particular standpoint in church, history, and culture of the one who undertakes to describe him. Hence one is tempted to speak redundantly, saying simply, "Jesus Christ is Jesus Christ," or to accept the method of Biblical positivism, pointing to the New Testament and foregoing all interpretation.

It is, however, as unnecessary as it is undesirable to confine ourselves to such assertions and gestures. If we cannot say anything adequately, we can say some things inadequately. If we cannot point to the heart and essence of this Christ, we can at least point to some of the phenomena in which his essence appears. Though every description is an interpretation, it can be an interpretation of the objective reality. Jesus Christ who is the Christian's authority can be described, though every description falls short of completeness and must fail to satisfy others who have encountered him.

For the purpose of such description a moralist may be permitted to choose the somewhat arbitrary device of pointing out and defining the virtues of Jesus Christ; though it will be evident that the resultant portrait needs to be complemented by other interpretations of the same subject, and that a moral description cannot claim to come closer to the essence than do metaphysical or historical descriptions. By the virtues of Christ we mean the excellences of character which on the one hand he exemplifies in his own life, and which on the other he communicates to his followers. For some Christians they are the virtues his example and law demand; for others they are gifts he bestows through regeneration, the dying and rising of the self with him, the first-born of many brothers. But whether Christians emphasize law or grace, whether they look to the Jesus of history or to the pre-existent and risen Lord, the virtues of Jesus Christ are the same.

The virtue of Christ which religious liberalism has magnified beyond all others is love.[13] The discernment of this excellence in him surely constitutes no aberration on the part of liberal thought, whatever may be said about the paucity of references to love in the Synoptic Gospels. The remainder of the New Testament and the witness of Christians in all ages confirm the affirmation that love is one of Jesus Christ's great virtues, and that what he demands of his disciples or makes possible to them is love. Yet when we examine the New Testament and study its portraits of Jesus we become dubious of the descriptive value of such phrases as "the absolutism and perfectionism of Jesus' love ethic"[14] or of such statements as the following:

What [Jesus] freed from its connexion with self-seeking and ritual elements, and recognized as the moral principle, he reduces to *one* root and to *one* motive—love. He knows no other, and love itself, whether it takes the form of love of one's neighbor or of one's enemy, or the love of the Samaritan, is of one kind only. It must completely fill the soul; it is what remains when the soul dies to itself.[15]

Jesus nowhere commands love for its own sake, and nowhere exhibits that complete dominance of the kindly over the aggres-

[13] Cf. esp. Harnack, A., *What is Christianity?* 1901, pp. 78 ff. Not only liberals magnify this virtue; Reinhold Niebuhr, for instance, agrees with Harnack in regarding love as the key to Jesus' ethics. Cf. *An Interpretation of Christian Ethics*, 1935, chap. II.

[14] Niebuhr, *op. cit.*, p. 39.

[15] Harnack, *op. cit.*, p. 78.

sive sentiments and emotions which seems indicated by the idea that in him and for him love "must completely fill the soul," or that his ethics is characterized by "the ideal of love." The virtue of love in Jesus' character and demand is the virtue of the *love of God and of the neighbor in God,* not the virtue of the love of love. The unity of this person lies in the simplicity and completeness of his direction toward God, whether the relation be one of love or of faith or of fear. Love, to be sure, is characterized by a certain extremism in Jesus, but its extremism is not that of a passion unmodified by any other passions; it is the extremism of devotion to the one God, uncompromised by love of any other absolute good. This virtue in him is disproportionate only in the polytheistic-monotheistic sense, not in the sense that it is unaccompanied by other virtues perhaps equally great; nor in an Aristotelian sense, as though it did not lie in the mean between excess and defect or between kindliness and anger. For Jesus there is no other finally love-worthy being, no other ultimate object of devotion, than God; He is the Father; there is none good save God; He alone is to be thanked; His kingdom alone is to be sought. Hence the love of God in Jesus' character and teaching is not only compatible with anger but can be a motive to it, as when he sees the Father's house made into a den of thieves or the Father's children outraged. Hence also it is right and possible to underscore the significance of this virtue in Jesus, while at the same time one recognizes that according to the Synoptic Gospels he emphasized in conduct and in teaching the virtues of faith in God and humility before Him much more than love.

If the nature of this virtue in Jesus is to be understood, some attention must be given to his theology. The tendency to describe Jesus wholly in terms of love is intimately connected with the disposition to identify God with love. Fatherhood is

regarded as almost the sole attribute of God, so that when God
is loved it is the principle of fatherhood that is loved.[16] Or God
is defined as "the final unity which transcends the world's chaos
as certainly as it is basic to the world's order." This "unity of
God is not static, but potent and creative. God is, therefore,
love." He is all-inclusive good-will.[17] Surely this does not represent the theology of Jesus. Though God is love, love is not God
for him; though God is one, oneness is not his God. God whom
Christ loves is the "Lord of heaven and earth"; He is the God
of Abraham, Isaac, and Jacob; He is the power who causes rain
and sun, without whose will and knowledge not a sparrow dies,
nor a city is destroyed, nor he himself crucified. The greatness
and the strangeness of Jesus' love of God does not appear in his
love of cosmic love, but in his loyalty to the transcendent power
that to all men of little faith seems anything but fatherlike. The
word "Father" on the lips of Jesus is a greater, more faithful,
and more heroic word than is evident when fatherhood and
deity are identified.

To this interpretation of the unique nature of the virtue of
love in Jesus as based on the single-mindedness of his devotion
to God it will be objected that he practices and teaches a double
love, of the neighbor as well as of God, and that his ethics has
two foci, "God, the Father, and the infinite value of the human
soul."[18] Such statements forget that the double commandment,
whether originally stated or merely confirmed by Jesus, by no
means places God and neighbor on a level, as though complete
devotion were due to each. It is only God who is to be loved
with heart, soul, mind and strength; the neighbor is put on the
same level of value that the self occupies. Moreover, the idea

[16] *Ibid.*, pp. 68 ff., 154 f.

[17] Niebuhr, *op. cit.*, pp. 38, 49, 56.

[18] So Harnack, *op. cit.*, pp. 55, 68-76. The phrase in many variations has
become the commonplace of liberal Protestantism.

of ascribing "infinite" or "intrinsic" value to the human soul seems wholly foreign to Jesus. He does not speak of worth apart from God. The value of man, like the value of sparrow and flower, is his value to God; the measure of true joy in value is the joy in heaven. Because worth is worth in relation to God, therefore Jesus finds sacredness in all creation, and not in humanity alone—though his disciples are to take special comfort from the fact that they are of more value to God than are the also valued birds. The virtue of neighbor-love in Jesus' conduct and teaching can never be adequately described if it is in any way abstracted from the primary love of God. Christ loves his neighbor not as he loves himself but as God loves him. Hence the Fourth Gospel, discerning that the Jewish statement "Love thy neighbor as thyself" fitted adequately neither Jesus' actions nor his requirements, changed the commandment to read, "Love one another as I have loved you."[19] Beyond that it became clear to the disciples that Jesus Christ's love of men was not merely an illustration of universal benevolence but a decisive act of divine *Agape*. For we must face the recognition that what the early Christians saw in Jesus Christ, and what we must accept if we look at him rather than at our imaginations about him, was not a person characterized by universal benignity, loving God and man. His love of God and his love of neighbor are two distinct virtues that have no common quality but only a common source. Love of God is adoration of the only true good; it is gratitude to the bestower of all gifts; it is joy in Holiness; it is "consent to Being." But the love of man is pitiful rather than adoring; it is giving and forgiving rather than grateful; it suffers for and in their viciousness and profaneness; it does not consent to accept them as they are, but calls them to repentance. The love of God is nonpossessive *Eros*; the love of

---

[19] John 13:34, 15:12. Cf. Mark 12:28-34, Mt. 22:34-40, Luke 10:25-28.

man pure *Agape*; the love of God is passion; the love of man, compassion. There is duality here, but not of like-minded interest in two great values, God and man. It is rather the duality of the Son of Man and Son of God, who loves God as man should love Him, and loves man as only God can love, with powerful pity for those who are foundering.

There seems then to be no other adequate way to describe Jesus as having the virtue of love than to say that his love was that of the Son of God. It was not love but God that filled his soul.

Similar statements must be made about the other excellences we find in him. The liberalism that magnified his love has been followed by eschatological interpretations that see him as the man of hope, and by an existentialism that describes him as radically obedient. It was preceded by an orthodox Protestantism for which he was the exemplar and the bestower of the virtue of faith, and by a monasticism which was astonished and charmed by his great humility. The Christ of the New Testament possesses each of these virtues, and each of them is expressed in his conduct and teaching in a manner that seems extreme and disproportionate to secular, cultural wisdom. But he practices none of them and requires none of them of his followers otherwise than in relation to God. Because these virtues are qualities of conduct on the part of men who always confront the Almighty and Holy One, therefore they seem extreme.

It is so with the virtue of *hope*. The eschatologists, of whom Albert Schweitzer is the best known spokesman, have attempted to describe Jesus as uniquely characterized by expectancy rather than love. He hoped so intensely, they assert, for the realization of the Messianic promise, for the great reversal in history through which evil would be finally overcome and God's reign would be established, that nothing mattered to him except

preparation for this event. "Is it not even *a priori* the only conceivable view," writes Schweitzer, "that the conduct of one who
looked forward to his Messianic 'parousia' in the near future
should be determined by that expectation?"[20] Jesus' teaching,
like his conduct, is explained by reference to this hope. "If the
thought of the eschatological realization of the Kingdom is the
fundamental factor in Jesus' preaching, his whole theory of
ethics must come under the conception of repentance as preparation for the coming of the Kingdom. . . . [Repentance] is a
moral renewal in prospect of the accomplishment of universal
perfection in the future. . . . Jesus' ethics . . . is oriented entirely
by the expected supernatural consummation."[21] What Jesus
communicated to his disciples, the eschatologist maintains, was
a similar expectancy, heightened now by the conviction that in
him the Messianic future had come very near. Hence the ethics
of early Christianity is set forth as the ethics of the great hope.

As in the case of the liberal interpretation of Jesus as a hero
of love, a deep truth is evidently presented here, and all modern
Christianity is in debt to the eschatologists for drawing attention to this virtue in Jesus and to its setting. Their work has
greatly helped toward the achievement of Schweitzer's aim "to
depict the figure of Jesus in its overwhelming heroic greatness
and to impress it upon the modern age and upon modern
theology."[22] There was an extremeness in the hopefulness of
Jesus that sets him apart from all other men who expect lesser
glories or more frequently, no glory at all. Average morality
presupposes complacency tempered by a little cynicism, or
resignation qualified by moderate expectations of good. Intense
anticipation of supernal good must result in a transformation
of ethics.

[20] Schweitzer, A., *The Quest of the Historical Jesus*, 1926, p. 349.
[21] Schweitzer, A., *The Mystery of the Kingdom of God*, 1914, pp. 94, 100.
[22] *Ibid.*, p. 274.

Yet the urgency in Jesus' expectancy is inexplicable, and the degree to which he communicates it to disciples in cultures remote from first-century Palestine is unintelligible, when it is forgotten, as eschatologists sometimes seem to forget, that his hope was in God and for God. What Jesus hoped *in,* they seem inclined to say, was a dogma; what he hoped *for* was a metamorphosis of nature, human and nonhuman—a transformation of the whole earthly form of existence. So Schweitzer defines eschatological interpretation as "a critical examination of the dogmatic element in the life of Jesus. . . . Eschatology is simply 'dogmatic history'—history as moulded by theological beliefs. . . . Dogmatic considerations . . . guided the resolutions of Jesus."[23] Hence he is thought to have staked his hope upon what turned out to be an erroneous belief about the shortness of time, and to have tried to force a stubborn course of events to conform to his dogmatic pattern. Though the Jesus described in the New Testament was clearly animated by an intense hope, yet it seems evident that the reality present to him as the author of the future was not a course of history, dogmatically conceived. His eschatological view of history did not differ from the doctrine of progress only or primarily by regarding time as short. He was not dealing with history at all in the first place, but with God, the Lord of time and space. He hoped in the living God, by whose finger demons were being cast out, whose forgiveness of sins was being made manifest. The times were in His hand, and therefore predictions about times and seasons were out of place. And was not the object of Jesus' intense expectancy God Himself, the manifestation of divine glory and the revelation of divine righteousness? The Kingdom of God for Jesus is less a happy state of affairs in the first place than God in his evident rulership. He rules now, but His rule is to

[23] *Quest of the Historical Jesus,* pp. 248, 249, 357.

become manifest to all. The ethics of Jesus does not seem to depend on his view of history any more than his view of history depends on his ethics; both are reflections of his faith in God. Hence also one must do violence to the New Testament account if one attempts to make extreme hopefulness, with the repentance it entails, the key virtue in his conduct and teaching. Many of his most radical statements are not closely connected at all with expectancy of the coming kingdom, but rather with realization of the present rule of God in the course of daily and natural events. So in the teaching about nonanxiety there is no reference to future catastrophe and renewal, but only to God's daily care; and the teaching about forgiveness of the enemy is connected with the daily and ordinary demonstration of God's mercy in sending rain and sun on just and unjust.[24] The heroic character of Jesus' hopefulness does not stand alone, it is mated with heroic love and heroic faith; and all these have their source in his relation to the God who is Now as well as Then. Not eschatology but sonship to God is the key to Jesus' ethics.

It is not otherwise with the *obedience* of Christ. The Christian existentialists of our time find Jesus characterized by the virtue of radical obedience, undertaking as their predecessors did to describe him and his teaching by centering on one great excellence. So Bultmann writes that one can understand Jesus' proclamation of the will of God and his ethics, in distinction from the Greek ideal of humanity and from the modern ethics of autonomy and value theory, only if one notes its relation to and its distinction from Jewish piety. Then one can say concisely that "the ethic of Jesus, exactly like the Jewish, is an ethic of obedience, and the single though fundamental difference is that Jesus has conceived radically the idea of obedience."[25] Bult-

[24] Mt. 6:25-34, 5:43-48.
[25] Bultmann, Rudolf, *Jesus and the Word*, 1934, pp. 72-73.

mann accounts for the radicalness of Jesus' obedience by pointing out that for him there was no mediate authority between
God and man, for "radical obedience exists only when a man
inwardly assents to what is required of him, when the thing
commanded is seen as intrinsically God's command. . . . So
long as obedience is only subjection to an authority which man
does not understand, it is not true obedience." Further, obedience is radical when the whole man is involved, so that "he is
not only *doing* something obediently but *is* essentially obedient,"
and when he confronts an either-or so that he no longer seeks
a neutral position but accepts the burden of decision between
good and evil.[26]

Again, as in the case of an interpretation in terms of love, we
must recognize the evident truth in such statements. Jesus was
obedient, and he was radically obedient—as the believers recognized from the beginning. They marvelled at his obedience
unto death, at his submission in the agony and prayer at
Gethsemane; they saw that he had come down from heaven not
to do his own will but the will of Him that sent him; they
rejoiced that through the obedience of the one, many will be
made righteous; and they were consoled by the thought that
they had a high priest in heaven who, though he was a Son, had
learned obedience by what he had suffered.[27] They discerned
that the radicalness of this obedience was connected with a
certain transcending of the mediate authority of the law, that
it was addressed to the whole man, including every thought and
motive as well as every overt deed, and that there was no escape
from the responsibility of obedience.

Yet something is lacking in the existentialist portrait of the
obedient Christ. Not only has one virtue been made the key to

[26] *Ibid.*, pp. 77, 78.
[27] Phil. 2:8, Mark 14:36, John 6:38, 15:10, Rom. 5:19, Hebrews 5:8.

all the others, but this virtue has been essentially abstracted
from that realization of God which makes all the virtues of
Jesus Christ radical. This existentialist Jesus is more Kantian
than Markan or Pauline or Johannine. Bultmann can find no
real content in the gospel idea of obedience. Jesus, he says, has
no doctrine "of duty or of the good. It is sufficient for a man
to know that God has placed him under the necessity of decision
in every concrete situation in life, in the here and now. And
this means that he himself must know what is required of him.
. . . Man does not meet the crisis of decision armed with a
definite standard; he stands on no firm base, but rather alone
in empty space. . . . He [Jesus] sees only the individual man
standing before the will of God. . . . Jesus teaches no ethics at
all in the sense of an intelligible theory valid for all men concerning what should be done and left undone."[28] Moreover,
although God is mentioned as the one whose will is to be obeyed,
the idea of God ascribed to Jesus is as empty and formal as the
idea of obedience. Just as for liberalism God is the counterpart
of human love, so in this existentialism He becomes the mere
counterpart of moral decision. He is "the Power which constrains man to decision," the one whom man can find "only in
the actual comprehension of his own existence"; "God Himself
must vanish for the man who does not know that the essence
of his own life consists in the full freedom of his decision."[29]
The animus of such existentialism against speculative and
naturalistic ideas of God can be understood, but the ascription
to Jesus of this twentieth century view of freedom results in a
caricature of the New Testament Christ. For the Jesus who is
radically obedient knows that the will of God is the will of the
Creator and Governor of all nature and of all history; that there

[28] *Op. cit.,* pp. 108, 85, 84. Cf. pp. 87-88.
[29] *Op. cit.,* pp. 103, 154.

is structure and content in His will; that He is the author of the
ten commandments; that He demands mercy and not sacrifice;
that He requires not only obedience to Himself but love and
faith in Him, and love of the neighbor whom He creates and
loves. This Jesus is radically obedient; but he also knows that
love and faith alone make obedience possible, and that God
is the bestower of all these gifts. His obedience is a relation to
a God who is much more than an "Unconditioned," met in the
moment of decision; its radical character is therefore not something that lies in itself, or something that is separable from
radical love and hope and faith. It is the obedience of a Son
whose sonship is not definable as just obedience to a principle
that constrains obedience.

Examination of Protestant concentration on the *faith* of
Jesus Christ, and of monastic interest in his great *humility,*
leads to the same result. He is indeed characterized by an
extreme faith and by a radical humility. But faith and humility
are not things in themselves; they are relations to persons—
habits of behavior in the presence of others. Now when we
look at Jesus from the point of view of his faith in men, he
seems a great skeptic who believes that he is dealing with an
evil and adulterous generation, with a people that stones its
prophets and then erects monuments to them. He puts no
trust in the enduring institutions and traditions of his society.
He shows little confidence in his disciples; he is convinced that
they will be offended in him, and that the sturdiest of them will
be unable to stand by him in the time of testing. Only romantic
fictionizing can interpret the Jesus of the New Testament as
one who believed in the goodness of men, and sought by trusting
it to bring out what was good in them. Yet despite his skepticism
he is remarkably free from anxiety. He is heroic in his faith in
God, calling the Lord of heaven and earth Father. He relies in

his poverty-stricken existence, without family, food, or lodging, on the one who gives the bread needful for the day; and in the end he commends his spirit to Him whom he knows to be responsible for his ignominious and shameful death. To Him also he entrusts his nation, believing that everything needful will be granted to folk who, turning away from self-defense, seek only the Kingdom of God. Such faith will always seem radical to human beings with their deep suspicion of the power which brought them forth, maintains them, and decrees their death. It is the faith of a Son of God, too extreme for those who conceive themselves as sons of nature, or of men, or of blind chance.

Jesus' humility is also inordinate. He lives with the sinners and pariahs; he washes the disciples' feet; he accepts indignities and scurrilities from priests and soldiers. When he is recognized as the living, risen Lord, the magnificence of his lowliness astounds and staggers his believers. Though he was rich, he had become poor that he might enrich many; though he was in the form of God, he had taken the form of a slave; the Word through whom all things were made had become flesh; the life which was the light of men had entered their darkness. There is indeed something disproportionate about the humility of Jesus Christ; it would not be surprising if a new school of interpreters arose in the wake of existentialists with an attempt to understand him as the man of radical humility. But the humility of Jesus is humility before God, and can only be understood as the humility of the Son. He neither exhibited nor commended and communicated the humility of inferiority-feeling before other men. Before Pharisees, high priests, Pilate, and "that fox" Herod he showed a confidence that had no trace of self-abnegation. Whatever may be true of his Messianic self-consciousness, he spoke with authority and acted with confidence of power.

When he repudiated the title of "Good Master" he did not defer
to other rabbis better than himself, but said, "No one is good
but God alone." There is no condescension in his life toward
the sinners, such as might mark an insecure or apologetic man.
His humility is of the sort that raises to a new sense of dignity
and worth those who have been humiliated by the defensive
pretentions of the "good" and the "righteous." It is a kind of
proud humility and humble pride, which can be called paradoxical only if the relation to God as the fundamental relation
in his life is left out of account. If it is wholly different from all
the modesties and diffidences that mark men's efforts to accommodate themselves to their own and each others' superiority-
feelings, it is also wholly different from that wise Greek virtue
of remaining within one's limits lest the jealous gods destroy
their potential rivals. The humility of Christ is not the modera-
tion of keeping one's exact place in the scale of being, but rather
that of absolute dependence on God and absolute trust in Him,
with the consequent ability to remove mountains. The secret
of the meekness and the gentleness of Christ lies in his relation
to God.

Thus any one of the virtues of Jesus may be taken as the key
to the understanding of his character and teaching; but each is
intelligible in its apparent radicalism only as a relation to God.
It is better, of course, not to attempt to delineate him by describing one of his excellences but rather to take them all together,
those to which we have referred and others. In either case, however, it seems evident that the strangeness, the heroic stature,
the extremism and sublimity of this person, considered morally,
is due to that unique devotion to God and to that single-hearted
trust in Him which can be symbolized by no other figure of
speech so well as by the one which calls him Son of God.

Hence belief in Jesus Christ by men in their various cultures always means belief in God. No one can know the Son without acknowledging the Father. To be related in devotion and obedience to Jesus Christ is to be related to the One to whom he undeviatingly points. As Son of God he points away from the many values of man's social life to the One who alone is good; from the many powers which men use and on which they depend to the One who alone is powerful; from the many times and seasons of history with their hopes and fears to the One who is Lord of all times and is alone to be feared and hoped for; he points away from all that is conditioned to the Unconditioned. He does not direct attention away from this world to another; but from all worlds, present and future, material and spiritual, to the One who creates all worlds, who is the Other of all worlds.

Yet this is only half the meaning of Christ, considered morally. The other half has been indicated above by what was said about his love of men in relation to his love of God. Because he is the moral Son of God in his love, hope, faith, obedience, and humility in the presence of God, therefore he is the moral mediator of the Father's will toward men. Because he loves the Father with the perfection of human *eros,* therefore he loves men with the perfection of divine *agape*, since God is *agape*. Because he is obedient to the Father's will, therefore he exercises authority over men, commanding obedience not to his own will but to God's. Because he hopes in God, therefore he gives promises to men. Because he trusts perfectly in God who is faithful, therefore he is trustworthy in his own faithfulness towards men. Because he exalts God with perfect human humility, therefore he humbles men by giving them good gifts beyond all their deserts. Since the Father of Jesus Christ is what He is, sonship to Him involves the Son not in an ambiguous but in an ambivalent process. It involves the double movement—with men toward God, with God toward men; from the world to the

Other, from the Other to the world; from work to Grace, from Grace to work; from time to the Eternal and from the Eternal to the temporal. In his moral sonship to God Jesus Christ is not a median figure, half God, half man; he is a single person wholly directed as man toward God and wholly directed in his unity with the Father toward men. He is mediatorial, not median. He is not a center from which radiate love of God and of men, obedience to God and to Caesar, trust in God and in nature, hope in divine and in human action. He exists rather as the focusing point in the continuous alternation of movements from God to man and man to God; and these movements are qualitatively as different as are *agape* and *eros,* authority and obedience, promise and hope, humiliation and glorification, faithfulness and trust.

Other approaches besides the moral one must be taken if Jesus Christ is to be described adequately. Yet as the history of the church and its theologies indicate, each such approach tends toward the same issue. The power and attraction Jesus Christ exercises over men never comes from him alone, but from him as Son of the Father. It comes from him in his Sonship in a double way, as man living to God and God living with men. Belief in him and loyalty to his cause involves men in the double movement from world to God and from God to world. Even when theologies fail to do justice to this fact, Christians living with Christ in their cultures are aware of it. For they are forever being challenged to abandon all things for the sake of God; and forever being sent back into the world to teach and practice all the things that have been commanded them.

III. Toward the Definition of Culture

From this inadequate definition of the meaning of Christ we turn now to the task of defining, in similarly tenuous fashion, the meaning of culture. What do we mean in our use of this word when we say that the Christian church enduringly struggles with the problem of Christ and culture?

A theologian's definition of the term must, in the nature of the case, be a layman's definition, since he cannot presume to enter into the issues raised by professional anthropologists; yet it must also, at least initially, be a definition of the phenomenon without theological interpretation, for it is just this theological interpretation which is the point at issue among Christians. For some of them culture is essentially Godless in the purely secular sense, as having neither positive nor negative relation to the God of Jesus Christ; for others it is Godless in the negative sense, as being anti-God or idolatrous; for others it seems solidly based on a natural, rational knowledge of God or His law. Christian disinterestedness forbids the adoption at least at the outset—of any one of these evaluations.

The culture with which we are concerned cannot be simply that of a particular society, such as the Graeco-Roman, the medieval, or the modern Western. Some theologians, like some anthropologists, do, indeed, think of Christian faith as integrally related to Western culture, whether this term be used to designate one continuous historical society beginning not later than the first century A.D., or a series of distinct and affiliated civilizations as in Toynbee's scheme. So Ernst Troeltsch believes that Christianity and Western culture are so inextricably intertwined that a Christian can say little about his faith to members of other civilizations, and the latter in turn cannot encounter Christ save as a member of the Western world.[30] Troeltsch himself, however, is highly aware of the tension between Christ and Western culture, so that even for the Westerner Jesus Christ is

[30] Troeltsch, Ernst, *Christian Thought*, 1923, esp. pp. 21-35; cf. also his *Die Absolutheit des Christentums*, 1929 (3d ed.) and *Gesammelte Schriften*, Vol. II, 1913, pp. 779 ff.

never merely a member of his cultural society. Furthermore, Christians in the East, and those who are looking forward to the emergence of a new civilization, are concerned not only with the Western Christ but with one who is to be distinguished from Western faith in him and who is relevant to life in other cultures. Hence culture as we are concerned with it is not a particular phenomenon but the general one, though the general thing appears only in particular forms, and though a Christian of the West cannot think about the problem save in Western terms.

Neither may we define culture narrowly by taking into view some special phase of human social organization and achievement. This is done when the problem is stated in terms of Christ's relation to science and philosophy, as in the question of revelation and reason, or of his relation to political organization, as in the question of church and state. It is also done when, with Jakob Burkhardt, "culture" is distinguished from both religion and state. He regards these three powers, religion, state, and culture, as "supremely heterogeneous to each other." Culture, in his usage, is distinguished from the other two powers by its nonauthoritarian character. It is "the sum of all that has *spontaneously* arisen for the advancement of material life and as an expression of spiritual and moral life—all social intercourse, technologies, arts, literature and sciences. It is the realm of the variable, free, not necessarily universal, of all that cannot lay claim to compulsive authority."[31] The spearhead of such culture is speech, he says; the foremost expressions of its spirit are found in the arts. Doubtless the relation of Christ to these elements in civilization raises special problems, yet we can find no clear demarcation between them and those that arise in political and religious society; nor are authoritarianism and

[31] *Force and Freedom,* 1943, p. 107; cf. 140 ff.

freedom distributed as Burkhardt seems to think. It is especially
arbitrary and confusing to define culture as though it excluded
religion, and the latter as though it included Christ, since the
problems with which we are concerned are often most difficult
in the realm of religion, where we must ask about the connection of Christ with our social faiths. Again, culture is too narrowly defined for our purposes if it is distinguished from
civilization, the latter term being used to designate the more
advanced, perhaps more urban, technical and even senescent
forms of social life.[32]

What we have in view when we deal with Christ and culture
is that total process of human activity and that total result of
such activity to which now the name *culture,* now the name
civilization, is applied in common speech.[33] Culture is the "artificial, secondary environment" which man superimposes on the
natural. It comprises language, habits, ideas, beliefs, customs,
social organization, inherited artifacts, technical processes, and
values.[34] This "social heritage," this "reality sui generis," which
the New Testament writers frequently had in mind when they
spoke of "the world," which is represented in many forms but
to which Christians like other men are inevitably subject, is
what we mean when we speak of culture.

Though we cannot venture to define the "essence" of this
culture, we can describe some of its chief characteristics. For
one thing, it is inextricably bound up with man's life in society;
it is always *social.* "The essential fact of culture, as we live and
experience it, as we can observe it scientifically," writes Malin-

[32] Malinowski, Bronislaw, art. "Culture," *Encyclopedia of Social Sciences,*
Vol. IV, pp. 621 ff.; Dawson, Christopher, *Religion and Culture,* 1947, p. 47,
Spengler, Oswald, *The Decline of the West,* 1926, Vol. I, pp. 31 f., 351 ff.

[33] Cf. Robinson, James Harvey, art. "Civilization," *Encyclopedia Britannica,*
14th ed., Vol. V, p. 735; Brinkmann, Carl, art. "Civilization," *Encyclopedia of
Social Sciences,* Vol. III, pp. 525 ff.

[34] Malinowski, *loc. cit.*

owski, "is the organization of human beings into permanent groups."[35] Whether or not this is the essential fact, it is an essential part of the fact. Individuals may use culture in their own ways; they may change elements in their culture, yet what they use and change is social.[36] Culture is the social heritage they receive and transmit. Whatever is purely private, so that it neither derives from nor enters into social life, is not a part of culture. Conversely, social life is always cultural. Anthropology, it seems, has completely scotched the romantic idea of a purely natural society, not characterized by highly distinct and acquired habits, customs, forms of social organization, etc. Culture and social existence go together.

Culture, secondly, is *human achievement*. We distinguish it from nature by noting the evidences of human purposiveness and effort. A river is nature, a canal culture; a raw piece of quartz is nature, an arrowhead culture; a moan is natural, a word cultural. Culture is the work of men's minds and hands. It is that portion of man's heritage in any place or time which has been given us designedly and laboriously by other men, not what has come to us via the mediation of nonhuman beings or through human beings insofar as they have acted without intention of results or without control of the process. Hence it includes speech, education, tradition, myth, science, art, philosophy, government, law, rite, beliefs, inventions, technologies. Furthermore, if one of the marks of culture is that it is the result of past human achievements, another is that no one can possess it without effort and achievement on his own part. The gifts of nature are received as they are communicated without human intent or conscious effort; but the gifts of culture cannot be possessed without striving on the part of the recipient. Speech

[35] Malinowski, *A Scientific Theory of Culture and Other Essays*, 1944. p. 43.
[36] On individual and society in relation to culture see Benedict, Ruth, *Patterns of Culture*, 1934, chapters VII and VIII.

must be laboriously acquired; government cannot be maintained without constant effort; scientific method must be re-enacted and reintended with every generation. Even the material results of cultural activity are useless unless they are accompanied by a learning process that enables us to employ them as they were intended to be employed. Whether we try to interpret the signs of ancient culture or to solve problems of contemporary civilization, this characteristic feature will always be brought to our attention: we are dealing with what man has purposefully wrought and with what man can or ought to do. The world so far as it is man-made and man-intended is the world of culture.

These human achievements, in the third place, are all designed for an end or ends; the world of culture is a *world of values*. Whether or not we should ask value-questions about nature or pass value-judgments on natural occurrences is a moot question. But with respect to culture phenomena this problem never arises. What men have made and what they make, we must assume, is intended for a purpose; it is designed to serve a good.[37] It can never be described without reference to ends in minds of designers and users. Primitive art interests us because it indicates human interest in form, rhythm, and color, in meanings and symbols, and because we are interested in these things. Potsherds are studied that they may reveal what ancient men intended and what methods they had devised to achieve their ends. We judge science and philosophy, technology and education, whether in past or present, always with reference to the values that were intended by them and to the values that attract us. To be sure, the ends that human achievements serve may change; what was intended for utility may be preserved for

[37] So Malinowski uses as a central concept in his theory of culture the idea of "an organized system of purposive activities." *A Scientific Theory of Culture*, chaps. V and VI.

the sake of aesthetic satisfaction or of social harmony; yet the value-relation is inescapable wherever we encounter culture.

Further, the values with which these human achievements are concerned are dominantly those of the *good for man.* Philosophers in cultural societies may argue whether the ends that are to be served by culture are ideal or natural, whether they are ideas of value given to spiritual vision or natural goods, that is, ends interesting man as biological being. In either case, however, they seem to agree that man must serve his own good, that he is the measure of all things.[38] In defining the ends that his activities are to realize in culture, man begins with himself as the chief value and the source of all other values. What is good is what is good for him. It seems self-evident in culture that animals are to be domesticated or annihilated so far as these measures serve man's good, that God or the gods are to be worshiped so far as this is necessary or desirable for the sake of maintaining and advancing human life, that ideas and ideals are to be served for the sake of human self-realization. Though the search of the good-for-man is dominant in the work of culture, it is not evident that this anthropocentrism is of an exclusive sort. It is not only conceivable that men should undertake to labor and produce for the sake of some other being's good, but it seems true that they do indeed in their cultures often seek to serve causes transcending human existence. From totemic to modern societies they identify themselves with orders of being that include more than men. They regard themselves as representatives of life, so that social organization and laws as well as art and religion show some respect for life even in nonhuman beings. They define themselves as representatives of the

[38] Nikolai Hartmann's *Ethics,* 1932, which is from one point of view a great philosophy of culture, presents at one and the same time a strong argument for the transcendent, objective character of values and a defence of the primacy of human value.

order of rational beings, and seek to realize what is good-for-reason. They also serve the gods. And yet the pragmatic tendency to do all these things for the sake of men seems inconquerable. It must at once be added, however, that no culture is really humanistic in the broad sense, for there are only particular cultures, and in each of them a particular society or a particular class in that society tends to regard itself as the center and source of value, seeking to achieve what is good for it, though justifying that endeavor by claiming for itself a special status as the representative of something universal.

Again, culture in all its forms and varieties is concerned with the *temporal and material realization of values*. This does not mean that the goods that human effort seeks to realize are necessarily temporal or material, however much the concern for these is a part of all cultural achievement. It is fallacious to think of culture as materialistic in the sense that what men labor to achieve is always the satisfaction of their needs as physical and temporal beings. Even the economic interpretations of culture recognize that beyond material goods—that is, values relative to man's physical existence, beyond food, drink, clothing, progeny, and economic order—men in culture seek to gain less tangible values. But even the immaterial goods must be realized in temporal and material form; even the good-for-man as mind and person must be given "a local habitation and a name." Prestige and glory on the one hand, beauty, truth, and goodness on the other—to use the unsatisfactory symbols of spiritual-value theory—are presented to feeling, imagination, or intellectual vision; and human effort presses on to embody in concrete, tangible, visible, and audible forms what has been imaginatively discerned. The harmony and proportion, the form, order and rhythm, the meanings and ideas that men intuit and trace out as they confront nature, social events, and the

world of dreams, these by infinite labor they must paint on wall
or canvas, print on paper as systems of philosophy and science,
outline in carved stone or cast in bronze, sing in ballad, ode,
or symphony. Visions of order and justice, hopes of glory, must
at the cost of much suffering be embodied in written laws
dramatic rites, structures of government, empires, ascetic lives

Because all these actualizations of purpose are accomplished
in transient and perishing stuff, cultural activity is almost as
much concerned with the *conservation of values* as with their
realization. Much of the energy which men in their societies
expend at any time is given to this complicated task of preserv-
ing what they have inherited and made. Their houses, schools,
and temples, their roads and machines, stand in constant need
of repair. The desert and the jungle threaten every cultivated
acre. Even greater are the dangers of decay that surround the
less material achievements of the past. The systems of laws and
liberties, the customs of social intercourse, the methods of
thought, the institutions of learning and religion, the techniques
of art, of language, and of morality itself—these cannot be conserved by keeping in repair the walls and documents that are
their symbols. They need to be written afresh generation by
generation "on the tables of the heart." Let education and training lapse for one generation, and the whole grand structure of
past achievements falls into ruin. Culture is social tradition
which must be conserved by painful struggle not so much against
nonhuman natural forces as against revolutionary and critical
powers in human life and reason.[39] But whether customs or
artifacts are in question, culture cannot be maintained unless

[39] Henri Bergson in *The Two Sources of Morality and Religion*, 1935, offers
an illuminating and persuasive interpretation of the role of conservatism in
culture. Cf. chaps. I and II. Cf. also Lecomte du Nüoy, *Human Destiny*, 1947,
chaps. IX and X.

men devote a large part of their efforts to the work of conservation.

Finally, attention must be directed to the *pluralism* that is characteristic of all culture. The values a culture seeks to realize in any time or place are many in number. No society can even try to realize all its manifold possibilities; each is highly complex, made up of many institutions with many goals and interweaving interests.[40] The values are many, partly because men are many. Culture is concerned with what is good for male and female, child and adult, rulers and ruled; with what is good for men in special vocations and groups, according to the customary notions of such good. Moreover, all the individuals have their special claims and interests; and everyone in his individuality is a complex being with desires of body and mind, with self-regarding and other-regarding motives, with relations to other men, nature and supernatural beings. Even if economic or biological interpretations of culture are maintained, still all that can be claimed is that economic or biologic values are fundamental, while the vast superstructure of other interests must be recognized.[41] But in culture as we meet it and live it not even such unity as these interpretations claim is recognizable. The values we seek in our societies and find represented in their institutional behavior are many, disparate, and often incomparable, so that these societies are always involved in a more or less laborious effort to hold together in tolerable conflict the many efforts of many men in many groups to achieve and conserve many goods. The cultures are forever seeking to combine peace with prosperity, justice with order, freedom

[40] Cf. Benedict, Ruth, *Patterns of Culture*, 1934, chap. II; Malinowski, B., *A Scientific Theory* etc., chaps. X and XI.

[41] Cf. for instance Friedrich Engels' statement about the relative independence of the superstructure in his letter of Sept. 21, 1890, to Joseph Bloch. Adoratsky, V., *Karl Marx, Selected Works*, Vol. I, p. 381.

with welfare, truth with beauty, scientific truth with moral good, technical proficiency with practical wisdom, holiness with life, and all these with all the rest. Among the many values the kingdom of God may be included—though scarcely as the one pearl of great price. Jesus Christ and God the Father, the gospel, the church, and eternal life may find places in the cultural complex, but only as elements in the great pluralism.

These are some of the obvious characteristics of that culture which lays its claim on every Christian, and under the authority of which he also lives when he lives under the authority of Jesus Christ. Though sometimes we state the fundamental human problem as that of grace and nature, in human existence we do not know a nature apart from culture. In any case we cannot escape culture any more readily than we can escape nature, for "the man of nature, the *Naturmensch,* does not exist,"[42] and "no man ever looks at the world with pristine eyes."[43]

IV. The Typical Answers

Given these two complex realities—Christ and culture—an infinite dialogue must develop in the Christian conscience and the Christian community. In his single-minded direction toward God, Christ leads men away from the temporality and pluralism of culture. In its concern for the conservation of the many values of the past, culture rejects the Christ who bids men rely on grace. Yet the Son of God is himself child of a religious culture, and sends his disciples to tend his lambs and sheep, who cannot be guarded without cultural work. The dialogue proceeds with denials and affirmations, reconstructions, compromises, and new denials. Neither individual nor church can come to a stopping-

[42] Malinowski in *Encyclopedia of Social Sciences,* Vol. IV, p. 621.
[43] Ruth Benedict, *op. cit.,* p. 2

place in the endless search for an answer which will not provoke a new rejoinder.

Yet it is possible to discern some order in this multiplicity, to stop the dialogue, as it were, at certain points; and to define typical partial answers that recur so often in different eras and societies that they seem to be less the product of historical conditioning than of the nature of the problem itself and the meanings of its terms. In this way the course of the great conversation about Christ and culture may be more intelligently followed, and some of the fruits of the discussion may be garnered. In the following chapters such typical answers are to be set forth and illustrated by reference to such Christians as John and Paul, Tertullian and Augustine, Thomas Aquinas and Luther, Ritschl and Tolstoy. At this point brief and summary descriptions of these typical answers is offered as a guide to what follows. Five sorts of answers are distinguished, of which three are closely related to each other as belonging to that median type in which both Christ and culture are distinguished and affirmed; yet strange family resemblances may be found along the whole scale.

Answers of the first type emphasize the *opposition* between Christ and culture. Whatever may be the customs of the society in which the Christian lives, and whatever the human achievements it conserves, Christ is seen as opposed to them, so that he confronts men with the challenge of an "either-or" decision. In the early period of church history Jewish rejection of Jesus, defended by Klausner, found its counterpart in Christian antagonism to Jewish culture, while Roman outlawry of the new faith was accompanied by Christian flight from or attack upon Graeco-Roman civilization. In medieval times monastic orders and sectarian movements called on believers living in what purported to be a Christian culture to abandon the

"world" and to "come out from among them and be separate."
In the modern period answers of this kind are being given by
missionaries who require their converts to abandon wholly the
customs and institutions of so-called "heathen" societies, by
little groups of withdrawing Christians in Western or "Christianized" civilization, and in partial manner, by those who
emphasize the antagonism of Christian faith to capitalism and
communism, to industrialism and nationalism, to Catholicism
and Protestantism.

Recognition of a fundamental *agreement* between Christ and
culture is typical of the answers offered by a second group. In
them Jesus often appears as a great hero of human culture history; his life and teachings are regarded as the greatest human
achievement; in him, it is believed, the aspirations of men toward their values are brought to a point of culmination; he
confirms what is best in the past, and guides the process of
civilization to its proper goal. Moreover, he is a part of culture
in the sense that he himself is part of the social heritage that
must be transmitted and conserved. In our time answers of this
kind are given by Christians who note the close relation between
Christianity and Western civilization, between Jesus' teachings
or the teachings about him and democratic institutions; yet there
are occasional interpretations that emphasize the agreement between Christ and Eastern culture as well as some that tend to
identify him with the spirit of Marxian society. In earlier times
solutions of the problem along these lines were being offered
simultaneously with the solutions of the first or "Christ-against-
culture" type.

Three other typical answers agree with each other in seeking
to maintain the great differences between the two principles
and in undertaking to hold them together in some unity. They
are distinguished from each other by the manner in which

each attempts to combine the two authorities. One of them, our third type, understands Christ's relation to culture somewhat as the men of the second group do: he is the fulfillment of cultural aspirations and the restorer of the institutions of true society. Yet there is in him something that neither arises out of culture nor contributes directly to it. He is discontinuous as well as continuous with social life and its culture. The latter, indeed, leads men to Christ, yet only in so preliminary a fashion that a great leap is necessary if men are to reach him or, better, true culture is not possible unless beyond all human achievement, all human search for values, all human society, Christ enters into life from above with gifts which human aspiration has not envisioned and which human effort cannot attain unless he relates men to a supernatural society and a new value-center. Christ is, indeed, a Christ of culture, but he is also a *Christ above culture*. This *synthetic* type is best represented by Thomas Aquinas and his followers, but it has many other representatives in both early and modern times.

Another group of median answers constitutes our fourth type. In these the duality and inescapable authority of both Christ and culture are recognized, but the opposition between them is also accepted. To those who answer the question in this way it appears that Christians throughout life are subject to the tension that accompanies obedience to two authorities who do not agree yet must both be obeyed. They refuse to accommodate the claims of Christ to those of secular society, as, in their estimation, men in the second and third groups do. So they are like the "Christ-against-culture" believers, yet differ from them in the conviction that obedience to God requires obedience to the institutions of society and loyalty to its members as well as obedience to a Christ who sits in judgment on that society.

Hence man is seen as subject to two moralities, and as a citizen of two worlds that are not only discontinuous with each other but largely opposed. In the *polarity* and *tension* of Christ and culture life must be lived precariously and sinfully in the hope of a justification which lies beyond history. Luther may be regarded as the greatest representative of this type, yet many a Christian who is not otherwise a Lutheran finds himself compelled to solve the problem in this way.

Finally, as the fifth type in the general series and as the third of the mediating answers, there is the *conversionist* solution. Those who offer it understand with the members of the first and the fourth groups that human nature is fallen or perverted, and that this perversion not only appears in culture but is transmitted by it. Hence the opposition between Christ and all human institutions and customs is to be recognized. Yet the antithesis does not lead either to Christian separation from the world as with the first group, or to mere endurance in the expectation of a transhistorical salvation, as with the fourth. Christ is seen as the converter of man in his culture and society, not apart from these, for there is no nature without culture and no turning of men from self and idols to God save in society. It is in Augustine that the great outlines of this answer seem to be offered; John Calvin makes it explicit; many others are associated with these two.

When the answers to the enduring problem are stated in this manner it is apparent that a construction has been set up that is partly artificial. A type is always something of a construct, even when it has not been constructed prior to long study of many historic individuals and movements. When one returns from the hypothetical scheme to the rich complexity of individual events, it is evident at once that no person or group ever conforms completely to a type.[44] Each historical figure will show characteristics that are more reminiscent of some other family than the one by whose name he has been called, or traits will appear that seem wholly unique and individual. The method of typology, however, though historically inadequate, has the advantage of calling to attention the continuity and significance of the great *motifs* that appear and reappear in the long wrestling of Christians with their enduring problem. Hence also it may help us to gain orientation as we in our own time seek to answer the question of Christ and culture.

[44] C. J. Jung's *Psychological Types*, 1924, is suggestive and illuminating as an example of typological method. On the applicability to individuals of type descriptions see especially pp. 10 f., 412 ff.

※

Christ Against Culture

I. THE NEW PEOPLE AND "THE WORLD"

The first answer to the question of Christ and culture we shall consider is the one that uncompromisingly affirms the sole authority of Christ over the Christian and resolutely rejects culture's claims to loyalty. It seems to be both logically and chronologically entitled to the first position: logically, because it appears to follow directly from the common Christian principle of the Lordship of Jesus Christ; chronologically, because it is widely held to be the typical attitude of the first Christians. Both claims are subject to question, yet it must be conceded that the answer was given at a very early time in the history of the church, and that on the surface it seems to be logically more consistent than the other positions.

While various New Testament writings evince something of this attitude, none presents it without qualification. The first gospel contrasts the new law with the old, yet contains very explicit statements about the Christians' obligations to be obedient not only to the code of Moses but also to the requirements of the leaders of Jewish society.[1] The book of Revelation is radical in its rejection of "the world," but here the problem is complicated by the persecution situation in which Christians

---

[1] Mt. 5:21-48, 5:17-20; 23:1-3.

find themselves. Among the other writings, the First Letter of John contains the least ambiguous presentation of this point of view.

This little classic of devotion and theology has been treasured by Christians for its profound understanding and beautiful statement of the doctrine of love. It achieves the simple summary of Christian theology: "God is love," and the equally concise formulation of Christian ethics: "Love one another." It presents in their inseparable relation and in fugue-like manner the three themes of love: God's love for man, and man's for God, and brother's for brother. "In this is love, not that we loved God but that he loved us. . . . We love because he first loved us. . . . Beloved, if God so loved us, we ought also to love one another. . . . If any one says, 'I love God,' and hates his brother, he is a liar. . . . No man has ever seen God; if we love one another God abides in us and his love is perfected in us. . . . He who does not love his brother whom he has seen, cannot love God, whom he has not seen."[2] The central interest of the writer, however, is quite as much the Lordship of Christ as the idea of love. Indeed, Christ is the key to the whole kingdom of love, for "in this the love of God was made manifest among us, that God sent his only Son into the world, so that we might live through him"; and "by this we know love, that he laid down his life for us; and we ought to lay down our lives for the brethren."[3] The Christ who makes human love for God and neighbor possible by his demonstration of the greatness of God's love for man, the Christ who loves men to the point of laying down his life for them and who is their advocate in heaven, is also the one who requires what he has made possible. The writer of I John insists on obedience to the commandment of Jesus Christ

[2] I John 4, vv. 10-12 combined with vv. 19-20.
[3] *Ibid.*, 4:9; 3:16.

no less than on confidence in the love of God.[4] The gospel and the new law are here thoroughly united.[5] Hence God requires two things: "This is his commandment, that we should believe in the name of his Son Jesus Christ and love one another, just as he has commanded us."[6] The dual commandment of love of God and neighbor, which the writer well knows,[7] has here undergone a certain transformation as a result of the recognition that the first movement of love is not from man to God but from God to man and that the first requirement of the Christian life is therefore a faith in God that is inseparable from the believing acceptance of Jesus Christ as his Son. It is exceedingly important for the First Letter of John that Christians be loyal to no merely spiritual Christ but to a visible and tangible Jesus Christ of history, who is, however, not only the Jesus of history but the Son of God, inseparably united with the unseen Father in love and righteousness, in the power to achieve and the authority to command.[8] With these two themes of love and faith in Jesus Christ, other ideas, such as those of the forgiveness of sin, the gift of the Spirit and of eternal life, are closely connected; nevertheless these two define the Christian life; no one can be a member of the Christian fellowship who does not acknowledge Jesus as the Christ and the Son of God and who does not love the brothers in obedience to the Lord.

This succinct statement of the positive meaning of Christianity is, however, accompanied by an equally emphatic negation. The counterpart of loyalty to Christ and the brothers is the rejection of cultural society; a clear line of separation is

---

[4] *Ibid.*, 2:3-11; 3:4-10, 21-24; 4:21; 5:2-3.
[5] Dodd, C. H., *The Johannine Epistles*, 1946, p. xxxi.
[6] I John, 3:23.
[7] *Ibid.*, 4:21.
[8] Cf. *ibid.*, 1:1-3; 2:1-2; 2:22-24; 3:8b; 4:2-3, 9-10, 14-15; 5:1-5; cf. also Dodd, *op. cit.*, pp. xxx-xxxvi; 1-6; 55-58.

drawn between the brotherhood of the children of God and the world. Save in two instances[9] the word "world" evidently means for the writer of this letter the whole society outside the church, in which, however, the believers live.[10] The injunction to Christians is, "Do not love the world or the things in the world. If any one loves the world, love for the Father is not in him."[11] That world appears as a realm under the power of evil; it is the region of darkness, into which the citizens of the kingdom of light must not enter; it is characterized by the prevalence in it of lies, hatred, and murder; it is the heir of Cain.[12] It is a secular society, dominated by the "lust of the flesh, the lust of the eyes and the pride of life," or, in Prof. Dodd's translation of these phrases, it is "pagan society, with its sensuality, superficiality and pretentiousness, its materialism and its egoism."[13] It is a culture that is concerned with temporal and passing values, whereas Christ has words of eternal life; it is a dying as well as a murderous order, for "the world passes away and the lust of it."[14] It is dying, however, not only because it is concerned with temporal goods and contains the inner contradictions of hatred and lie, but also because Christ has come to destroy the works of the devil and because faith in him is the victory which overcomes the world.[15] Hence the loyalty of the believer is directed entirely toward the new order, the new society and its Lord.

The "Christ-against-culture" position is not set forth here in its most radical form. Though love of neighbor has been interpreted to mean love of the brother—that is, the fellow believer

---

[9] I John 2:2; 4:14.
[10] Cf. Dodd, *op. cit.*, pp. 27, 39-45.
[11] I John 2:15.
[12] *Ibid.*, 5:19; 1:6; 2:8-9, 11; 3:11-15.
[13] *Op. cit.*, p. 42.
[14] I John 2:17; cf. 2:8.
[15] *Ibid.*, 3:8; 5:4-5.

—it is also taken for granted that Jesus Christ has come to expiate the sins of the world, which probably means in I John the expiation of the sins of all men, regarded more or less individually. Though there is no statement here that the Christian is obliged to participate in the work of the social institutions, to maintain or convert them, neither is there any express rejection of the state or of property as such. Doubtless the end of "the world" seemed so near to the writer that he found no occasion for counsel on these points; all that was required under the circumstances was loyalty to Jesus Christ and to the brotherhood, without concern for the transitory culture.

Similar, though less profound, expressions of the same attitude are to be found in other Christian writings of the second century, while Tertullian stated it in radical fashion. The best-loved books of the time, such as *The Teaching of the Twelve*, *The Shepherd of Hermas*, *The Epistle of Barnabas*, and the *First Epistle of Clement*, present Christianity as a way of life quite separate from culture. Some of them are more legalistic than I John, setting forth the meaning of Christ's Lordship almost solely in terms of the laws given by him or in Scriptures, and regarding the new life under divine mercy more as a reward to be earned by obedience than as free gift and present reality.[16] But whether grace or law is emphasized as the essence of the Christian life, in any case it is life in a new and separated community. The idea which is common to second-century statements of this type is the conviction that Christians constitute a new people, a third "race" besides Jews and Gentiles. So Clement writes, "God, who seeth all things and who is the ruler of all spirits and the Lord of all flesh . . . chose our Lord Jesus Christ and us through him to be a peculiar people."[17] As

[16] Cf. Lietzmann, H., *The Beginnings of the Christian Church*, 1937, pp. 261-273.
[17] *I Clement* lxiv, 1; cf. *Epistle of Barnabas*, xiii-xiv.

Harnack has summarized the beliefs of these early Christians,
they were persuaded that "1) our people is older than the
world; 2) the world was created for our sakes; 3) the world is
carried on for our sakes; we retard the judgment of the world;
4) everything in the world is subject to us and must serve us;
5) everything in the world, the beginning and course and end
of all history, is revealed to us and lies transparent to our eyes;
6) we shall take part in the judgment of the world and ourselves
enjoy eternal bliss."[18] The fundamental conviction, however,
was the idea that this new society, race, or people, had been
established by Jesus Christ, who was its lawgiver and King. The
corollary of the whole conception was the thought that whatever
does not belong to the commonwealth of Christ is under the
rule of evil. This came to expression in the doctrine of the two
ways: "two ways there are, one of life and one of death, but
there is a great difference between the two ways."[19] The way
of life was the Christian way. It was expounded by the rehears-
ing of the commandments of the new law, such as the commandments to love God and neighbor, the Golden Rule, the counsels
to love the enemy and not to resist evil; certain injunctions
drawn from the Old Testament were, however, also included.
The way of death was described simply as the vicious course of
life, so that the plain alternative was to be either a Christian
or a wicked man. There seems to be in this Christian ethic no
recognition of the fact that in a society where gospel rules are
not acknowledged some rules are nevertheless in force; and that

[18] Harnack, A., *Mission and Expansion of Christianity in the First Three
Centuries*, 1904, Vol. I, p. 302; cf. Gavin, Frank, *Church and Society in the Second Century*, 1934, which draws a picture of primitive Christian life—chiefly on
the basis of Hippolytus' *Apostolic Tradition*—as dominated by the sense of its
"corporate and social quality." "It was as if to say that the proudest boast of the
believer was that he was a 'member.' His most essential quality was that he
'belonged.'" P. 3; cf. pp. 5, 8.

[19] *The Teaching of the Twelve Apostles*, i, 1; cf. *Barnabas*, xix-xx; *Shepherd
of Hermas*, Mand. 6, i.

as there are virtues and vices in the domain of Christ so there are also virtues and vices relative to the standards of non-Christian culture. The line was sharply drawn between the new people and the old society, between obedience to the law of Christ and simple lawlessness; though some concession to the presence of divine government in and over cultural institutions is to be found in Clement's prayer "that we may be obedient to thy almighty and glorious name, and to our rulers and governors upon the earth." He recognized, as he goes on to say, that "Thou, Master, hast given the power of sovereignty to them through thy excellent and inexpressible might, that we may know the glory and honor given to them by thee, and be subject to them, in nothing resisting thy will."[20]

The most explicit and, apart from New Testament writers, doubtless the greatest representative in early Christianity of the "Christ-against-culture" type was Tertullian. One must hasten to add that he does not wholly conform to our hypothetical pattern, but demonstrates traits that relate him to other families and types. He is a Trinitarian who understands that the God Who reveals Himself in Jesus Christ is the Creator and the Spirit also; but within that context he maintains the absolute authority of Jesus Christ, "the supreme Head and Master of [God's promised] grace and discipline, the Enlightener and Trainer of the human race, God's own Son."[21] Tertullian's loyalty to Christ can express itself in such radical terms as the following: "Christ Jesus our Lord (may he bear with me a moment in thus expressing myself!), whosoever he is, of what God soever he is the Son, of what substance soever he is man and God, of what faith soever he is the teacher, of what reward soever he is the promiser, did, whilst he lived on earth himself

[20] *I Clement* lx, 4-lxi, 1.
[21] *Apology*, chap. xxi. This and the following quotations are taken from the translation of Tertullian's works in *Ante-Nicene Fathers*, Vols. III and IV.

declare what he was, what he had been, what the Father's will was which he was administering, what the duty of man was which he was prescribing."[22] In every case the primary Christian reference is to Christ "as the Power of God and the Spirit of God, as the Word, the Reason, the Wisdom and the Son of God," and the Christian confession is, "We say, and before all men we say, and torn and bleeding under . . . tortures we cry out, 'We worship God through Christ.' "[23] With this concentration on the Lordship of Jesus Christ Tertullian combines a rigorous morality of obedience to his commandments, including not only love of the brothers but of enemies, nonresistance to evil, prohibitions of anger and the lustful look. He is as strict a Puritan in his interpretation of what Christian faith demands in conduct as one can find.[24] He replaces the positive and warm ethics of love which characterizes the First Letter of John with a largely negative morality; avoidance of sin and fearsome preparation for the coming day of judgment seem more important than thankful acceptance of God's grace in the gift of his Son.

Tertullian's rejection of the claims of culture is correspondingly sharp. The conflict of the believer is not with nature but with culture, for it is in culture that sin chiefly resides. Tertullian comes very close to the thought that original sin is transmitted through society, and that if it were not for the vicious customs that surround a child from its birth and for its artificial training its soul would remain good. The universe and the soul are naturally good, for God is their maker, yet "we must not consider merely by whom all things were made, but by whom they have been perverted," and that "there is a vast difference

---

[22] *The Prescription Against Heretics*, chap. xx.
[23] *Apology*, xxiii, xx.
[24] Cf. *Apology*, xxxix, xlv; *De Spectaculis*; *De Corona*; *On Repentance*.

between the corrupted state and that of primal purity."[25] How much corruption and civilization coincide in Tertullian's thought is partly indicated in the reflection that Christ came not to bring "boors and savages . . . into some civilization . . . ; but as one who aimed to enlighten men already civilized, and under illusions from their very culture, that they might come to the knowledge of the truth."[26]

It becomes more evident when one notes what the vices are that he condemns and what the worldliness is that the Christian is required to shun. The most vicious thing, of course, is social, pagan religion, with its polytheism and idolatry, its beliefs and rites, its sensuality and its commercialization.[27] Such religion, however, is interfused with all the other activities and institutions of society, so that the Christian is in constant danger of compromising his loyalty to the Lord. Tertullian, to be sure, rejects the charge that believers are "useless in the affairs of life," for, he says, "we sojourn with you in the world, abjuring neither forum, nor shambles, nor bath, nor booth, nor inn, nor weekly market, nor any other places of commerce." He even adds, "We sail with you, and fight with you, and till the ground with you; and in like manner we unite with you in your traffickings—even in the various arts we make public property of our works for your benefit."[28] This, however, is said in defense. When he admonishes believers his counsel is to withdraw from many meetings and many occupations, not only because they are corrupted by their relation to pagan faith but because they

[25] The quotation is from *De Spectaculis,* ii. For the doctrine of the natural goodness of the soul see *Apology,* xvii, *The Soul's Testimony,* and *A Treatise on the Soul,* chapter xxxix of which speaks of the corruption of the soul through customs; but cf. chap. xli.

[26] *Apology,* xxi.

[27] *On Idolatry; Apology,* x-xv.

[28] *Apology,* xlii.

require a mode of life contrary to the spirit and the law of
Christ.

So political life is to be shunned. "As those in whom all ardor
in the pursuit of honor and glory is dead," writes Tertullian
even in defense, "we have no pressing inducement to take part
in your public meetings; nor is there aught more entirely foreign to us than affairs of state."[29] There is an inner contradic-
tion between the exercise of political power and Christian faith.
Military service is to be avoided because it involves participation
in pagan religious rites and the swearing of an oath to Caesar,
but chiefly because it violates the law of Christ, who, "in dis-
arming Peter, unbelted every soldier." How "shall the son of
peace take part in battle when it does not become him even to
sue at law?"[30] Trade cannot be prohibited with equal rigor,
and there may even be some righteousness in business, yet it
is scarcely "adapted for a servant of God," for apart from covet-
ousness, which is a species of idolatry, there is no real motive
for acquiring.[31]

When Tertullian turns to philosophy and the arts he is, if
anything, more drastic in pronouncing prohibitions than he is
in the case of the soldier's occupation. He has no sympathy with
the efforts of some Christians of his time to point out positive
connections between their faith and the ideas of the Greek
philosophers. "Away,' he exclaims, "with all attempts to produce a mottled Christianity of Stoic, Platonic and dialectic
composition. We want no curious disputation after possessing
Jesus Christ. . . . With our faith we desire no further belief."[32]

[29] *Ibid.*, xxxviii. Elsewhere, in chap. xxi, Tertullian remarks that "Caesars
too would have believed in Christ, if either the Caesars had not been necessary
for the world, or if Christians could have been Caesars."
[30] *On Idolatry*, xix; *De Corona*, xi.
[31] *On Idolatry*, xi.
[32] *Prescription Against Heretics*, vii; *Apology*, xlvi.

In Socrates' daimon he discovers an evil demon; the disciples of Greece have for him nothing in common with "the disciples of heaven"; they corrupt the truth, they seek their own fame, they are mere talkers rather than doers. In so far as he must concede the presence of some truth in these non-Christian thinkers, he believes that they derived their insights from the Scriptures. The stain of corruption pervades the arts also. Literary erudition, to be sure, cannot be wholly avoided, therefore "learning literature is allowable for believers"; but teaching it must be discountenanced, for it is impossible to be a professor of literature without commending and affirming "the praises of idols interspersed therein."[33] As for the theater, not only the games with their levity and brutality, but tragedy and even music are ministers of sin. Tertullian seems to delight in his vision of the last judgment, when the illustrious monarchs who had been deified by men, the wise men of the world, the philosophers, poets, and tragedians, along with play-actors and wrestlers, will groan in the lowest darkness or be tossed in the fiery billows, while the carpenter's son they despised is exalted in glory.[34]

The great North African theologian seems, then, to present the epitome of the "Christ-against-culture" position. Yet he sounds both more radical and more consistent than he really was.[35] As we shall have occasion to note, he could not in fact emancipate himself and the church from reliance on and participation in culture, pagan though it was. Nevertheless he remains one of the foremost illustrations of the anticultural movement to be found in the history of the church.

[33] *On Idolatry*, x.
[34] *De Spectaculis*, xxx.
[35] Cf. Cochrane, C. N., *Christianity and Classical Culture*, 1940, pp. 222 ff., 227 ff., 245 f. For further discussions of Tertullian's ethics see Guignebert, Charles, *Tertullien, Étude sur ses Sentiments a l'Égard de l'Empire et de la Societé Civile*, 1901, and Brandt, Theodor, *Tertullians Ethik*, 1929.

II. Tolstoy's Rejection of Culture

We shall not undertake to describe how this *motif* in early Christianity was developed in the monastic movement, with its withdrawal from the institutions and societies of civilization, from family and state, from school and socially established church, from trade and industry. Eventually, of course, many sorts of monasticism arose and some of the varieties occupied positions quite distinct from those of Tertullian and the First Letter of John. Yet the main stream of the movement, as represented for instance by the *Rule of St. Benedict*, remained in the tradition of exclusive Christianity. Whatever contributions it eventually made to culture, including the recognized social religion, were incidental byproducts which it did not intend. Its intention was directed to the achievement of a Christian life, apart from civilization, in obedience to the laws of Christ, and in pursuit of a perfection wholly distinct from the aims that men seek in politics and economics, in sciences and arts. Protestant sectarianism—to use that term in its narrow, sociological meaning—has given the same sort of answer to the question of Christ and culture. Out of the many sects that arose in the sixteenth and seventeenth centuries, protesting against the worldly church, both Catholic and Protestant, and seeking to live under the Lordship of Christ alone, only a few survive. The Mennonites have come to represent the attitude most purely, since they not only renounce all participation in politics and refuse to be drawn into military service, but follow their own distinctive customs and regulations in economics and education. The Society of Friends, never as radical, represents the type less adequately; though the family resemblance can be noted, especially in connection with the practice of brotherly love and the abstention from military service. By and large, however, the modern Quaker shows greater affinity to the opposite attitude in Christianity, the one which regards Christ as the representative of culture.[36] Hundreds of other groups, many of them evanescent, and thousands of individuals, have felt themselves compelled by loyalty to Christ to withdraw from culture and to give up all responsibility for the world. We meet them in all times and in many lands. In the nineteenth and early twentieth centuries they did not attract much attention, for most Christians seemed to believe that another answer to their problem had been finally established. But there was one man who in his own way and under the circumstances of his own time and place stated the radical position as vehemently and consistently as Tertullian. That man was Leo Tolstoy. He is worth our special attention, because of the great and dramatic manner in which he presented his convictions in life and art, and because of the pervasiveness of his influence in West and East, in Christianity and beyond it.

The great crisis Tolstoy met in his middle years was resolved, after many painful struggles, when he accepted the Jesus Christ of the Gospels as his sole and explicit authority. Noble by birth, wealthy by inheritance, famous by his own achievements as the author of *War and Peace* and *Anna Karenina*, he yet found himself threatened in his own life by the meaninglessness of existence and the tawdriness of all the values that his society esteemed. He could not rise from this despair into tranquillity, and from the full stoppage of life into new activity, until he recognized the fallibility of all other authorities and acknowledged the teaching of Jesus as inescapable truth, founded on

---

[36] The best discussion, within the compass of one work, of the ethics of medieval and modern sectarianism is to be found in Troeltsch, E., *The Social Teachings of the Christian Churches*, 1931, pp. 328 ff., 691 ff.

reality.[37] Jesus Christ was for Tolstoy always the great lawgiver, whose commandments were in accordance with man's true nature and with the demands of uncorrupted reason. His conversion centered in the realization that what Jesus had really done was to give men a new law, and that this law was based on the nature of things. "I have understood," he writes in describing the great change in his life, "Christ's teaching in his commandments and I see that their fulfillment offers blessedness to me and to all men. I have understood that the execution of these commandments is the will of that Source of all from which my life also has come. . . . In its fulfillment lies the only possibility of salvation. . . . And having understood this, I understood and believed that Jesus is not only the Messiah, the Christ, but that he is really the Saviour of the world. I know that there is no other exit either for me or for all those who together with me are tormented in this life. I know that for all, and for me together with them, there is no way of escape except by fulfilling those commands of Christ which offer to all humanity the highest welfare of which I can conceive."[38] The literalness with which Tolstoy interpreted the new law, as found particularly in the fifth chapter of the Gospel according to St. Matthew, and the rigorousness of his obedience to it, made his conversion a very radical event. In the little book entitled *What I Believe* or *My Religion* he relates the story of his effort to understand the New Testament, and of his release from struggle when he at last discovered that Jesus' words were to be literally interpreted, with all ecclesiastical glosses on the text eliminated. Then it became clear that Christ's commandments were a statement of

[37] Cf. Preface to "The Christian Teaching," Vol. XII, pp. 209 ff. of *The Tolstoy Centenary Edition*, London, 1928-37. (This edition will hereafter be cited as *Works*.) Cf. also "A Confession," *Works*, Vol. XI, pp. 3 ff.; "What I Believe," Vol. XI, pp. 307 ff.

[38] "What I Believe," *Works*, Vol. XI, pp. 447, 448.

God's eternal law, that he had abolished the law of Moses, and had not come, as the church inclined to say, to reinforce the old law or to teach that he was the second person of the Trinity.[39] Tolstoy believed that he was interpreting the gospel faithfully when he undertook to summarize this new law in five definite injunctions. The first commandment was: "Live at peace with all men and never consider your anger against any man justified. . . . Try in advance to destroy any enmity between yourself and others that it may not flame up and destroy you." The second: "Do not make the desire for sexual relations an amusement. Let every man have a wife and each wife a husband and let the husband have only *one* wife and the wife only *one* husband, and under no pretext infringe the sexual union of one with the other." The "definite and practicable third commandment is clearly expressed: Never take an oath to anyone, anywhere, about anything. Every oath is extorted for evil ends." The fourth commandment destroys "the stupid and bad" social order in which men live, for simply, clearly, and practically it says: "Never resist the evildoer by force, do not meet violence with violence. If they beat you, endure it; if they take your possessions, yield them up; if they compel you to work, work; and if they wish to take from you what you consider to be yours, give it up." The final commandment, enjoining love of the enemy, Tolstoy understood as the "definite, important, and practicable rule . . . : not to make distinctions between one's own and other nations and not to do all the things that flow from making such distinctions; not to bear enmity to foreign nations; not to make war or to take part in warfare; not to arm oneself for war, but to behave to all men, of whatever race they may be, as we behave to our own people."[40] Through the

[39] *Ibid.,* pp. 353 ff., 370 ff.
[40] *Ibid.,* pp. 376 f., 386, 390, 392 f., 398, 404. Cf. "The Gospel in Brief," *Works,* Vol. XI, pp. 163-167.

promulgation of these five laws, Tolstoy believed, Christ had established the kingdom of God; though it is clear that the law of nonresistance was for him the key to the whole.

As in the case of other examples of this type which we have considered, the counterpart of such devotion to the commandments of Jesus Christ is a thoroughgoing opposition to the institutions of culture. To Tolstoy these seem to be founded on a complex foundation of errors, including the acceptance of the inevitability of evil in man's present life, the belief that life is governed by external laws so that men cannot attain blessedness by their own efforts, the fear of death, the identification of true life with personal existence, and, above all, the practice of and belief in violence. Even less than Tertullian does he think that human corruption is resident in human nature; the evil with which men contend is in their culture only. Moreover, Tolstoy seems to have little understanding of the extent and depth to which culture enters into human nature. Hence he can center his attack on the conscious beliefs, the tangible institutions, and the specious customs of society. He is not content simply to withdraw from these himself and to live a semimonastic life; he becomes a crusader against culture under the banner of the law of Christ.

Every phase of culture falls under indictment. Though state, church, and property system are the citadels of evil, philosophy and sciences and arts also come under condemnation. There is no such thing as good government for Tolstoy. "The revolutionaries say: 'The government organization is bad in this and that respect; it must be destroyed and replaced by this and that.' But a Christian says: 'I know nothing about the governmental organization, or in how far it is good or bad, and for the same reason I do not want to support it.' . . . All the state obligations are against the conscience of a Christian: the oath of allegiance, taxes, law proceedings and military service."[41] The state and Christian faith are simply incompatible; for the state is based on love of power and the exercise of violence, whereas the love, humility, forgiveness, and nonresistance of Christian life draw it completely away from political measures and institutions. Christianity does not so much make the state unnecessary as sap its foundations and destroy it from within. The argument of such Christians as Paul who contend that the state performs an interim function in restraining evil does not appeal to Tolstoy, for he sees the state as the chief offender against life.[42] Against its evil there is no defense except complete nonparticipation, and nonviolent striving for the conversion of all men to peaceful, anarchic Christianity.

Though the churches call themselves Christian, they are equally far removed from the Christianity of Jesus. Tolstoy regards them as self-centered organizations that assert their own infallibility; servants of the state, defenders of the reign of violence and privilege, of inequality and property; obscurers and falsifiers of the gospel. "The Churches as Churches . . . are anti-Christian institutions," utterly hostile in their "pride, violence, and self-assertion, immobility and death" to the "humility, penitence, meekness, progress and life" of Christianity.[43] As in the case of states, reformation of such institutions is wholly inadequate. Christ did not found them, and comprehension of his doctrine will not reform but will "destroy the churches and their significance."[44] To this theme, as to the criticism of the state, Tolstoy returns again and again. The church is an invention of the devil; no honest man believing the gospel can remain priest or preacher; all the churches are alike in their

---

[41] "The Kingdom of God Is Within You," *Works*, Vol. XX, pp. 275 f.
[42] *Ibid.*, pp. 281 ff.
[43] *Ibid.*, p. 82.
[44] *Ibid.*, pp. 69, 101.

betrayal of Christ's law; churches and states together represent the institutionalization of violence and fraud.[45]

Tolstoy's attack on economic institutions is equally intransigent. His own effort to renounce property while yet retaining some responsibility for its administration constitutes part of his personal tragedy. He believed that property claims were based on robbery and maintained by violence. More radical than second-century radical Christians and than most monks, he turned even against the subdivision of labor in economic society. It seemed to him to be the means by which privileged persons, such as artists, intellectuals, and their kind, absorbed the labor of others, justifying themselves by the belief that they were beings of a higher order than workingmen, or that their contribution to society was so great that it compensated for the harm they did by overburdening manual workers with their claims. The first supposition has been exploded by Christian teaching about human equality; the contribution made to society by the privileged is dubious when it is not patently mischievous. Hence Tolstoy urges the intellectuals, as well as landlords and military men in society, to stop deceiving themselves, to renounce their own righteousness, advantages, and distinctions, to labor with all their power to sustain their own lives and those of others by manual labor. Following his own principles, he attempted to be his own tailor and cobbler, and would have liked to be his own gardener and cook.[46]

Like Tertullian, Tolstoy also turned against philosophy and

[45] Cf. "The Restoration of Hell," a remarkable little fable in which the re-establishment of the reign of evil on earth after Christ's victory is explained particularly by the invention of the church. The devil who invented it explains to Beelzebub, "I have arranged it so that men do not believe in Christ's teaching but in mine, which they call by his name." *Works*, Vol. XII, pp. 309 ff. Cf. also "Religion and Morality," "What is Religion?" "Church and State," "An Appeal to the Clergy," in the same volume.

[46] "What Then Must We Do?" *Works*, Vol. XIV, pp. 209 ff., 269 ff., 311 ff.

the sciences and arts in which he had been nurtured. The first
two are not only useless, because they fail to answer the fundamental questions of man about the meaning and conduct of
life, but are bad because they rest on falsehood. The experi-
mental sciences devote great energies to confirm a dogma that
makes the whole enterprise false, namely the dogma that "matter and energy exist," while they do nothing to ameliorate man's
actual life. "I am convinced," writes Tolstoy, "that a few centuries hence the so-called 'scientific' activity of our belauded
recent centuries of European humanity will furnish an inex-
tinguishable fund of mirth and pity to future generations."[47]
Philosophy leads us no further than to the knowledge that all is
vanity; but "what is hidden to the wise and prudent is revealed
to babes." The common peasant who follows the Sermon on
the Mount knows what the great and wise cannot understand.
"Special talents and intellectual gifts are needed, not for the
knowledge and statement of truth but for the invention and
statement of falsehood."[48] The artist Tolstoy could not make
quite as complete a break with the arts. He at least made a
distinction between good art and bad. To the latter category
he consigned all his own former work, save for two small stories,
all "genteel" art designed for the privileged classes, and even
Hamlet and the *Ninth Symphony.* But he allowed a place for
an art that was a sincere expression and communication of feeling, that had universal appeal, was comprehensible by the
masses of men, and was in accord with Christian moral consciousness.[49] Hence in so far as he did not devote his great
literary talents to the writing of homilies and tracts on non-

[47] "What I Believe," *Works,* Vol. XI, p. 420; cf. "A Confession," Vol. XI, pp.
23 ff.; "On Life," Vol. XII, pp. 12 f.
[48] "Reason and Religion," *Works,* Vol. XII, p. 202; cf. "A Confession," Vol.
XI, pp. 56 ff., 73 f.
[49] "What Is Art?" *Works.* Vol. XVIII, pp. 291 ff.

resistance and true religion, he produced parables and stories such as "Where Love Is There God Is" and "Master and Man."

Tolstoy of course no more conforms completely to our type than any other great individual conforms to a pattern. He is like the author of I John in his praise of love and his rejection of the "lust of the flesh, the lust of the eyes, and the pride of life." He is like Tertullian in the vehemence of his attack on social institutions. He is like the monks in his personal withdrawal into a life of poverty. But he differs from all these in his relation to Jesus Christ, for one finds in them a personal devotion to a personal Lord which is strangely lacking in Tolstoy. For him the law of Christ is much more significant than the person of the lawgiver. Maxim Gorky has remarked that when Tolstoy spoke of Christ there was "no enthusiasm, no feeling in his words, and no spark of real fire."[50] The writings in general bear out that judgment. Moreover, Tolstoy shows little understanding for the meaning of the grace of God manifested in Jesus Christ, for the historical nature of Christian revelation, for the psychological, moral, and spiritual depths of both corruption and salvation. Hence he was more of a legalist than even the legal Tertullian. Yet in modern history and under the conditions of the modern culture of which he was in part a product, Tolstoy remains a clear-cut example of anticultural Christianity.[51]

It would be easy to multiply illustrations of the type. Described one after the other they would constitute a very diverse group, including Eastern and Western Catholics, orthodox and sectarian Protestants, millenarians and mystics, ancient and medieval and modern Christians. Yet their unity of spirit would also be apparent in their common acknowledgment of the sole

[50] Gorky, Maxim, *Reminiscences of Leo Nikolaevich Tolstoy*, 1920, p. 5.
[51] For full descriptions of Tolstoy's life and works see Aylmer Maude's *Life of Tolstoy* and Ernest J. Simmon's *Leo Tolstoy*.

authority of Jesus Christ and the common rejection of the prevailing culture. Whether that culture calls itself Christian or not is of no importance, for to these men it is always pagan and corrupt. Neither is it of first-rate significance whether such Christians think in apocalyptic or in mystical terms. As apocalyptics they will prophesy the early passing of the old society and the coming into history of a new divine order. As mystics they will experience and announce the reality of an eternal order hidden by the specious temporal and cultural scene. The significant question to be asked about Christians in this respect is not whether they think historically or mystically about the kingdom of God; but rather whether they are convinced of its nearness and are governed by this conviction, or whether they think of it as relatively remote in time or space and relatively ineffective in power. Neither are the differences between Protestants and Catholics decisive. Monastic characteristics reappear in Protestant sectarians; and a Lutheran Kierkegaard attacks the Christendom of post-Reformation culture with the same intransigence that marks a Wiclif's thrust against medieval social faith. Various and diverse though these men and movements are, they give a recognizably common answer to the problem of Christ and culture.

III. A Necessary and Inadequate Position

It is easy to raise objections to this solution of the Christian dilemma. Yet intelligent Christians who cannot conscientiously take this position themselves will recognize the sincerity of most of its exponents, and its importance in history and the need for it in the total encounter of church and world.

Half-baked and muddle-headed men abound in the anticultural movement as well as elsewhere; doubtless hypocrisy flourishes here too. Yet the single-heartedness and sincerity of the great representatives of this type are among their most attractive qualities. There has been a kind of Kierkegaardian "reduplication" in their lives, for they have expressed in their actions what they said in words. They have not taken easy ways in professing their allegiance to Christ. They have endured physical and mental sufferings in their willingness to abandon homes, property, and the protection of government for the sake of his cause. They have accepted the derision and animosity which societies inflict on nonconformists. From the persecutions of Christians under Domitian to the imprisonment of Jehovah's Witnesses in national-socialist Germany and democratic America, such people have been subject to martyrdom. In so far as Christian pacifists in our time belong to this group—not all of them do—their sufferings will seem to themselves and others to be more evidently due to obedience to Jesus Christ than is the case when a Christian soldier suffers and dies. Part of the appeal of the "Christ-against-culture" answer lies in this evident reduplication of profession in conduct. When we make it we seem to be proving to ourselves and others that we mean what we say when we say that Jesus Christ is our Lord.

In history these Christian withdrawals from and rejections of the institutions of society have been of very great importance to both church and culture. They have maintained the distinction between Christ and Caesar, between revelation and reason, between God's will and man's. They have led to reformations in both church and world, though this was never their intention. Hence men and movements of this sort are often celebrated for their heroic roles in the history of a culture which they rejected. What Montalembert said of Benedict of Nursia applies in one way or another to almost all the great representatives of exclusive Christianity: "Historians have vied in praising his genius and clear-sightedness; they have supposed that he intended to regenerate Europe, to stop the dissolution of society, to prepare the reconstitution of political order, to re-establish public education, and to preserve literature and the arts. . . . I firmly believe that he never dreamt of regenerating anything but his own soul and those of his brethren, the monks."[52] Doubtless the individualistic ideal of soul-regeneration is not an adequate key to the attitude of radical Christians; but neither is the hope of social reform. In social reform they accomplish what they did not intend. Second-century believers who had no interest in the rule of Caesar prepared the way for the social triumph of the church and the conversion of the pagan world into a Christian civilization. Monasticism eventually became one of the great conservers and transmitters of cultural tradition; it trained many great ecclesiastical and political leaders of society; it strengthened the institutions from which its founders had withdrawn. Protestant sectarians made important contributions to political customs and traditions, such as those which guarantee religious liberty to all members of a society. Quakers and Tolstoyans, intending only to abolish all methods of coercion, have helped to reform prisons, to limit armaments, and to establish international organizations for the maintenance of peace through coercion.

Now that we have recognized the importance of the role played by anticultural Christians in the reform of culture, we must immediately point out that they never achieved these results alone or directly but only through the mediation of believers who gave a different answer to the fundamental question. Not Tertullian, but Origen, Clement of Alexandria, Ambrose, and Augustine initiated the reformation of Roman culture. Not Benedict, but Francis, Dominic, and Bernard of Clairvaux accomplished the reform of medieval society often credited to

[52] De Montalembert, *The Monks of the West*, 1896, Vol. I, p. 436.

Benedict. Not George Fox, but William Penn and John Woolman, changed social institutions in England and America. And in every case the followers did not so much compromise the teachings of the radicals as follow another inspiration than the one deriving from an exclusive loyalty to an exclusive Christ.

Yet the radically Christian answer to the problem of culture needed to be given in the past, and doubtless needs to be given now. It must be given for its own sake, and because without it other Christian groups lose their balance. The relation of the authority of Jesus Christ to the authority of culture is such that every Christian must often feel himself claimed by the Lord to reject the world and its kingdoms with their pluralism and temporalism, their makeshift compromises of many interests, their hypnotic obsession by the love of life and the fear of death. The movement of withdrawal and renunciation is a necessary element in every Christian life, even though it be followed by an equally necessary movement of responsible engagement in cultural tasks. Where this is lacking, Christian faith quickly degenerates into a utilitarian device for the attainment of personal prosperity or public peace; and some imagined idol called by his name takes the place of Jesus Christ the Lord. What is necessary in the individual life is required also in the existence of the church. If Romans 13 is not balanced by I John, the church becomes an instrument of state, unable to point men to their transpolitical destiny and their suprapolitical loyalty; unable also to engage in political tasks, save as one more group of power-hungry or security-seeking men. Given Jesus Christ with his authority, the radical answer is inevitable; not only when men are in despair about their civilization, but also when they are complacent, not only as they hope for a kingdom of God, but also as they shore up the crumbling walls of temporal societies for the sake of the men who might be buried under their ruins. So long as eternity cannot be translated into temporal terms nor time into eternity, so long as Christ and culture cannot be amalgamated, so long is the radical answer inevitable in the church.

It is an inevitable answer; but it is also inadequate, as members of other groups in the church can easily point out. It is inadequate, for one thing, because it affirms in words what it denies in action; namely, the possibility of sole dependence on Jesus Christ to the exclusion of culture. Christ claims no man purely as a natural being, but always as one who has become human in a culture; who is not only in culture, but into whom culture has penetrated. Man not only speaks but thinks with the aid of the language of culture. Not only has the objective world about him been modified by human achievement; but the forms and attitudes of his mind which allow him to make sense out of the objective world have been given him by culture. He cannot dismiss the philosophy and science of his society as though they were external to him; they are in him—though in different forms from those in which they appear in the leaders of culture. He cannot rid himself of political beliefs and economic customs by rejecting the more or less external institutions; these customs and beliefs have taken up residence in his mind. If Christians do not come to Christ with the language, the thought patterns, the moral disciplines of Judaism, they come with those of Rome; if not with those of Rome, then with those of Germany, England, Russia, America, India, or China. Hence the radical Christians are always making use of the culture, or parts of the culture, which ostensibly they reject. The writer of I John employs the terms of that Gnostic philosophy to whose pagan use he objects.[53] Clement of Rome uses semi-Stoic ideas. In almost every utterance Tertullian makes

53 Cf. Dodd, C. H., *op. cit.,* xx, xxix, xlii, *et passim.*

evident that he is a Roman, so nurtured in the legal tradition and so dependent on philosophy that he cannot state the Christian case without their aid.[54] Tolstoy becomes intelligible when he is interpreted as a nineteenth century Russian who participates, in the depths of his unconscious soul as well as consciously, in the cultural movements of his time, and in the Russian mystic sense of community with men and nature. It is so with all the members of the radical Christian group. When they meet Christ they do so as heirs of a culture which they cannot reject because it is a part of them. They can withdraw from its more obvious institutions and expressions; but for the most part they can only select—and modify under Christ's authority —something they have received through the mediation of society.

The conservation, selection, and conversion of cultural achievements is not only a fact; it is also a morally inescapable requirement, which the exclusive Christian must meet because he is a Christian and a man. If he is to confess Jesus before men, he must do so by means of words and ideas derived from culture, though a change of meaning is also necessary. He must use such words as "Christ" or "Messiah" or "Kyrios" or "Son of God" or "Logos." If he is to say what "love" means he must choose among such words as *"eros," "philanthropia"* and *"agape,"* or "charity," "loyalty," and "love"—seeking one that comes close to the meaning of Jesus Christ, and modifying it by use in context. These things he must do, not only that he may communicate, but also that he may himself know whom and what he believes. When he undertakes to fulfill the demands of Jesus Christ, he finds himself partly under the necessity of translating into the terms of his own culture what was commanded

[54] Cf. Shortt, C. De Lisle, *The Influence of Philosophy on the Mind of Tertullian,* and Beck, Alexander, *Roemisches Recht bei Tertullian und Cyprian.*

in the terms of another, partly under the requirement of giving precision and meaning to general principles by adopting specific rules relevant to his social life. What is the meaning of Jesus' statements about the Sabbath in a society which does not celebrate such a day? Is it to be introduced and modified, or left aside as a part of an alien, non-Christian culture? What is the meaning of praying to a Father in heaven, in a culture with a cosmology differing radically from that of Palestine in the first century? How shall demons be cast out where they are not believed to exist? There is no escape from culture here; the alternative seems to be between the effort to reproduce the culture in which Jesus lived, or to translate his words into those of another social order. Furthermore, the command to love the neighbor cannot be obeyed except in specific terms that involve cultural understanding of the neighbor's nature, and except in specific acts directed toward him as a being who has a place in culture, as member of family or religious community, as national friend or enemy, as rich or poor. In his effort to be obedient to Christ, the radical Christian therefore reintroduces ideas and rules from non-Christian culture in two areas: in the government of the withdrawn Christian community, and in the regulation of Christian conduct toward the world outside.

The tendency in exclusive Christianity is to confine the commandments of loyalty to Christ, of love of God and neighbor, to the fellowship of Christians. Here also the other gospel requirements are to be enforced. But, as Martin Dibelius among many others has pointed out, "the words of Jesus were not intended as ethical rules for a Christian culture, and even if they were applied as such they were not sufficient to supply an answer to all the questions of daily life."[55] Other helps were needed; and they were found by early Christians in Jewish and

[55] Dibelius, Martin, *A Fresh Approach to the New Testament*, p. 219.

Hellenistic-Jewish popular ethics. It is remarkable to what extent the ethics of second-century Christianity—as summarized for instance in *The Teaching of the Twelve* and the *Epistle of Barnabas*—contains material extraneous to the New Testament. These Christians, who thought of themselves as a new "race" distinct from Jews and Gentiles, borrowed from the laws and customs of those from whom they had separated what they needed for the common life but had not received from their own authority. The situation is similar in the case of the monastic rules. Benedict of Nursia seeks Scriptural foundation for all his regulations and counsels; but the New Testament does not suffice him, nor does the Bible as a whole; and he must find, in old reflections on human experience in social life, rules by means of which to govern the new community. The spirit in which both Scriptural and non-Scriptural regulations are presented also shows how impossible it is to be only a Christian without reference to culture. When Tertullian recommends modesty and patience, Stoic overtones are always present; and when Tolstoy speaks of nonresistance, Rousseauistic ideas are in the context. Even if no use were made of another inheritance besides that derived from Jesus Christ, the needs of the withdrawn community would lead to the development of a new culture. Invention, human achievement, temporal realization of value, organization of the common life—all must go on in it. When the dogmas and rites of social religion have been abandoned, a new dogma and a new ritual must be developed, if religious practice is to go on at all. Therefore monks work out their own rituals in their monasteries, and Quaker silences become as formalized as masses; Tolstoy's dogmas are as confidently uttered as are those of the Russian church. When the state has been rejected, the exclusively Christian community has necessarily developed some political organization of its own;

and has done so with the aid of other ideas than those derived from the injunction that the first shall be the servant of all. It has called its leaders prophets or abbots, its governing assemblies quarterly meetings or congregations; it has enforced uniformity by means of popular opinion and banishment from the society; but in any case it has sought to maintain internal order, not only generally but in a specific way of life. Prevailing property institutions have been set aside; but something more than the counsel to sell all and give to the poor has been necessary, since men had to eat and be clothed and sheltered even in poverty. Hence ways and means of acquiring and distributing goods were devised, and a new economic culture was established.

In dealing with the society which he regards as pagan, but from which he never succeeds in separating himself completely, the radical Christian has also always been required to take recourse to principles he could not derive directly from his conviction of Christ's Lordship. His problem here has been that of living in an interim. Whether exclusive Christians are eschatologists or spiritualists, in either case they must take account of the "meanwhile," the interval between the dawning of the new order of life and its victory, the period in which the temporal and material has not yet been transformed into the spiritual. They cannot separate themselves completely, therefore, from the world of culture around them, nor from those needs in themselves which make this culture necessary. Though the whole world lies in darkness, yet distinctions must be made between relative rights and wrongs in that world, and in Christian relations to it. So, Tertullian writing to his wife advises her to remain a widow if he should die first. He disclaims any motive of jealousy or possessiveness, for such carnal motives will be eliminated in the resurrection, and "there will at that day be no resumption of voluptuous disgrace between us." She is to re-

main a widow because Christian law permits only one marriage
and because virginity is better than marriage. Marriage is not
really good but only not evil; indeed, when Jesus says " 'They
were marrying and buying' He sets a brand on the very leading
vices of the flesh and the world, which call men off the most from
divine disciplines." Hence Tertullian counsels his wife to accept
his death as God's call to the great good of a life of continence.
But thereafter he wrote a second letter in which he gave the
"next best advice," to the effect that if she needed to remarry
she should at least "marry in the Lord," that is, marry a Christian and not an unbeliever.[56] In the end one can find in Tertullian a whole scale of relative goods and evils in his estimation of
orders in man's sex-life in the interval before the resurrection.
Compared with virginity, marriage is relatively evil; a single
marriage in a lifetime, however, is relatively good as compared
with second marriage; yet if the evil of second marriage does
take place, marriage with a believer is relatively good. If Tertullian were pressed he might concede that if there were to be
marriage with an unbeliever, a monogamous marriage would
still be a better wickedness than polygamy; and even that in a
disordered world polygamy might be relatively good compared
to wholly irresponsible sex relations.

Other illustrations of the necessity for recognizing laws relative to the time of the interim and to the existence of a pagan
society can be found in the history of Friends who are concerned that since there is a vicious institution of slavery slaves
should be treated "justly"; and since there is buying and selling
a fixed-price policy should prevail. One thinks, too, of Christian
pacifists, who, having rejected the institutions and practices of
warfare as wholly evil, yet seek to have armaments limited and

[56] "To His Wife," (*Ante-Nicene Fathers,* Vol. IV); cf. also "On Monogamy";
"On Exhortation to Chastity."

certain weapons banned. Count Tolstoy's daughter has told the story of her father's tragedy, which was at least in part the tragedy of an exclusive Christian whose responsibilities did not allow him to escape the problems of the "meanwhile." For himself he could choose the life of poverty, but not for wife and children, who did not share his convictions; he did not want the protection of police, and did not need it; but he was a member of a family that required the guardianship of force. So the poor man lived on his own rich estate, unwillingly and with ambiguous responsibility; the nonresister was protected against mobs even at his death. Countess Alexandra relates a story that presents the problem dramatically, and indicates how even Tolstoy needed to recognize that conscience and the rule of right lay their claims on man in the midst of bad institutions. Since he had renounced property but remained bound to his family, responsibility for the management of the estate fell on his wife, who was poorly equipped for the task. Under her inadequate supervision, incompetent or dishonest stewards allowed the property to fall into general disorder. A horrible accident occurred as a result of maladministration—a peasant was buried alive in a neglected sandpit. "I seldom saw father so upset," writes his daughter. " 'Such things can't happen, they can't happen,' he was telling mother. 'If you want an estate you must manage it well, or else give it up altogether.' "[57]

Stories of this sort, which illustrate the adjustments of radical Christians to a rejected and evil but inescapable culture, can be multiplied; and they delight their critics. But surely the delight is premature and unfounded, for such stories only underscore the common Christian dilemma. The difference between the radicals and the other groups is often only this: that the

[57] Tolstoy, Countess Alexandra, *The Tragedy of Count Tolstoy*, 1933, p. 65. cf. pp. 161-165, and Simmons, *op. cit.*, 631 ff., 682 f. *et passim*.

radicals fail to recognize what they are doing, and continue to speak as though they were separated from the world. Sometimes the contradictions are quite explicit in their writings; as in the case of Tertullian, who seems to argue against himself on such subjects as the value of philosophy and government. Often they are implicit, and come to expression only in contradictory conduct. In either case the radical Christian confesses that he has not solved the problem of Christ and culture, but is only seeking a solution along a certain line.

IV. Theological Problems

There are indications in the Christ-against-culture movement that the difficulties the Christian faces as he deals with his dilemma are not only ethical but theological; and that ethical solutions depend quite as much on theological understanding as vice versa. Questions about divine and human nature, about God's action and man's, arise at every point, as the radical Christian undertakes to separate himself from the cultural society, and as he engages in debate with members of other Christian groups. Four of these questions with their radical answers may be briefly sketched here.

The first of these is the problem of reason and revelation. There is a tendency in the radical movement to use the word "reason" to designate the methods and the content of knowledge to be found in cultural society; "revelation" to indicate that Christian knowledge of God and duty that is derived from Jesus Christ and resident in the Christian society. These definitions, then, are connected with the denigration of reason and the exaltation of revelation.[58] Even in I John, the least extreme

[58] The opposition of reason and revelation to each other in this manner is of course not confined to members of the Christ-against-culture movement. Christians who take other positions than the radical one in political or economic matters may adopt the exclusive attitude in dealing with the problem of knowledge.

of our examples, something of this contrast appears, in the opposition of the world of darkness to the realm of light in which Christians walk; and Christians are said to know all things because they have been anointed by the Holy One. Tertullian, of course, is the stock example in history of the position that substitutes revelation for reason. Though he did not say, "I believe because it is absurd," in the sense in which that statement is usually ascribed to him, he did write, "You will not be 'wise' unless you become a 'fool' to the world, by believing 'the foolish things of God.' . . . The Son of God was crucified; I am not ashamed because men must needs be ashamed of it. The Son of God died; it is by all means to be believed, because it is absurd [*prorsus credibile est, quia ineptum es*]. And He was buried and rose again; the fact is certain, because it is impossible."[59] But it is not so much the vigor of this confession of belief in the common Christian doctrine that makes him the great exponent of the antirational defense of revelation, as those attacks on philosophy and cultural wisdom to which we have previously referred. A similar attitude toward cultural reason is to be found in many monastics, in the early Quakers and other Protestant sectarians; it is characteristic of Tolstoy. Human reason as it flourishes in culture is for these men not only inadequate because it does not lead to knowledge of God and the truth necessary to salvation; but it is also erroneous and deceptive. Yet it is true that few of them find the rejection of reason and the acceptance of revelation in its stead sufficient. With Tertullian and Tolstoy, they distinguish between the simple, "natural" knowledge that the uncorrupted human soul possesses, and the vitiated understanding that is to be found in culture; furthermore, they tend to make a distinction between the revelation given by the spirit or the inner light, and that

[59] *On the Flesh of Christ*, ch. v.

which is historically given and transmitted through the Scriptures. They cannot solve their problem of Christ and culture without recognizing that distinctions must be made both with respect to the reasoning that goes on outside the Christian sphere and to the knowledge that is present in it.

Secondly, the question about the nature and prevalence of sin is involved in the answer to the Christ-and-culture question. The logical answer of the radical seems to be that sin abounds in culture, but that Christians have passed out of darkness into the light, and that a fundamental reason for separation from the world is the preservation of the holy community from corruption. Some of them, for instance certain Friends and Tolstoy, regard the doctrine of original sin itself as a measure by means of which a compromising Christianity justifies itself. The tendency is—and here these men make an important contribution to theology—to explain in social terms the inheritance of sin among men. The corruption of the culture in which a child is reared, not the corruption of its uncultivated nature, is responsible for the long history of sin. Yet this solution of the problem of sin and holiness is found, by the exclusive Christians themselves, to be inadequate. For one thing, the demands of Christ for holiness of life meet resistance in the Christian himself; not apparently because he has inherited culture, but because he has been given a certain nature. The ascetic practices of the radicals, from Tertullian to Tolstoy, in dealing with sex, eating and fasting, anger, and even sleep, indicate how great their awareness is that temptation to sin arises out of nature as well as culture. More significant is their understanding that one of the distinctions between Christianity and secularism is just this, that the Christian faces up to the fact of his sinfulness. "If we say we have no sin," writes John, "we deceive ourselves and the truth is not in us." Tolstoy comes close to the same fundamental idea when he addresses himself to landowners, judges, priests, and soldiers, asking them to do one thing above all, to refuse to recognize the lawfulness of their crimes. To give up the land and to abdicate all advantages is a heroic act; "but it may be, as is most likely, that you have not the strength. . . . But to recognize the truth as a truth and avoid lying about it is a thing you can always do." The truth they must confess is that they are not serving the common good.[60] If the greatest sin is the refusal to acknowledge one's sinfulness, then it becomes impossible to make the line between Christ's holiness and man's sinfulness coincide with the line drawn between the Christian and the world. Sin is in him, not outside his soul and body. If sin is more deeply rooted and more extensive than the first answer of radical Christianity indicates, then the strategy of Christian faith in gaining victory over the world needs to include other tactics than those of withdrawal from culture and defense of new-won holiness.

Closely connected with these problems is the question about the relations of law and grace. Opponents of the exclusive type frequently accuse its representatives of legalism, and of neglecting the significance of grace in Christian life and thought; or of so emphasizing the character of Christianity as a new law for a select community that they forget its gospel to all men. This much is true, that they all insist on the exhibition of Christian faith in daily conduct. How can a follower of Jesus Christ know that he is a disciple if his conduct in love of the brothers, in self-denial, in modesty, in nonresistance, and in voluntary poverty does not distinguish him from other men? The emphasis on conduct may lead to the definition of precise rules, concern for one's conformity to such rules, and concentration on one's own will rather than on the gracious work of God. As we have

---

[60] "The Kingdom of God Is Within You," *Works*, Vol. XX, p. 442.

noted, I John combines grace and law, and emphasizes the primacy of that divine love that alone enables men, in response to its great attraction, to love both God and neighbor. Tertullian, however, is in all respects, more legally minded, and so are many of the monastics, against whose "works-righteousness" Protestantism then objects. Tolstoy represents the extreme, since for him Jesus Christ is really only the teacher of the new law, since this law is statable in precise commandments, and since the problem of obedience may be solved by summoning up within oneself the resident power of one's good will. Mated with such leanings toward legalism, however, one finds in Tertullian, monastics, sectarians and even Tolstoy reflections that Christians are just like other men, needing to rely wholly on the gracious forgiveness of their sins by God-in-Christ, that Christ is by no means the founder of a new closed society with a new law but the expiator of the sins of the whole world, that the only difference between Christians and non-Christians lies in the spirit with which Christians do the same things as non-Christians. "Eating the same food, wearing the same attire, having the same habits, under the same necessities of existence," sailing together, ploughing together, even holding property together and fighting together, the Christian does everything with a difference; not because he has a different law, but because he knows grace and hence reflects grace; not because he must distinguish himself, but because he does not need to distinguish himself.[61]

The knottiest theological problem raised by the Christ-against-culture movement is the problem of the relation of Jesus Christ to the Creator of nature and Governor of history as well as to the Spirit immanent in creation and in the Chris-

---

[61] Tertullian, *Apology*, xlii; cf. Tolstoy, "Kingdom of God," *Works*, Vol. XX, pp. 452 ff.

tian community. Some exponents of radical Christianity, such as certain sectarians and Tolstoy, regard the doctrine of the Trinity as having no ethical meaning, and as the corrupt invention of a corrupt church. But they cannot escape the problem with which it deals and they try to solve it in their own way. Others, such as the author of I John and Tertullian, belong among the founders of the orthodox doctrine. The positive and negative interest of these strongly ethical and practical Christians in the problem and its solution indicates that Trinitarianism is by no means as speculative a position and as unimportant for conduct as is often maintained. Practically the problem arises for radical Christians when, in their concentration on the Lordship of Christ, they seek to defend his authority, to define the content of his commandment, and to relate his law or reign to that power which governs nature and presides over the destinies of men in their secular societies. The extreme temptation the radicals meet when they deal with these questions is that of converting their ethical dualism into an ontological bifurcation of reality. Their rejection of culture is easily combined with a suspicion of nature and nature's God; their reliance on Christ is often converted into a reliance on the Spirit immanent in him and the believer; ultimately they are tempted to divide the world into the material realm governed by a principle opposed to Christ and a spiritual realm guided by the spiritual God. Such tendencies are evident in Tertullian's Montanism, in Spiritual Franciscanism, in the inner light doctrine of the Quakers, and in Tolstoy's spiritualism. At the edges of the radical movement the Manichean heresy is always developing. If on the one hand this tendency leads exclusive Christianity to obscure the relation of Jesus Christ to nature and to the Author of nature, it leads on the other to loss of contact with the historical Jesus Christ of history, for whom a spiritual principle is substituted. Hence George Fox's radical reform of a Christianity that had compromised, as he thought, with the world, was connected with an emphasis on the spirit that led in some parts of his movement to the virtual abandonment of the Scriptures and the Scriptural Jesus Christ, and the enthronement, as man's supreme authority, of private conscience. Tolstoy substitutes for the Jesus Christ of history the spirit immanent in Buddha, in Jesus, in Confucius, and in himself. Why radical Christians should be so subject to the temptation of a spiritualism that leads them away from the principle with which they begin, namely Christ's authority, is difficult to fathom. Perhaps it is indicated that Christ cannot be followed alone, as he cannot be worshipped alone; and that radical Christianity, important as one movement in the church, cannot itself exist without the counterweight of other types of Christianity.

CHAPTER 3

The Christ of Culture

1. Accommodation to Culture in Gnosticism and Abelard

In every culture to which the Gospel comes there are men who hail Jesus as the Messiah of their society, the fulfiller of its hopes and aspirations, the perfecter of its true faith, the source of its holiest spirit. In the Christian community they seem to stand in direct opposition to the radicals, who reject the social institutions for Christ's sake; but they are far removed from those "cultured among the despisers" of Christian faith who reject Christ for the sake of their civilization. These men are Christians not only in the sense that they count themselves believers in the Lord but also in the sense that they seek to maintain community with all other believers. Yet they seem equally at home in the community of culture. They feel no great tension between church and world, the social laws and the Gospel, the workings of divine grace and human effort, the ethics of salvation and the ethics of social conservation or progress. On the one hand they interpret culture through Christ, regarding those elements in it as most important which are most accordant with his work and person; on the other hand they understand Christ through culture, selecting from his teaching and action as well as from the Christian doctrine about him such points as seem to agree with what is best in civilization. So they harmonize Christ and culture, not without excision, of course, from New Testament and social custom, of stubbornly discordant features. They do not necessarily seek Christian sanction for the whole of prevailing culture, but only for what they regard as real in the actual; in the case of Christ they try to disentangle the rational and abiding from the historical and accidental. Though their fundamental interest may be this-worldly, they do not reject other-worldliness; but seek to understand the transcendent realm as continuous in time or character with the present life. Hence the great work of Christ may be conceived as the training of men in their present social existence for the better life to come; often he is regarded as the great educator, sometimes as the great philosopher or reformer. Just as the gulf between the worlds is bridged, so other differences between Christ and culture that seem like chasms to radical Christians and anti-Christians are easily passed over by these men. Sometimes they are ignored, sometimes filled in with convenient material derived from historical excavations or demolitions of old thought-structures. Such Christians have been described psychologically by F. W. Newman and William James as constituting the company of the "once-born" and the "healthy-minded." Sociologically they may be interpreted as nonrevolutionaries who find no need for positing "cracks in time"—fall and incarnation and judgment and resurrection. In modern history this type is well-known, since for generations it has been dominant in a large section of Protestantism. Inadequately defined by the use of such terms as "liberal" and "liberalism," is is more aptly named Culture-Protestantism;[1] but appearances of the type have not been confined to the modern world nor to the churches of the Reformation.

[1] Karl Barth, I believe, invented the term. See especially his *Protestantische Theologie im 19. Jahrhundert*, 1947, chap. iii.

There were movements of this sort in the earliest days of Christianity, as it arose in the midst of Jewish society, was carried into the Graeco-Roman world by Paul and other missionaries, and became involved in the complex interactions of the many cultural ingredients that bubbled in the Mediterranean melting pot. Among Jewish Christians doubtless all the variations appeared that we find among ancient and modern Gentile Christians as they wrestle with the Christ-culture problem. Paul's conflict with the Judaizers and later references to Nazarenes and Ebionites indicate that there were groups or movements which were more Jewish than Christian, or which, it might be better to say, sought to maintain loyalty to Jesus Christ without abandoning any important part of current Jewish tradition or giving up the special Messianic hopes of the chosen people.[2] Jesus was for them not only the promised Messiah but the Messiah of the promise, as this was understood in their society.

In early Gentile Christianity many modifications of the Christ-culture theme combined more or less positive concern for culture with fundamental loyalty to Jesus. Radical Christians of a later time have been inclined to relegate them all to the undifferentiated limbo of compromise or apostate Christianity; but there were great differences among them. The extreme attitude, which interprets Christ wholly in cultural terms and tends to eliminate all sense of tension between him and social belief or custom, was represented in the Hellenistic world by the Christian Gnostics. These men—Basilides, Valentinus, the author of *Pistis Sophia*, and their like—are heretics in the eyes of the main body of the church as well as of radical Christians. But they seem to have thought of themselves as loyal believers.

[2] On Jewish Christianity see Lietzmann, H., *The Beginnings of the Christian Church*, pp. 235 ff.; Weiss, J., *History of Primitive Christianity*, Vol. II, pp. 707 ff.

They "started from Christian ideas, they were attempting to formulate a Christian theory of God and man; the contest between Catholics and Gnostics was a struggle between persons who felt themselves to be Christians, not between Christians and heathens."[3]

Prof. Burkitt has argued persuasively that in the thought of such Gnostics "the figure of Jesus is essential, and without Jesus the systems would drop to pieces," that what they sought to do was to reconcile the gospel with the science and philosophy of their time. As nineteenth-century defenders of the faith tried to state the doctrine of Jesus Christ in terms of evolution, so these men undertook to interpret it in the light of the fascinating ideas that had been suggested to enlightened minds by Ptolemaian astronomy and by the psychology of the day with its catchwords *soma-sema*, its theory that the body was the soul's tomb.[4] Nothing is as evanescent in history as the pansophic theories that flourish among the illuminati of all times under the bright sunlight of the latest scientific discoveries; and nothing can be more easily dismissed by later periods as mere speculation. But we may well believe that the Gnostics were no more inclined to fantasy than are those folk in our day who find in psychiatry the key to the understanding of Christ, or in nuclear fission the answer to the problems of eschatology. They sought to disentangle the gospel from its involvement with barbaric and outmoded Jewish notions about God and history; to raise Christianity from the level of belief to that of intelligent knowledge, and so to increase its attractiveness and its power.[5] Emancipated as they were from the crude forms of polytheism

[3] Burkitt, F. C., *Church and Gnosis*, 1932, p. 8; cf. also *Cambridge Ancient History*, Vol. XII, pp. 467 ff.; McGiffert, A. C., *History of Christian Thought*, Vol. I, pp. 45 ff.

[4] Burkitt, *op. cit.*, pp. 29-35; 48; 51; 57 f.; 87-91.

[5] Ehrhard, Albert, *Die Kirche der Maertyrei*, 1932, p. 130.

and idolatry, and cognizant of profound spiritual depths of being, they set forth a doctrine according to which Jesus Christ was a cosmic savior of souls, imprisoned and confounded in the fallen, material world, the revealer of the true, redeeming wisdom, the restorer of right knowledge about the abyss of being and about the ascent as well as the descent of man.[6] This is the most obvious element in the effort of the Gnostics to accommodate Christianity to the culture of their day: their "scientific" and "philosophic" interpretation of the person and work of Christ. What is less obvious is that this attempt entailed his naturalization in the whole civilization. Christianity so interpreted became a religious and philosophic system, regarded doubtless as the best and the only true one, yet one among many. As a religion dealing with the soul it laid no imperious claim on man's total life. Jesus Christ was spiritual savior, not the Lord of life; his Father was not the source of all things nor their Governor. For the church, the new people, there was substituted an association of the enlightened who could live in culture as those who sought a destiny beyond it but were not in strife with it. Participation in the life of culture was now a matter of indifference; it involved no great problems. A Gnostic had no reason for refusing to pay homage to Caesar or to participate in war; though perhaps he had no compelling reason, apart from social pressure, for yielding to the mores and the laws. If he was too enlightened to take seriously the popular and official worship of idols, he was also too enlightened to make an issue out of its rejection; and martyrdom he scorned.[7] In the Gnostic version, knowledge of

[6] Cf. Burkitt, *op. cit.,* pp. 89 f. The thought of the Gnostics will seem less strange and foreign to those modern students of theology who have become acquainted with the ideas of Nicolai Berdyaev, who calls himself a Christian Gnostic. See especially his *Freedom and the Spirit,* 1935.

[7] Irenaeus, *Against Heretics,* IV, xxxiii, 9; cf. Ehrhard, *op. cit.,* pp. 162, 17c f.

Jesus Christ was an individual and spiritual matter, which had its place in the life of culture as the very pinnacle of human achievement. It was something that advanced souls could attain; and it was the advanced, the religious, attainment of such souls. Doubtless it was connected with ethics—sometimes with very rigoristic conduct of life, sometimes with indulgence and even license; but the ethics was grounded not upon Christ's commandment nor upon the loyalty of the believer to the new community. It was rather the ethics of individual aspiration after a destiny highly exalted above the material and the social world, and at the same time an ethics of individual adjustment to this indifferent world. From the point of view of the culture problem, the effort of the Gnostic to reconcile Christ with the science and philosophy of his day was not an end but a means. What he accomplished for himself—wittingly and designedly or unwittingly—as the corollary of this effort, was the easing of all tensions between the new faith and the old world. How much of the gospel he retained is another question, though it must be pointed out that the Gnostic was selective in his attitude toward culture as well as toward Christ. He rejected, for himself at least, what seemed ignoble in it, and cultivated what appeared to be most religious and most Christian.[8]

The movement represented by Gnosticism has been one of the most powerful in Christian history, despite the fact that its extreme representatives have been condemned by the church. At its center is the tendency to interpret Christianity as a religion rather than as church, or to interpret church as religious association rather than as new society. It sees in Jesus

[8] Another kind of cultural Christianity in the early period is represented by Lactantius and those theologians and statesmen who, at the time of the Constantinian settlement, sought to amalgamate Romanism and the new faith. It has been excellently described by Cochrane in his *Christianity and Classical Culture*, Pt. II, especially chapter V.

Christ not only a revealer of religious truth but a god. the object of religious worship; but not the Lord of all life, and not the son of the Father who is the present Creator and Governor of all things. It is too easy to say that Gnosticism retains the religion and drops the ethics of Christianity; the acceptance of the terms "religion" and "ethics" as characteristics of Christianity is itself an acceptance of the cultural point of view, of a pluralistic conception of life in which activity can be added to activity. The difficulty involved appears partly in the fact, evident in the case of the Gnostics, that when what is called religion is separated from ethics it becomes something very different from what it is in the church: it is now a metaphysics, a "Gnosis," a mystery cult rather than a faith governing all life.

The problems raised by Gnosticism regarding the relations of Christ to religion and of religion to culture became more rather than less acute with the development of so-called Christian civilization. There can be no doubt that medieval society was intensely religious, and that its religion was Christianity; yet the question whether Christ was the Lord of this culture is not answered by reference to the pre-eminence of the religious institution in it, nor even by reference to the pre-eminence of Christ in that institution. In this religious society the same problems about Christ and culture appeared that perplexed Christians in pagan Rome, and similarly divergent efforts at solution resulted. If some varieties of monasticism and some of the medieval sects followed Tertullian, then in an Abélard we may discern the attempt to answer the question somewhat as the Christian Gnostics answered it in the second century. Though the content of Abélard's thought is very different from that of the Gnostics, in spirit he is much akin to them. He seems to quarrel only with the church's way of stating its belief; since this prevents Jews and other non-Christians, especially those who revere and follow the Greek philosophers, from accepting something with which in their hearts they agree.[9] But in stating the faith, its beliefs about God and Christ and its demands on conduct, he reduces it to what conforms with the best in culture. It becomes a philosophic knowledge about reality, and an ethics for the improvement of life. The moral theory of the atonement is offered as an alternative not only to a doctrine that is difficult for Christians as Christians but to the whole conception of a once-and-for-all act of redemption. Jesus Christ has become for Abélard the great moral teacher who "in all that he did in the flesh . . . had the intention of our instruction,"[10] doing in a higher degree what Socrates and Plato had done before him. Of the philosophers he says that "in their care for the state and its citizens, . . . in life and doctrine, they give evidence of an evangelic and apostolic perfection and come little or nothing short of the Christian religion. They are, in fact, joined to us by this common zeal for moral achievement."[11] Such a remark is revelatory not only of a broad and charitable spirit toward non-Christians, but, more significantly, of a peculiar understanding of the gospel, markedly different surely from that of radical Christians. Abélard's ethics reveals the same attitude. One seeks in vain in his *Scito te Ipsum* for a recognition of the hard demand which the Sermon on the Mount makes on the Christian. What is offered here is kindly and liberal guidance for good people who want to do right and for their spiritual directors.[12] All conflict between Christ and culture is gone; the

---

[9] Cf. McCallum, J. R., *Abélard's Christian Theology*, 1948, p. 90.

[10] *Ibid.*, p. 84.

[11] *Ibid.*, p. 62; cf. De Wulf, Maurice, *History of Medieval Philosophy*, 1925, Vol. I, pp. 161-166.

[12] McCallum, J. R., *Abailard's Ethics*, 1935.

tension that exists between church and world is really due, in the estimation of an Abélard, to the church's misunderstanding of Christ.

II. "CULTURE-PROTESTANTISM" AND A. RITSCHL

In medieval culture Abélard was a relatively lonely figure; but since the 18th century his followers have been numerous, and what was heresy became the new orthodoxy. A thousand variations of the Christ-of-culture theme have been formulated by great and little thinkers in the Western world, by leaders of society and of the church, by theologians and philosophers. It appears in rationalistic and romantic, in conservative and liberal versions; Lutherans, Calvinists, sectarians, and Roman Catholics produce their own forms. From the point of view of our problem, the catchwords "rationalism," "liberalism," "fundamentalism," etc., are not highly significant. They indicate what lines of division there are within a cultural society, but obscure the fundamental unity that obtains among men who interpret Christ as a hero of manifold culture.

Among these many men and movements one may name a John Locke for whom *The Reasonableness of Christianity* commended itself to all who not only used their reason but used it in the "reasonable" manner characteristic of an English culture that found the middle way between all extremes. Leibnitz belongs here; and fundamentally Kant, with his translation of the gospel into a *Religion Within the Limits of Reason*, for in this case also the word "reason" means the particular exercise of man's analytical and synthetic intellectual power characteristic of the best culture of the time. Thomas Jefferson is one of the group. "I am a Christian," he declared, "in the only sense in which he [Jesus Christ] wished any one to be," but he made that declaration after he had carefully excerpted from the New Testament the sayings of Jesus which commended themselves to him. Though Jesus' doctrines, in the sage of Monticello's judgment, have not only come down to us in mutilated and corrupted form but were defective in their original pronouncement, yet "notwithstanding these disadvantages, a system of morals is presented to us, which, if filled up in the style and spirit of the rich fragments he left us, would be the most perfect and sublime that has ever been taught by man." Christ did two things: "1. He corrected the Deism of the Jews, confirming them in their belief in one only God, and giving them juster notions of his attributes and government. 2. His moral doctrines relating to kindred and friends, were more pure and perfect than those of the most correct of the philosophers, and greatly more so than those of the Jews; and they went far beyond both in inculcating universal philanthropy, not only to kindred and friends, to neighbors and countrymen, but to all mankind, gathering all into one family, under the bonds of charity, peace, common wants and common aids."[13] The philosophers, statesmen, reformers, poets, and novelists who acclaim Christ with Jefferson all repeat the same theme; Jesus Christ is the great enlightener, the great teacher, the one who directs all men in culture to the attainment of wisdom, moral perfection, and peace. Sometimes he is hailed as the great utilitarian, sometimes as the great idealist, sometimes as the man of reason, sometimes as the man of sentiment. But whatever the categories are by means of which he is understood, the things for which he stands are fundamentally the same—a peaceful, co-operative society achieved by moral training.

[13] From a letter to Dr. Benjamin Rush, Apr. 21, 1803; in Foner, P. S., *Basic Writings of Thomas Jefferson*, pp. 660-662. Cf. also Thomas Jefferson, *The Life and Morals of Jesus of Nazareth, extracted textually from the Gospels.*

Many of the leading theologians of the church in the nineteenth century joined the movement. The Schleiermacher of the *Speeches on Religion* participated in it, though he does not so evidently represent it in his writing of *The Christian Faith*. The former, youthful utterance is characteristically directed to "the cultured among the despisers of religion." Though the word "culture" here means the specialized attainment of the most self-consciously intellectual and aesthetic group in society, yet it is also indicated that Schleiermacher is directing himself, like the Gnostics and Abélard before him, to the representatives of culture in the broad sense. Like them also he believes that what they find offensive is not Christ but the church with its teachings and ceremonies; and again he conforms to the general pattern by dealing with Christ in terms of religion. For Christ is in this presentation less the Jesus Christ of the New Testament than the principle of mediation between finite and infinite. Christ belongs in culture, because culture itself, without "sense and taste for the infinite," without a "holy music" accompanying all its work, becomes sterile and corrupt. This Christ of religion does not call upon men to leave homes and kindred for his sake; he enters into their homes and all their associations as the gracious presence which adds an aura of infinite meaning to all temporal tasks.[14]

Karl Barth, in a brilliant appreciation and critique, emphasizes the duality and unity of Schleiermacher's two interests: he was determined to be both a Christo-centric theologian and a modern man, participating fully in the work of culture, in the development of science, the maintenance of the state, the cultivation of art, the ennoblement of family life, the advancement of philosophy. And he carried out this double task without a

[14] *On Religion.* Translated by John Oman, 1893; cf. pp. 246, 249, 178 *et passim*.

sense of tension, without the feeling that he served two masters. Perhaps Barth sees Schleiermacher as too much of one piece; but certainly in the *Speeches on Religion*, as well as in his writings on ethics, he is a clear-cut representative of those who accommodate Christ to culture while selecting from culture what conforms most readily to Christ.[15]

As the nineteenth century moved on from Kant, Jefferson, and Schleiermacher to Hegel, Emerson, and Ritschl, from the religion within the limits of reason to the religion of humanity, the Christ-of-culture theme was sounded over and over again in many variations, was denounced by cultural opponents of Christ and by radical Christians, and merged into other answers that sought to maintain the distinction between Christ and civilization while yet maintaining loyalty to both. Today we are inclined to regard the whole period as the time of cultural Protestantism; though even as we do so we make our criticism of its tendencies with the aid of such nineteenth century theologians as Kierkegaard and F. D. Maurice. The movement toward the identification of Christ with culture doubtless reached its climax in the latter half of the century; and the most representative theologian of that time, Albrecht Ritschl, may be taken as the best modern illustration of the Christ-of-culture type. Unlike Jefferson and Kant, Ritschl stays close to the New Testament Jesus Christ. Indeed, he is partly responsible for the intense concentration of modern scholarship on the study of the Gospels and the history of the early church. He retains a much larger share of the creed of the church than do the cultured lovers of Christ and despisers of the church.

[15] Barth, K., *Die Protestantische Theologie im 19. Jahrhundert*, 1947, pp. 387 ff.; cf. also Barth, K., "Schleiermacher" in his *Die Theologie und die Kirche*, 1928, pp. 136 ff.; Brandt, Richard B., *The Philosophy of Schleiermacher*, 1941, pp. 166 ff. The unity of Christian and philosophical ethics is asserted most unambiguously by Schleiermacher in his essay "On the Philosophical Treatment of the Idea of Virtue," in *Saemmtliche Werke* (Reimer), Pt. III, Vol. II, pp. 350 ff.

He counts himself a member of the Christian community; and believes that only in its context can one speak significantly about sin and salvation. Yet he also takes seriously his responsibility in the community of culture, and stands at the opposite extreme from his contemporary Tolstoy in his attitude toward science and state, economic life and technology.

Ritschl's theology had two foundation stones: not revelation and reason, but Christ and culture. He resolutely rejected the idea that we could or should begin our Christian self-criticism by seeking out some ultimate truth of reason, self-evident to all; or by accepting the dogmatic pronouncement of some religious institution; or by looking into our own experience for some persuasive feeling or sense of reality. "Theology," he wrote, "which ought to set forth the authentic content of Christian religion in positive form, needs to draw its content from the New Testament and from no other source."[16] The Protestant dogma of the authority of Scriptures verifies but does not constitute the ground for this necessity; the church is not the foundation of Christ, but Christ is the founder of the church. "The Person of its Founder is . . . the key to the Christian view of the world, and the standard of Christians' self-judgment and moral effort," as well as the standard which shows how such specifically religious acts as prayer should be carried on.[17] Thus Ritschl begins his theological task resolutely as a member of the Christian community, which has no other beginning than Jesus Christ as set forth in the New Testament.

In fact, however, he had another starting point in the community of culture, which has as its principle the will of man to gain mastery over nature. As a modern man and as a Kantian, Ritschl understands the human situation fundamentally in

[16] Ritschl, A., *Rechtfertigung und Versoehnung*, 3d ed., 1889, Vol. II, p. 18.
[17] Ritschl, A., *The Christian Doctrine of Justification and Reconciliation: The Positive Development of the Doctrine*, 1900, p. 202.

terms of man's conflict with nature. Popular thought celebrates as the greatest human achievement the victories of applied science and technology over natural forces. Doubtless Ritschl was also impressed by these conquests; but what concerned him more as a moral thinker and as a Kantian was the effort of the ethical reason to impress on human nature itself the internal law of the conscience; to direct individual and social life toward the ideal goal of virtuous existence in a society of free yet interdependent virtuous persons. In the ethical realm man faces a double problem: he needs not only to subdue his own nature, but also to overcome the despair which arises from his understanding of the indifference of the external natural world to his own lofty interests. What Ritschl accepts as given is "man's self-distinction from nature and his endeavours to maintain himself against it or over it."[18] Man must regard personal life, whether in himself or another, as an end in itself. All the work of culture has its source in the conflict with nature, and its goal in the victory of personal, moral existence; in the achievement, to use Kantian terms, of the kingdom of ends—or, in the New Testament phrase, of the kingdom of God.

With these two starting points Ritschl might have become a Christian of the median sort, who sought to combine two distinct principles by accepting polar tensions or grades of existence or otherwise. There may be, here and there in his writings, indications of tendencies toward such solutions. But on the whole he found no problem. The difficulties other Christians encountered seemed to him to be due to erroneous interpretations of God, of Christ, and of the Christian life; they were due, for instance, to the use of metaphysical ideas rather than of those critical methods that enabled men to understand the true doctrine of God and the true meaning of for-

[18] *Ibid.*, p. 219; cf. 222 ff.

giveness. In his own views there were dualities, to be sure, but no real conflicts save between culture and nature. Christianity itself needed to be regarded as an ellipse with two foci, rather than as a circle with one center. One focus was justification or the forgiveness of sins; the other, ethical striving for the attainment of the perfect society of persons. But there was no conflict between these ideas; for forgiveness meant the divine companionship that enabled the sinner after every defeat to arise again and resume his work at the ethical task. There was the duality of the church and the cultural community; but here also Ritschl found no conflict, and attacked most sharply monastic and pietistic practices in separating the church from the world.[19] If the Christian church was the community in which everything was referred to Jesus Christ, it was also the true form of ethical society, in which members of different nations are combined together in mutual love and for the sake of achieving the universal kingdom of God.[20] There is the duality of Christian calling and Christian vocation, but only medieval Catholicism finds conflict here. The Christian can exercise his calling to seek the kingdom of God if, motivated by love of neighbor, he carries on his work in the moral communities of family and economic, national, and political life. Indeed "family, private property, personal independence and honor (in obedience to authority)" are goods that are essential to moral health and the formation of character. Only by engagement in civic work for the sake of the common good, by faithfulness in one's social calling, is it possible to be true to the example of Christ.[21] There is duality in Ritschl's thought be-

[19] Cf. his *Geschichte des Pietismus*, 3 vols. 1880-1886.

[20] *Unterricht in der christlichen Religion*, 1895, p. 5; *Justification and Reconciliation*, pp. 133 ff.

[21] *Unterricht in der christlichen Religion*, pp. 53 f.; cf. *Justification and Reconciliation*, pp. 661 ff.

tween the work of God and the work of man; but it is not of such a sort that the strictures of anti-Christian exponents of culture regarding Christian reliance on God rather than on personal effort are in any sense validated. For God and man have in common the task of realizing the kingdom; and God works within the human community through Christ and through conscience, rather than on it from without. There is duality, finally, in Christ himself; for he is both priest and prophet, he belongs both to the sacramental and praying community of those who depend on grace, and to the cultural community which through ethical striving in many institutions labors for the victory of free men over nature. But there is no conflict and no tension here either; for the priest mediates forgiveness in order that the prophet's ideal may be realized, and the founder of the Christian community is at the same time the moral hero who marks a great advance in the history of culture.[22]

It is largely by means of the idea of the kingdom of God that Ritschl achieved the complete reconciliation of Christianity and culture. When we attend to the meaning he attaches to that term, we become aware of the extent to which he has interpreted Jesus as a Christ of culture, in both senses: as the guide of men in all their labor to realize and conserve their values, and as the Christ who is understood by means of nineteenth-century cultural ideas. "The Christian idea of the Kingdom of God," writes Ritschl, "denotes the association of mankind—an association both extensively and intensively the most comprehensive possible—through the reciprocal moral action of its members, action which transcends all merely natural and particular considerations.[23] If Jesus' eschatological hope in the

[22] *Justification and Reconciliation*, chap. VI.
[23] *Ibid.*, p. 284.

manifestation of God is lacking here, so also is his noneschato-
logical faith in the present rule of the transcendent Lord of
heaven and earth. All the references are to man and to man's
work; the word "God" seems to be an intrusion, as perhaps
those later Ritschlians recognized who substituted the phrase
"brotherhood of man" for "kingdom of God." This statement
of the end of human striving in cultural work is, moreover,
wholly in line with the thought of the nineteenth century. As
we have noted, the conception of the kingdom of God Ritschl
ascribes to Jesus Christ is practically the same as Kant's idea of
the kingdom of ends; it is closely related to Jefferson's hope for
a mankind gathered into one family "under the bonds of
charity, peace, common wants and common aids"; in its political
aspects it is Tennyson's "Parliament of Man and Federation of
the World"; it is the synthesis of the great values esteemed by
democratic culture: the freedom and intrinsic worth of individuals, social co-operation, and universal peace.

Yet it must be said, in fairness to Ritschl, that if he interpreted Christ through culture he also selected from culture
those elements which were most compatible with Christ. Many
other movements were present in the flourishing civilization
of the late nineteenth century besides the highly ethical Kantian
idealism that was for Ritschl the key to culture. He did not find
or seek as some did, to establish contact between Jesus Christ
and the capitalistic or the nationalistic or the materialistic
tendencies of the time. If he used Christianity as a means to an
end, he chose an end more compatible with Christianity than
were many other goals of the contemporary culture. If he
selected among the attributes of the God of Jesus Christ the
one quality of love at the expense of his attributes of power and
of justice, still the resultant theology, though a caricature, was
recognizably Christian. Moreover, Ritschl sought to do justice

to the fact that Christ accomplished some things for men which they could never accomplish for themselves in culture, even by imitation of the historic example. He mediated and mediates the forgiveness of sin; and he brings to light the immortality that no human labor and wisdom can achieve. Man's lordship over the world has its limits; he is limited by his own corporeal nature, and by the multitude of natural forces he cannot tame, "and the multitude of hindrances which he has to tolerate from those on whose support he is reckoning." Though he "identifies himself with the advancing forces of human civilization," he cannot hope to conquer by his labor the system of nature that opposes him. In this situation, religion and Jesus Christ, as a teacher of high religion—assure man that he stands close to the supramundane God, and give him the certainty that he is destined for a supramundane goal.[24] Of course this also sounds more like the gospel according to St. Immanuel than according to St. Matthew or St. Paul.

It is not necessary to develop in further detail Ritschl's solution of the problem of Christ and culture; to show how loyalty to Jesus leads to active participations in every cultural work, and to care for the conservation of all the great institutions. The general outlines are familiar to most modern Christians, especially to Protestants, whether or not they have ever heard of Ritschl, not to speak of having read his works. Partly because of his influence, but even more because he was a representative man who made explicit ideas that were widespread and deeply rooted in the world before the Wars, his understanding of Christ and culture has been reproduced in essence by scores of leading theologians and churchmen. Walter Rauschenbusch's social gospel presents the same general interpretation of Christ and the gospel, though with greater moral

[24] *Ibid.*, pp. 609 ff.

force and less theological depth. Harnack in Germany, Garvie in England, Shailer Matthews and D. C. Macintosh in America, Ragaz in Switzerland, and many others, each in his own way, find in Jesus the great exponent of man's religious and ethical culture. Popular theology condenses the whole of Christian thought into the formula: The Fatherhood of God and the Brotherhood of Man.

Back of all these Christologies and doctrines of salvation is a common notion that is part of the generally accepted and unquestioned climate of opinion. It is the idea that the human situation is fundamentally characterized by man's conflict with nature. Man the moral being, the intellectual spirit, confronts impersonal natural forces, mostly outside himself but partly within him. When the issue in life is so conceived, it is almost inevitable that Jesus Christ should be approached and understood as a great leader of the spiritual, cultural cause, of man's struggle to subdue nature, and of his aspirations to transcend it. That man's fundamental situation is not one of conflict with nature but with God, and that Jesus Christ stands at the center of that conflict as victim and mediator—this thought, characteristic of the church as a whole, culture-theology never seems to entertain. In its view, those Christians who so understand the human dilemma and its solution are obscurantists in man's cultural life and perverters of the gospel of the kingdom.

III. In Defense of Cultural Faith

The widespread reaction against cultural Protestantism in our time tends to obscure the importance of answers of this type to the Christ-and-culture problem. But we are warned against cavalier treatment of the position by the reflection that some of its severest critics share the general attitude they purport to reject; and by the recognition that as a perennial move-

ment the acculturation of Christ is both inevitable and profoundly significant in the extension of his reign.

How often the Fundamentalist attack on so-called liberalism
—by which cultural Protestantism is meant—is itself an expression of a cultural loyalty, a number of Fundamentalist interests
indicate. Not all though many of these antiliberals show a
greater concern for conserving the cosmological and biological
notions of older cultures than for the Lordship of Jesus Christ.
The test of loyalty to him is found in the acceptance of old
cultural ideas about the manner of creation and the earth's
destruction. More significant is the fact that the mores they
associate with Christ have at least as little relation to the New
Testament and as much connection with social custom as have
those of their opponents. The movement that identifies obedience to Jesus Christ with the practices of prohibition, and
with the maintenance of early American social organization, is
a type of cultural Christianity; though the culture it seeks to
conserve differs from that which its rivals honor. The same
thing is true of the Marxian-Christian criticism of the "bourgeois Christianity" of democratic and individualistic liberalism.
Again, Roman Catholic reaction against the Protestantism of
the nineteenth and twentieth centuries seems often to be
animated by a desire to return to the culture of the thirteenth;
to the religious, economic, and political institutions and to the
philosophical ideas of another civilization than ours. In so far as
the contemporary attack on Culture-Protestantism is carried on
in this way, it is a family quarrel between folk who are in
essential agreement on the main point; namely, that Christ
is the Christ of culture, and that man's greatest task is to maintain his best culture. Nothing in the Christian movement is so
similar to cultural Protestantism as is cultural Catholicism,
nothing more akin to German Christianity than American

Christianity, or more like a church of the middle class than a workers' church. The terms differ, but the logic is always the same: Christ is identified with what men conceive to be their finest ideals, their noblest institutions, and their best philosophy.

As in the case of the radical answer, there are values in this position that are hidden to its opponents. One cannot doubt that the acculturation of Jesus Christ has contributed greatly in history to the extension of his power over men. The statement that the blood of the martyrs is the seed of the church is probably something of a half-truth. If in ancient times men were impressed by the constancy of Christians who refused to yield to popular and official demand for conformity to custom, they were also attracted by the harmony of the Christian message with the moral and religious philosophy of their best teachers, and by the agreement of Christian conduct with that of their exemplary heroes.[25] For that matter, culture has its martyrs as well as the church; and their graves have also been seed-plots of regenerative movements in society. Hellenists were able to find a likeness between Jesus and Socrates, as Indians in our time discern a similarity between the death of Christ and Gandhi's. Though the aim of many of the Christians who interpret Christ as the Messiah of a culture is the salvation or reform of that culture rather than the extension of Christ's power, they contribute greatly to the latter by helping men to understand his gospel in their own language, his character by means of their own imagery, and his revelation of God with the aid of their own philosophy. They rarely if ever succeed in doing this by themselves; for other Christian wrestlers with the Christ-and-culture problem, apart from the culture-reject-

[25] The duality in the attraction of Christianity for pagans in the second century has been well described by Prof. H. Lietzmann in his *The Founding of the Church Universal*, 1938, pp. 193 ff. Cf. also Nock, A. D., *Conversion*, 1933.

ing radicals, carry on the largest part of the enterprise; yet the cultural Christians give a strong impetus in this direction. That the translation of the gospel into the "vulgar tongue" has its dangers the aberrations of this group make evident, but it is also clear that to avoid such perils by leaving the gospel untranslated is to invite the danger of letting it be buried in the dead language of an alien society. Those critics of cultural Protestantism who urge return to Biblical ways of thought sometimes seem to forget that many cultures are represented in the Bible; and that as there is no single Biblical language there is also no single Biblical cosmology or psychology. The word of God as it is uttered to men comes in human words; and human words are cultural things, along with the concepts with which they are associated. If the writers of the New Testament needed to use such words as "Messiah," "Lord," and "Spirit" in speaking of Jesus, the Son of God, their interpreters and the interpreters of Jesus Christ himself serve the same cause by using words like "Reason," "Wisdom," "Emancipator," and "Avatar."

One contribution to the extension of the reign of Jesus Christ which the cultural Christians make is grudgingly acknowledged, if at all, by those who make Christ's appeal to the humble a source of pride. The cultural Christians tend to address themselves to the leading groups in a society; they speak to the cultured among the despisers of religion; they use the language of the more sophisticated circles, of those who are acquainted with the science, the philosophy, and the political and economic movements of their time. They are missionaries to the aristocracy and the middle class, or to the groups rising to power in a civilization. In these circumstances they may—though they do not need to—participate in the class consciousness of many whom they address; and they may take pains to show that they do not belong to the vulgar herd of the unenlightened followers of the Master. That is a sorry fault; but it is the same sin into which those fall who take pride in their lowly position in society, and thank Christ less for sharing their humble lot than for casting down the mighty from their seats. Apart from such considerations, it seems true that the conversion to Christianity of the leading groups in a society has been as significant in the mission of the church as the direct conversion of the masses. Paul is a symbolic figure, representing, in his conversion and his power, scores and hundreds of former cultured despisers of Christ who became his servants.

The Christ-of-culture position appears in these and other similar ways to make effective the universal meaning of the gospel, and the truth that Jesus is the savior, not of a selected little band of saints, but of the world. It also brings into sharp focus elements in the teaching and life of the New Testament Jesus Christ that the radical Christians pass over. He was relevant to his time; he affirmed the laws of his society; he sought and sent his disciples to seek out the lost sheep of his own house of Israel. He not only pointed to the end of the ages, but also to temporal judgments, such as the fall of the tower of Siloam and the destruction of Jerusalem. He took issue with the political parties of his nation and time. Though he was more than a prophet, he was also a prophet who like an Isaiah showed concern for the peace of his own city. He thought no temporal value as great as the life of the soul; but he healed the sick in body when he forgave their sins. He made distinctions between fundamental principles and traditions of little worth. He found some wise men in his day nearer the kingdom of God than others. Though he commanded his disciples to seek the kingdom above all else, he did not advise them to scorn other goods; nor was he indifferent to the institution of the family, to order in the temple, to the freedom of the temporally oppressed, and to the fulfillment of duty by the powerful. The other-world-liness of Jesus is always mated with a this-worldly concern; his proclamation and demonstration of divine action is inseparable from commandments to men to be active here and now; his future kingdom reaches into the present. If it is an error to interpret him as a wise man teaching a secular wisdom, or a reformer concerned with the reconstruction of social institutions, such interpretations serve at least to balance the opposite mistakes of presenting him as a person who had no interest in the principles men used to guide their present life in a damned society because his eye was fixed on the Jerusalem that was to come down from heaven.

For the radical Christian the whole world outside the sphere where Christ's Lordship is explicitly acknowledged is a realm of equal darkness; but cultural Christians note that there are great differences among the various movements in society; and by observing these they not only find points of contact for the mission of the church, but also are enabled to work for the reformation of the culture. The radicals reject Socrates, Plato, and the Stoics, along with Aristippus, Democritus, and the Epicureans; tyranny and empire seem alike to them; highwaymen and soldiers both use violence; figures carved by Phidias are more dangerous temptations to idolatry than those made by a handy man; modern culture is all of one piece, individualistic and egoistic, secularistic and materialistic. The cultural Christian, however, understands that there are great polarities in any civilization; and that there is a sense in which Jesus Christ affirms movements in philosophy toward the assertion of the world's unity and order, movements in morals toward self-denial and the care for the common good, political concerns for justice, and ecclesiastical interests in honesty in religion. Therefore they make contact with culture; presenting Jesus as the wise man, the prophet, the true high priest, the incorruptible judge, the reformer with a passion for the good of the common man; and at the same time they encourage the forces that are fighting against secular corruption. The Gnostics help to keep the church from becoming a withdrawn sect; Abélard prepares the way for the philosophical and scientific enlightenment of medieval society and for the reform of the penitential system; the Culture-Protestants are preachers of repentance to an industrial culture endangered by its peculiar corruptions.

To all this it will be objected that culture is so various that the Christ of culture becomes a chameleon; that the word "Christ" in this connection is nothing but an honorific and emotional term by means of which each period attaches numinous quality to its personified ideals. Now this word designates a wise man, a philosopher, now a monk, now a reformer, now a democrat, and again a king. Doubtless this objection has much validity. What similarity is there between the wonder-working, supernatural hero of a Christianized mystery cult and "Comrade Jesus" who "has his red card"? Or between the teacher of a better than Stoic wisdom and "The Man Nobody Knows"? Yet two things may be said in rejoinder, and in defence of the Christ-of-culture Christians. The first is, of course, that Jesus Christ has indeed many aspects, and that even caricatures sometimes help to call attention to features otherwise ignored. The other point is this: the fact that Christians have found kinship between Christ and the prophets of the Hebrews, the moral philosophers of Greece, the Roman Stoics, Spinoza and Kant, humanitarian reformers and Eastern mystics, may be less indicative of Christian instability than of a certain stability in human wisdom. Though apart from Christ it is difficult to find unity in what is sometimes called the great tradition of culture, with his aid such a unity can be discerned. One is tempted to formulate this notion theologically, saying that the Spirit proceeds not only from the Son but from the Father also, and that with the aid of the knowledge of Christ it is possible to discriminate between the spirits of the times and the Spirit which is from God.

IV. Theological Objections

Not only churchmen, but also non-Christians to whom Jesus has been so presented as the Christ of culture, raise objections to the interpretation. The Christian Gnostics are assailed by pagan writers as well as by the orthodox. Christian liberalism is rejected by a John Dewey as well as by a Barth. Marxists dislike Christian socialism as much as orthodox Calvinists and Lutherans do. It is not our task to analyze these objections that are made from the side of culture. It is relevant, however, to point out that cultural Christianity is not, evidently, more effective in gaining disciples for Christ than Christian radicalism is. In so far as part of its purpose is always that of recommending the gospel to an unbelieving society, or to some special group, such as the intelligentsia, or political liberals or conservatives, or workingmen, it often fails to achieve its end because it does not go far enough, or because it is suspected of introducing an element that will weaken the cultural movement. It seems impossible to remove the offense of Christ and his cross even by means of these accommodations; and cultural Christians share in the general limitation all Christianity encounters whether it fights or allies itself with the "world."

If the evangelists of the Christ of culture do not go far enough to meet the demands of men whose loyalty is primarily to the values of civilization, they go too far in the judgment of their fellow believers of other schools. These point out that

the cultural answers to the Christ-culture problem show a
consistent tendency to distort the figure of the New Testament
Jesus. In their efforts at accommodation, Gnostics and cultural
Protestants find it strangely desirable to write apocryphal
gospels and new lives of Jesus. They take some fragment of the
complex New Testament story and interpretation, call this the
essential characteristic of Jesus, elaborate upon it, and thus
reconstruct their own mythical figure of the Lord. Some choose
the opening verses of the Fourth Gospel, some the Sermon on
the Mount, some the announcement of the kingdom, as the key
to Christology. It is always something that seems to agree with
the interests or the needs of their time. The point of contact
they seek to find with their hearers dominates the whole sermon; and in many instances the resultant portrait of Christ is
little more than the personification of an abstraction. Jesus
stands for the idea of spiritual knowledge; or of logical reason;
or of the sense for the infinite; or of the moral law within;
or of brotherly love. Ultimately these fanciful descriptions are
destroyed by the force of the Biblical story. With or without the
official actions of bishops and councils, the New Testament
witness maintains itself against them. In the second century the
formation of the New Testament canon, in the nineteenth and
twentieth the continuous work of Biblical scholars, make it
evident that Jesus Christ is not like this. He is greater and
stranger than these portraits indicate. These apocryphal gospels
and lives contain elements foreign to him; the Biblical Christ
says and does things that are not found in them. Sooner or later
it becomes apparent that the supernatural being was a man
of flesh and blood; the mystic a teacher of morals; the moral
teacher one who cast out demons by the power of God; the
incarnate spirit of love a prophet of wrath; the martyr of a good
cause the Risen Lord. It is clear that his commandments are

more radical than the Ritschlian reconciliation of his law with the duties of one's calling allows; and that his conception of his mission can never be forced into the pattern of an emancipator from merely human oppressions.

The number of special objections of this sort that are raised against the Christ-of-culture interpretations can be multiplied; but whether few or many they become the basis of the charge that loyalty to contemporary culture has so far qualified the loyalty to Christ that he has been abandoned in favor of an idol called by his name. The indictment is often too sharply drawn and contains too many counts. Moreover, no human court, least of all a Christian court, is entitled to estimate the loyalty and treason of disciples. Yet because an evident danger is present in the cultural Christian position, the major part of the Christian movement has consistently rejected it; and has done so with greater firmness than it has displayed in refusing to adopt the opposite, radical attitude.

As in the case of the exclusive believers, cultural Christianity encounters theological problems that indicate how much theories of sin and grace and the Trinity are involved in what seem to be only practical questions. Extremes meet; and the Christ-of-culture folk are strangely like the Christ-against-culture people, both in their general attitude toward the theology of the church, and in the specific theological positions they take. They suspect theology, as the radicals do, though for the opposite reason; since the latter regard it as an intrusion of worldly wisdom into the sphere of revelation, and the former believe it to be irrational. Like their opponents, the cultural Christians tend to separate reason and revelation, but evaluate the two principles differently. Reason, they think, is the highroad to the knowledge of God and salvation; Jesus Christ is for them the great teacher of rational truth and goodness, or the emergent genius in the history of religious and moral reason. Revelation, then, is either the fabulous clothing in which intelligible truth presents itself to people who have a low I. Q.; or it is the religious name for that process which is essentially the growth of reason in history. This is the general tendency in the thought of the cultural Christians; but as the radicals cannot rid themselves of some dependence on reason, so these men cannot proceed in their reasoning without reliance on the purely given historical fact, and without references to an action of self-disclosure on the part of that Being with which reason is concerned when it deals with the Infinite and the moral law. The Christian Gnostic parts company with the pagan in the confession that the Word became flesh, and in a stubborn dependence on the Jesus who suffered under Pontius Pilate. Christianity is all very reasonable to John Locke; yet it requires one thing which goes beyond reason, and which this reasonable man cannot reasonably refuse—the acknowledgment that Jesus is the Christ. Though Ritschlians see that Jesus belongs in the story of man's developing practical reason, they confess that his forgiveness of their sins has in it a superrational element; and though to call him Son of God is an intelligible value-judgment, he must also be called that in another not so intelligible sense if the first phrase is to have meaning. A surd remains; and this surd is not—as the pagans often maintain— due to the cowardice of rationalists who bow to church authority or popular Christian custom for the sake of irrelevant, personal advantage. It is rather due to the fact that their own reasoning is not only historically conditioned by the presence of Jesus in their personal and social history, but also that it is logically dependent on the acceptance of a conviction that reason cannot give to itself.

The two points are closely related. We can try to state them in somewhat negative fashion by saying that Jesus Christ in history is an inevitable test case of all this Christian rationalism. If his appearance was an accident rather than the Word made flesh, a chance occurrence rather than a manifestation of the ultimate pattern and purpose in things, then all the reasoning of the Christian rationalists is wrong; and more or less explicitly they acknowledge this. If he is not the Christ, not the realization of all the promises and pointers in human history of the meaning of the story, not the one by whom what is truly promising and significant in that story may be selected—then this reasoning is in error, because it is not in agreement with the nature of things. If Jesus Christ, obedient to his own moral law with complete devotion, has not risen from the dead, if the end of love or of pure obedience was impotence and nothingness— then all this reasoning about what is required of man and what is possible to him flies in the face of fact. In these ways, at least, the cultural Christians encounter and partly recognize the presence of a revelation that cannot be completely absorbed into the life of reason.

Extremes seem to meet also in the radical and the cultural Christian views of sin, of grace and law, and of the Trinity. The idea of a depravity that is total in the sense of extending to all men, and in the other sense of involving all of human nature, is foreign to both groups; both also tend to locate sin on the one hand in the animal passions, on the other hand in certain social institutions. For the radical, all culture is involved; the cultural Christian may confine the evil to selected bad institutions, such as ignorant and superstitious religion, or the competitive customs that tempt all men to selfishness, or to other "super-personal forces of evil," as Rauschenbusch calls them. Yet both are inclined to posit a realm free from sin; in the one case the holy community, in the other a citadel of righteousness in the high place of the personal spirit. In the pure reason in the moment of *gnosis*, in the pure intention preceding the act, in the cleansed and forgiven personal religious life, or in prayer, man ascends above the world of sin; and from this retreat he goes forth to conquer evil in his nature and his society. But here too the warning is sounded that "if we say we have no sin we deceive ourselves." Kant discerns the radical evil that corrupts the intention, and Rudolf Otto brings to awareness the creaturely sense of uncleanness before the Holy God that created reason shares. As the cultural Christian approaches this knowledge he also approaches his fellow believers, who think less highly of human achievement even in morals and religion, and who are less confident that there is any place where man can find a leverage for his effort to lift the world out of its bitterness.

Like their radical counterparts, the Christ-of-culture believers incline to the side of law in dealing with the polarity of law and grace. By obedience to the laws of God and of reason, speculative and practical, men are able, they seem to think, to achieve the high destiny of knowers of the Truth and citizens of the Kingdom. The divine action of grace is ancillary to the human enterprise; and sometimes it seems as if God, the forgiveness of sins, even prayers of thanksgiving, are all means to an end, and a human end at that. Grace is a good thing to believe in if you want to attain deiformity or assert your lordship over nature. Cultural Christianity, in modern times at least, has always given birth to movements that tended toward the extreme of self-reliant humanism, which found the doctrine of grace—and even more the reliance upon it— demeaning to man and discouraging to his will. But there have also issued from it movements in the other direction; and this indicates how much it itself lives in the presence of what sounds like a paradox, namely, that we need to work out our salvation with fear and trembling, because it is God who works in us to will and to do. No matter how boldly rationalism announces that the theology of law and grace is irrational, it seems to come finally to the humble confession that the kingdom of God is both gift and task and thus simply states once more the old problem.

Finally, we must note how these efforts to interpret Jesus as the Christ of culture involve the Trinitarian problem. The radical Christians—of modern times at least—regard the development of Trinitarian theology to be a result of the introduction of a cultural philosophy into the Christian faith, rather than a consequence of believers' efforts to understand what they believe. But these Christian devotees of philosophy do not like the formula either. Gnostics need more than a Trinity, liberals less. All along the line the tendency in the movement is to identify Jesus with the immanent divine spirit that works in men. But then the question arises what the relation of this immanent, rational, spiritual, and moral principle is to nature and to the power that produces and governs it. The Gnostic seeks to solve the problem by means of intricate speculations; and the modern, having rejected all arguments from nature to God, raises at last the anxious question whether God exists, whether the value-judgments religious and moral man makes are also judgments about existence. For he cannot escape the problem of cultural and ethical life: whether there is any agreement between the power manifest in earthquake and fire and the one which speaks in the still, small, inner voice; whether that which transcends man as he confronts nature is pitiless and blind force, or the Father of Jesus Christ. The relation of Jesus Christ to the Almighty Creator of heaven and earth is ultimately no speculative question for the man concerned with the conservation of culture, but his fundamental problem. It arises for him not only in his eschatological visions, when he sees a "slow sure doom fall pitiless and dark on the world his ideals have fashioned," but also in all his construction when he discovers that his science and his architecture cannot stand unless they are ordered in a given order of nature. The spiritualism and idealism of cultural Christianity meets its challenge in naturalism; and sometimes it discovers in this encounter that it has hold on only a third of the truth when it says that God is Spirit. Other questions arise, as historical events manifest the presence in civilization of immanent spirits contradicting the spirit of Christ. It becomes more or less clear that it is not possible honestly to confess that Jesus is the Christ of culture unless one can confess much more than this.

CHAPTER 4

※

Christ Above Culture

I. THE CHURCH OF THE CENTER

Efforts at analysis in any sphere are subject to the temptation to distinguish just two classes of persons, things, or movements. Rightly to divide seems to mean to bisect. Existent things, we think, must be either spiritual or physical; the spiritual either rational or irrational, the physical either matter or motion. Therefore when we try to understand Christianity, we divide its adherents into the "once-born" and the "twice-born," its communities into churches or sects. This intellectual penchant may be connected with the primitive, unconquerable tendency to think in terms of in-group and out-group, of self and other. Whatever its causes, the result of such initial bisection is that we are always left with a large number of examples of mixture. When we begin with the distinction between black and white, most of the shades we are asked to identify will be grays. When we start our analysis of Christian communities with the church-sect division, most of them will seem to be hybrids. It is so with our present procedure. If Christ and culture are the two principles with which Christians are concerned, then most of them will seem to be compromising creatures who somehow manage to mix in irrational fashion an exclusive devotion to a Christ who rejects culture, with devotion to a culture that includes is at least founded on the "world" as nature, and cannot exist save as it is upheld by the Creator and Governor of nature.

There is agreement, too, among all the central groups that man is obligated in the nature of his being to be obedient to God—not to a Jesus separated from the Almighty Creator, nor to an author of nature separate from Jesus Christ, but to God-in-Christ and Christ-in-God—and that this obedience must be rendered in the concrete, actual life of natural, cultural man. In his sex life, in eating and drinking, in commanding and obeying other men, he is in the realm of God by divine ordering under divine orders. Since none of these activities can be carried on without the use of human intelligence and will, on a purely instinctive level, since man as created is endowed and burdened with freedom as he moves among necessities, culture is itself a divine requirement. As created and ordered by God, man must achieve what has not been given him; in obedience to God he must seek many values. There is agreement on this in the central church; though there are varieties of conviction about the extent of asceticism which is to be mated with such living of the cultural life.

The main movement of the church is also characterized by a certain harmony of conviction about the universality and radical nature of sin. We have noted that radical Christians are tempted to exclude their holy commonwealths from the dominion of sin, and that cultural Christians tend to deny that it reaches into the depths of human personality. The Christians of the center are convinced that men cannot find in themselves, as persons or as communities, a holiness which can be possessed. Their agreement on the point is difficult to state, for Catholics and Protestants, Thomists and Lutherans, debate endlessly about it with each other—and doubtless misunderstand each other also. Yet the common use of the sacraments, and the com-

Christ. They will seem to represent various degrees of
tion between I John and the Gnostics, between Bened
Abélard, Tolstoy and Ritschl.

The great majority movement in Christianity, which
call the church of the center, has refused to take eitl
position of the anticultural radicals or that of the acc
dators of Christ to culture. Yet it has not regarded its ef
solution of the Christ-culture problem as compromising
ever sinful it knows all human efforts to be. For it the
mental issue does not lie between Christ and the world,
tant as that issue is, but between God and man. The
culture problem is approached from this point of view ar
this conviction. Hence, wide as are the divergences
various groups in the church of the center they agree on
points when they ask about their responsibility in the
life. The agreement is formulated in theological terms, a
relevance of such formulae to the practical questions of
tian life is often obscure both to radical critics and to un
followers. It is as great, however, as that of relativity and
tum theories to inventions, to medical and even p
practice, in which millions participate who have no
standing of the theories. One of the theologically state
victions with which the church of the center approach
cultural problem is that Jesus Christ is the Son of G
Father Almighty who created heaven and earth. Wit
formulation it introduces into the discussion about
and culture the conception of nature on which all cul
founded, and which is good and rightly ordered by the (
whom Jesus Christ is obedient and with whom he is insep
united. Where this conviction rules, Christ and the world
be simply opposed to each other. Neither can the "wor
culture be simply regarded as the realm of godlessness; s

mon hope for redemption by grace, and the common attitude toward the institutions of culture, point to a fundamental agreement of conviction about sin's universality and radical character, even when express statements are somewhat difficult to reconcile.

These believers who reject both of the extreme positions also hold in common a conviction about grace and law that distinguishes them from legalists of any sort. Once more there are differences; so that Catholics are accused by Protestants of practicing "works-righteousness," and Catholics regard modern Protestants as independent men who think they can build the kingdom of God with the aid of good social engineering. But these are the criticisms they direct against each others' Abélards and Ritschls. In their central positions there is greater agreement. Thomas and Luther are closer to each other on the subject of grace than either is to the Gnostics or the modernists of the social movements to which they belong. The Christians of the center all recognize the primacy of grace and the necessity of works of obedience; though their analyses vary of the relation of man's love of the brothers to that action of divine love which is always first. They cannot separate the works of human culture from the grace of God, for all those works are possible only by grace. But neither can they separate the experience of grace from cultural activity; for how can men love the unseen God in response to His love without serving the visible brother in human society?

Despite such common characteristics, the Christians of the center do not constitute one ordered group in their attack on the Christ-culture problem. There are at least three distinguishable families among them; and each of them may at special times or on certain specific issues find itself more closely allied to one of the extreme parties than to other movements in the central church. We have named them synthesists, dualists, and conversionists; and shall now try to give meaning to these terms by examining typical representatives of each. As we venture on this task we warn ourselves once more against the danger of confusing hypothetical types with the rich variety and the colorful individuality of historical persons. These men with whom we are now to be concerned do not allow themselves to be forced into our typical molds any more than did Tertullian, Abélard, Tolstoy, and Ritschl. Yet the simplification our procedure calls for does serve to call attention to prominent features and to guiding motivations.

II. THE SYNTHESIS OF CHRIST AND CULTURE

When Christians deal with the problem of Christ and culture, there are at all times some who see that they are not dealing with an "either-or" but with a "both-and" relation. Yet they cannot affirm both Christ and culture after the fashion of the culture Christians, since these achieve reconciliation between the spirit of Jesus Christ and the climate of current opinion by simplifying the nature of the Lord in a manner not justified by the New Testament record. As Gnostics living in a society that regards the visible world more or less unreal or deceptive, they make him a wholly other-worldly being; as modernists adjusted to a society that in thought and action discounts what eye has not seen and ear has not heard, they portray him as man of this world. But the synthesist affirms both Christ and culture, as one who confesses a Lord who is both of this world and of the other. The accommodator of Christ to the views of the time erases the distinction between God and man by divinizing man or humanizing God, and worships either a divine or a human Jesus Christ. The synthesist maintains the distinction, and with it the paradoxical conviction, that Jesus, his Lord, is both God

and man, one person with two "natures" that are neither to be
confused nor separated. For the cultural Christian reconciliation of the gospel with the spirit of the times is made possible
by its presentation either as a revelation of speculative truth
about being, or of practical knowledge of value; but the true
synthesist will have nothing to do with easy subordinations of
value to being or being to value. He sees Jesus Christ as both
Logos and Lord. Hence, when he affirms both Christ and culture, he does so as one who knows that the Christ who requires
his loyalty is greater and more complex in character than the
easier reconciliations envisage. Something of the same sort is
true of his understanding of culture; which is both divine and
human in its origin, both holy and sinful, a realm of both
necessity and freedom, and one to which both reason and revelation apply. As his understanding of the meaning of Christ
separates him from the cultural believer, so his appreciation of
culture divides him from the radical.

There is in the synthesist's view a gap between Christ and
culture that accommodation Christianity never takes seriously
enough, and that radicalism does not try to overcome. The goal
of other-worldly salvation to which Christ points cannot be
indicated in the oratorio of the gospel by means of a few grace
notes, as modernism does with its hard-to-find paragraphs on
immortality or personal religion; it is a major theme. Neither
may God's demand for present action, relevant to the crises
of social life and to the establishment of just right relations
between men, be put on a par with the tithing of anise and
mint, as something also to be done. The commandments of
Christ to sell everything for the sake of following him, to give
up judging our fellows, to turn the other cheek to the violent,
to humble ourselves and become the servants of all, to abandon
family and to forget tomorrow, cannot, the synthesist sees, be

made to rhyme with the requirements of human life in civilized
society by allegorizing them or by projecting them into the future, when changed conditions will make them possible, or by
relegating them to the sphere of personal disposition and good
intention. They are too explicit for that. Yet, because he knows
that God is the creator, he cannot evade responsibility for meeting requirements that are given in the nature of man, and
which his reason discerns as commandments to his free will. H.
must procreate children, not because the sex urge is unconquerable by reason alone, but because he was made for this end
among others, and cannot be disobedient to the requirement
given with nature prior to any culture without denying what
nature affirms and he affirms by living. He must organize social
relations, because he is created social, intelligent, and free,
inescapably a member of a group yet never an ant in its hill or
a molecule in the crystal. There are other laws besides the laws
of Jesus Christ; and they are also imperative, and also from
God. To deal with this duality as cultural Christianity or radical
faith do, is to take neither Christ nor culture seriously enough;
for they fail to do justice either to the earnestness of Christ or
to the constancy of the Creator, and each failure involves the
other. We cannot say, "Either Christ or culture," because we
are dealing with God in both cases. We must not say, "Both
Christ and culture," as though there were no great distinction
between them; but we must say, "Both Christ and culture," in
full awareness of the dual nature of our law, our end, and our
situation.

So far the synthesist agrees in large part with other types of
central Christian faith. His distinction from them arises as he
analyzes the nature of the duality in Christian life, and combines in a single structure of thought and conduct the distinctly
different elements. Some description of examples of the type

may help to clarify its methods. Illustrations may be found in many periods and many groups—in the early church, the medieval and the modern, in Roman and in Anglican Catholicism, and even, though less plainly, in Protestantism. The New Testament contains no document that clearly expresses the synthetic view; but there are many statements in gospels and epistles which sound the *motif* or which can be interpreted, without violence to the text, as containing this solution of the Christ-and-culture problem. Among them are the following: "Think not that I have come to abolish the law and the prophets; I have not come to abolish them but to fulfill them. For truly, I say to you, till heaven and earth pass away, not an iota, not a dot, will pass from the law until all is accomplished. Whoever then relaxes one of the least of these commandments and teaches men so, shall be called least in the kingdom of heaven; but he who does them and teaches them shall be called great in the kingdom of heaven."[1] "Render to Caesar the things that are Caesar's, and to God the things that are God's."[2] "Let every person be subject to the governing authorities. For there is no authority except from God, and those that exist have been instituted by God. . . . The authorities are ministers of God."[3]

Tentative efforts to state the synthetic answer, particularly in connection with the problem of revelation and philosophic wisdom, are to be found in the Apologists of the second century, particularly in Justin Martyr. Tertullian's contemporary, Clement of Alexandria, is the first great representative of the type. How he tries to do justice to sharp injunctions of Jesus, and also to the claims of nature as culture discerns them, is indicated in his little pamphlet on the subject *Who is the Rich Man That Shall be Saved*, and becomes more fully apparent in his

[1] Mt. 5:17-19; cf. 23:2.
[2] Mt. 22:21
[3] Romans 12:1, 6.

Instructor and *The Miscellanies.* In dealing with the problem of wealth, he is concerned lest the church so use Christ's commandments to the rich and promises to the poor as to drive rich men to despair of salvation. Hence the spiritual meaning of such statements must be understood, and the rich man be assisted to cultivate, in the midst of his wealth, the detached Stoic attitude of one not dependent on possessions and the Christian virtue of thankful generosity. Such a one "is blessed by the Lord and called poor in spirit, a meet heir for the kingdom of heaven, not one who could not live rich."[4] So far Clement agrees with the cultural Christian; but to this Stoicized Christianity or Christianized Stoicism he adds a new note. Over and above this gentle adjustment of the gospel to the needs of the rich, he issues a clear Christian call to respond to the love of the self-impoverished Lord. "For each of us he gave his life— the equivalent for all. This he demands of us in return, to give our lives for one another. And if we owe our lives to the brethren and have made such a mutual compact with the Savior, why should we any more hoard and shut up worldly goods, which are beggarly, foreign to us, and transitory?"[5] There are two motives, then, that should guide the Christian in his economic action; and two stages of life in economic society. Stoic detachment and Christian love are not contradictory, but they are distinct and lead to different though not contradictory actions; life among possessions by which one is not possessed and life without possessions are not identical, though not in disagreement with each other; yet these two states mark distinct stages on the way to salvation. The search for salvation by means of self-cultivation, and the response to Christ's saving act, are not one human action, but neither are they alien to each other.

[4] *Who is the Rich Man That Shall be Saved,* xvi (*Ante-Nicene Fathers.* Vol. II).
[5] *Ibid.,* xxxvii.

In writing his book called ,The Instructor, Clement, concerned with the training of Christians, presented the Lord as a
kindly and wise tutor whose aim it was to improve the souls of
his charges and to train them up to a virtuous life. Not only is
Christ's purpose the great cultural work of education; but the
kind of training he gives Christians, according to Clement,
differs scarcely at all from that which any morally serious and
wise pagan teacher of Alexandria in 200 A.D. would have given
his pupils.[6] Indeed, Clement, this first Professor of Christian
Ethics, delights in the ease with which he can refer to Plato and
Aristotle and Zeno, to Aristophanes and Menander, as guaran-
tors of the truth of his practical admonitions. Jesus Christ is
the Word, the Reason of God; his reasoning in practical affairs
is for Clement like all good, sound reasoning. Hence the Christian ethics and etiquette of The Instructor correspond closely
to the content of Stoic handbooks of morality current at the
time. Christian conduct in eating, drinking, the use of orna-
ments, the wearing of shoes, in the public baths, in sex relations,
at feasts, is minutely discussed. How to walk, how to sleep, how
to laugh in a manner befitting an heir of blessedness, is pre-
scribed with great seriousness. We read among many other
things that when we eat we must keep "hand and couch and
chin free from stains," and "guard against speaking anything
while eating, for the voice becomes disagreeable and inarticulate
when confined by full jaws"; that "we are to drink without
contortions of the face, . . . nor before drinking make the eyes
roll with unseemly motion," for "in what manner do you think
the Lord drank when he became a man for our sakes? Was it
not with decorum and propriety? Was it not deliberately? For
rest assured, he himself also partook of wine."[7] Clement always

---

[6] Cf. Lietzmann, H., The Founding of the Church Universal, chap. xiii.
[7] Op. cit., Book II, chaps, i, ii (Ante-Nicene Fathers, Vol. II).

seeks connection between his rules of decent, sober conduct and the example or words of Jesus Christ, but the relation is usually a strained one, and often made possible only by ascribing the whole Old Testament to Christ, the Logos of God. His use of bread and fish in feeding the five thousand indicates his preference for simple foods; if men are warned against shaving, it is not only because this practice goes against nature but because Jesus said " 'The very hairs of your head are all numbered'; those on the chin, too are numbered, and those on the whole body. There must be therefore no plucking out, contrary to God's appointment, which has counted them according to his will."[8] Apart from numerous trifles of this sort, which doubtless strike us as more puerile than they did the readers of Clement's day, the *Instructor* is concerned with training Christians to temperance, frugality, self-control. Whatever else is required of the disciple, the good, sound training the best culture affords, and the avoidance of that license that characterizes revolt against custom, are fundamental demands made upon him. Clement is well aware that if Christianity is in any sense against culture, it has nothing to do with that anticultural movement that arises out of individualistic contempt for the mores. He is in no danger of confusing the Sabbath-breaker who does not know what he is doing with the one who is fully aware of the meaning of his action; or a crucified thief with a crucified Christ because both are the victims of the state. Clement also knows that Christians are subject to all the ordinary temptations. His interest, therefore, in presenting the ethics of a sober, decorous, respectable life as the ethics of Christ is far removed from the interest of men who want to make discipleship easy. He is not at all concerned with the task of recommending Christ to the cultured, but wholly occupied with the problem of training the

[8] *Ibid.*, Book III, chap. iii.

immature wisely, since "it is not by nature but by learning that people become noble and good."[9] His example is Christ, the great shepherd of the sheep; and one wholly misunderstands Clement if one does not discern that all this prudent moral exhortation is the work of a man who, loving his Lord, has heard the commandment to feed the lambs.

A Christian, in Clement's view, must then first of all be a good man in accordance with the standard of good culture. Sobriety in personal conduct is to be accompanied by honesty in economic dealings, and by obedience to political authority. But this is by no means the whole of the Christian life. There is a stage of existence beyond the morally respectable life of the church-goer. Christ invites men to attain, and promises them the realization of a perfection even greater than that of the passionless wise man. It is a life of love of God for His own sake, without desire of reward or fear of punishment; a life of spontaneous goodness in which neighbors and enemies are served in response to divine love; a life in freedom, being beyond the law.[10] This sort of life is not of this world, and yet the hope of its realization and previsions of its reality fill present existence. All Clement's work as pastor and author is evidently directed toward this end of attaining and helping others to come to full knowledge of the God in whom he believes, and to a full realization in action of the love of Christ. His Christ is not against culture, but uses its best products as instruments in his work of bestowing on men what they cannot achieve by their own efforts. He exhorts them to exert themselves in self-culture and intellectual training, in order that they may be prepared for a life in which they no longer care for themselves, their culture,

[9] *The Miscellanies*, Book I, chap. vi.
[10] See the descriptions of the life of the true Gnostic in *The Miscellanies*, especially Book IV, chaps xxi-xxvi; Book V, i-iii, Book VII, x-xiv.

or their wisdom. Clement's Christ is both the Christ of culture and the Christ above all culture.

This synthesis of the New Testament and the demands of life in the world is carried out by Clement not only with regard to ethics but also in connection with philosophy and faith. He neither seeks to reinterpret the figure of Jesus so as to make him wholly compatible with the speculative systems of the day, nor does he reject as worldly wisdom the philosophy of the Greeks. It is rather "the clear image of truth, a divine gift to the Greeks"; it is "a school-master to bring 'the Hellenic mind,' as the law, the Hebrews, 'to Christ.' "[11] Had his interest led him to develop his ideas on other pursuits in culture, such as art, politics, and economics, Clement would doubtless have taken a similar attitude. God "admonishes us to use, but not to linger and spend time, with secular culture. For what was bestowed on each generation advantageously, and at seasonable time, is a preliminary training for the word of the Lord."[12]

Clement's attempt to combine appreciation of culture with loyalty to Christ was made at a time when the church was still outlawed. It represents more of a sense of responsibility in the church for the maintenance of sound morals and learning than the feeling of obligation for the continuance and improvement of the great social institutions. It is more concerned with the culture of Christians than with the Christianization of culture. Thomas Aquinas, who is probably the greatest of all the synthesists in Christian history, represents a Christianity that has achieved or accepted full social responsibility for all the great institutions. Partly because the full weight of the Roman Catholic church has been thrown into the scales in his favor, but largely because of the intellectual and practical adequacy of

[11] *Ibid.*, Book I, ii, v; cf. VI, vii-viii.
[12] *Ibid.*, Book I, v.

his system, his way of solving the problem of culture and Christ has become the standard way for hosts of Christians. Many a Protestant who has abandoned the Ritschlian answer is attracted to Thomism without being tempted to transfer his allegiance to the Roman church, while in Anglican thought and practice his system is normative for many; on the Christ-culture issue the lines drawn among Christians cannot be made to coincide with the historic distinctions among the great churches.

Thomas also answers the question about Christ and culture with a "both-and"; yet his Christ is far above culture, and he does not try to disguise the gulf that lies between them. His own manner of life indicates how he unites the two claims, the two hopes and beginnings. He is a monk, faithful to the vows of poverty, celibacy, and obedience. With the radical Christians, he has rejected the secular world. But he is a monk in the church which has become the guardian of culture, the fosterer of learning, the judge of the nations, the protector of the family, the governor of social religion. This great medieval organization, symbolized in the person of Thomas, itself represents the achievement of a remarkable practical synthesis. It is the secular church against which monasticism raised its radical protest in obedience to a Christ against culture. Yet this protest has now been incorporated into the church without losing its radical character. The synthesis was not easily attained or maintained; it was full of tensions and dynamic movements and subject to strains. Both sides of the church, the one in the world and the one in the cloister, were subject to corruption, but also served in each other's reformation. In reality the unity of church and civilization, of this world and the other, of Christ and Aristotle, of reformation and conservation, was doubtless far removed from the idealized picture later imagination and propaganda have devised. Yet it was a synthesis such as is not likely to be achieved in modern society; which lacks, among other things, two of its prerequisites—the presence of a widespread and profoundly serious radical Christianity protesting against the attenuation of the gospel by cultural religious institutions, and a cultural church great enough to accept and maintain in union with itself this loyal opposition.

Thomas Aquinas, like Albert the Great, represented this achievement rather than made it possible. Like Plato and Aristotle before him, he came at the end of the social development whose inner rationale he set forth; and his effectiveness, like theirs, was reserved for a later time. In his system of thought he combined without confusing philosophy and theology, state and church, civic and Christian virtues, natural and divine laws, Christ and culture. Out of these various elements he built a great structure of theoretical and practical wisdom, which like a cathedral was solidly planted among the streets and market-places, the houses, palaces, and universities that represent human culture, but which, when one had passed through its doors, presented a strange new world of quiet spaciousness, of sounds and colors, actions and figures, symbolic of a life beyond all secular concerns. Like Schleiermacher later, he spoke to the cultured among the despisers of Christian faith, with whom he shared the philosophy common to the advanced spirits of his time, the Aristotelianism which Moslems and Jews had rediscovered and developed. But with a Tertullian he acknowledged that what was hidden to the wise was revealed to babes.

We shall concentrate here on the manner in which Thomas sought to synthesize the ethics of culture with the ethics of the gospel. In his theories of man's end, of human virtues, and of law, as well as in other parts of his practical philosophy and practical theology, he combined into one system of divine demands and promises the requirements cultural reason discerned

and those which Jesus uttered, the hopes based on the purpose
in things as known by the cultivated mind and those grounded
on the birth, life, death, and resurrection of Christ. The whole
effort at synthesis here is informed by, if not grounded on, the
conviction of which Trinitarian doctrine is a verbal expression;
namely, that the Creator of nature and Jesus Christ and the
immanent spirit are of one essence. Man does not possess three
ways to truth, but has been given ways to three truths; and
these three truths form one system of truth. We leave aside here
the question of the spirit, and concern ourselves with what culture knows about nature and faith receives from Christ.[13]

The Christian—and any man—must answer the question
about what he ought to do by asking and answering a previous
question: What is my purpose, my end? His reasonable answer
to that query will discount all immediate wishes and desires,
while it seeks to discover the ultimate purpose of his nature,
his fundamental being. All nature as reason (that is, Greek and
Aristotelian reason, the reason of this culture) understands it,
is purposive in character; known as creation of God, its character is revelatory of God's purpose for man and of his requirements. When we regard this nature of ours with the reason that
is both God's gift and human activity, then we discern, Thomas
is certain, that the purpose implicit in our existence—since we
are made as intelligent, willing beings—is to realize our poten-
tialities completely, as intellects in the presence of universal
truth and wills in the presence of universal good. "Nothing
can set the will of man at rest but universal good, which is not
found in anything created, but in God alone. Hence God alone

---

[13] This discussion of Thomas' ethics is based on the *Summa Theologica,*
Part II, Section I, especially Qq. i-v, lv-lxx, xc-cviii; cf. also *Summa Contra
Gentiles,* Book III. All quotations are from the Dominican Fathers' translations
of these works. Cf. further, Gilson, E., *Moral Values and the Moral Life, The
System of St. Thomas Aquinas,* 1931.

can fill the heart of man."[14] And since what is at the heart of man, his best activity and best power, is the speculative understanding, the "last and perfect happiness of man cannot be otherwise than in the vision of the divine essence"; or, since "every intelligent being gains its last end by understanding it ... therefore, it is by understanding that the human intellect attains God as its end."[15] So far Thomas is a Christian Aristotelian, who has reproduced the philosopher's argument for the superiority of the contemplative life to the practical, but has named the object of intellectual vision God. He has enthroned the monastic life, not as a protest against the corrupt world, but as an effort to rise above the sensible and temporal world to contemplation of unchanging reality. With aspiration toward a last end so defined it is wholly possible for Thomas, as for Aristotle, to reconcile the efforts men direct in their practical life and noncontemplative societies toward the attainment of ordinary ends, such as health, justice, knowledge of temporal realities, economic goods. These goods are requisite to happiness, and "if we look at things rightly we may see that all human occupations seem to be ministerial to the contemplators of truth."[16] But Thomas adds to this dual ethics of a society consisting of practical men and contemplators an understanding of man's last end that is gained more from the New Testament than from Aristotle. "In the state of the present life perfect happiness is not to be had by man," for here he is subject to many evils and to transiency. What man can gain in his culture and by culture of God's original gifts in creation is only an imperfect happiness. Beyond that lies another end in eternity, for which all striving is an inadequate preparation. The attainment of that ultimate happiness is not within the range of

---

[14] *Summa Theologica, II-I,* Q. ii, art. viii.

[15] *Ibid.,* Q. iii, art. viii; *Summa contra Gentiles,* Book III, chap. xxv.

[16] *Summa Theologica, II-I,* Q. iv; *Summa contra Gentiles,* III, xxxvii.

human possibilities, but it is freely bestowed on men by God through Jesus Christ. It is bestowed, moreover, not only on those who have attained to the imperfect happiness of contemplation, but also on those who have done what they could to live rightly in unphilosophic and unmonastic surroundings. It is bestowed also on the sinners.[17] Thomas does not construct an easy synthesis of successive stages, so that man ascends from rectitude in the practical life to the imperfect happiness of contemplation and thence to the perfect happiness of eternal blessedness. The stages are there, but a leap is required as man advances from one to the other, and a leap may carry him across an intermediate stage. More than that, the steep ascent to heaven, though always involving human activity, proceeds only by power sacramentally bestowed from above.

As there is a double happiness for man, one in his life in culture and one in his life in Christ, and as the former is again a double happiness, one in practical activity and one in contemplation, so the ways to blessedness are many yet form one system of roads. There is the way of the culture of the moral life through training in good habits; and the way of intelligent self-direction; and the way of ascetic obedience to the radical counsels of Jesus; and the way of gracious, spontaneous love, faith, and hope; but this last way is not one that man can find, nor one on which he can walk by his own power. Thomas is keenly aware that moral goodness comes through effort, that society and each individual person must expend immense labor in order that the habits of action necessary to human and humane existence may be formed and maintained. Prudence, self-control, courage, justice, and specific habits of thought, speech, eating, and the other human actions are necessary to life, yet are not given to free souls as inviolable instincts are bestowed on

17 *Summa Theologica, II-I,* Q. iii. art. ii. Q. v.

animals. Man is not governed without his consent or co-opera‚ tion. What he has painfully acquired he must painfully transmit. The "merely moral life," which some exclusive Christians at least pretend to despise, is a great achievement, a product of man's freedom yet also a compulsive necessity if he is to live as a man. Without it the imperfect but required end of achieving happiness in social life is impossible; unless a man possesses the ordinary, civil, "Philistine," "bourgeois" virtues, he cannot begin to aspire after the virtues and happiness of the contemplative life. Though the cultivation of such good habits of action is man's responsibility, yet even in this sphere he is not on his own; for he is constantly being assisted and directed by the gracious God, who mediates His help through the great social institutions of family, state, and church. But now there is set before him through the gospel the other happiness "exceeding the nature of man, whereunto man can arrive only by a divine virtue involving a certain participation in the Deity. . . . Hence there must be superadded to man by the gift of God certain principles, whereby he may be put on the way to supernatural happiness, even as he is directed to his connatural end by natural principles, yet not without divine aid."[18] Thomas understands fully—as many a cultural Christian does not seem to do—how superb and superhuman is the goodness required by the commandments to love God with all one's heart, soul, mind, and strength, and to love one's neighbor as one's self. He recognizes that where faith is absent it cannot be produced by an act of will; and that the hope of glory, attractive as it appears in lives animated by it, will not come as a consequence of resolution. Yet they are not impossible virtues; neither are they accidental gifts of luck, or of a capricious nature that produces strange moral and spiritual geniuses now and again. They are

[18] *Ibid., II-I*, Q. xlii, art. i.

given and promised by God through Jesus Christ, given in a foretaste, promised in fullness. Those who receive them share in Christ's nature; they no longer live for themselves, but have been lifted out of themselves. Theirs is the active and effortless goodness of self-forgetful charity. However much men may aspire after those theological virtues, this Christlike living, they can only prepare receptive hearts; they cannot force the gift. And the gift may come to a thief on the cross before it is extended to the righteous citizen or the ascetic monk.

The same sort of synthetic combination is characteristic of Thomas' theory of the law. Man cannot live in freedom save under law, that is to say, in culture. But law must be true law, not derived from the will of the strong but discovered in the nature of things. Thomas does not seek to find a rule for human social life in the gospels. These rules must be found by reason. They constitute in their broad principles a natural law which all reasonable men living human lives under the given conditions of common human existence can discern, and which is based ultimately on the eternal law in the mind of God, the creator and ruler of all. Though the application of these principles in civil law will vary from time to time and place to place, the principles remain the same. Culture discerns the rules for culture, because culture is the work of God-given reason in God-given nature. Yet there is another law besides the law rational men discover and apply. The divine law revealed by God through His prophets and above all through His Son is partly coincident with the natural law, and partly transcends it as the law of man's supernatural life. "Thou shalt not steal" is a commandment found both by reason and in revelation; "Sell all that thou hast and give to the poor" is found in the divine law only. It applies to man as one who has had a virtue implanted in him beyond the virtue of honesty, and who has been directed in hope toward a perfection beyond justice in this mortal existence.[19]

On this basis Thomas provides not only for defense of the great social institutions, but also for their guidance in accordance with moral principles germane to their character. Private property, for instance, so suspect to the radical, is justified, for it "is not contrary to natural law, but an addition thereto devised by human reason. Yet reason discerns that though the private management of exterior goods is a fair and just arrangement their use for purely private, egoistic ends is indefensible."[20] Trade, involving profit, is lawful though not virtuous, and must be governed by principles of fair price and abstention from usury; not simply because the Bible prohibits usury but because it is unreasonable to sell "what is nonexistent."[21] Government, the state, and the use of political power are provided for in similar fashion;[22] for God has created man a social being, and society is impossible on the human level without direction in accordance with law. Beyond the state is the church, which not only directs men to their supernatural end and provides sacramental assistance, but also as custodian of the divine law assists in the ordering of the temporal life; since reason sometimes falls short of its possible performance and requires the gracious assistance of revelation, and since it cannot reach to the inner springs and motives of action.[23] The church, however, is also a double organization, the religious institution in the world and the monastic order. In Thomas' synthesis all these institutions are so organically related to each other that while each serves a particular end each also serves the others. It is

---

[19] For Thomas' theory of law see *Summa Theologica, II-I,* Qq. xc-cviii.
[20] *Ibid., II-II,* Q. lxvi, art. 2.
[21] *Ibid., II-II,* Qq. lxxvii, lxxviii.
[22] "On the Governance of Rulers."
[23] *Summa Theologica, II-I,* Qq. xcix, cviii.

easy to emphasize the hierarchical character of this structure, and to picture it as a military organization in which a chain of command extends from the Divine Lawgiver and Ruler through his vicegerent on earth, the church with its papal head, through subordinate princes and estates, and so on down the line till it reaches the final subjects, who have only to obey. There is no question about the hierarchical principle in Thomas' conception; since, as he said in his inaugural lecture as Master of Theology at Paris and repeated in many variations, his fundamental conviction was that "the King and Lord of the heavens ordained from eternity this law: that the gifts of his providence should reach to the lowest things by way of those that lie between."[24] But the synthesis would not be as attractive and successful as it is had Thomas not provided all along the line for a certain independence of each institution and of each individual, rational creature. Each has its own proper end, each its own understanding through common reason of the goal and the law of its actions, each its own will or principle of self-direction. The hierarchy is present, but it is not an Oriental satrapy; it presupposes the presence of a common mind and the consent of the governed, as well as a degree of independence in every group and person performing its own immediate task.

In so far as this common mind was present in the thirteenth century culture, and in so far as the institutions of the day formed a unity without serious strains among them, Thomas' synthesis was not only an intellectual achievement but the philosophical and theological representation of a social unification of Christ and culture. That unity was broken as soon as it was achieved, not by the Reformation and the Renaissance but apart from them, in all the conflicts and stresses of the fourteenth century. When we examine later periods of Christian

[24] So quoted by Gerald Vann in his *St. Thomas Aquinas*, pp. 45 f.

history for similar examples of the Christianity of synthesis, we are hard put to it to find adequate illustrations of the type. One is tempted to interpret Tolstoy's and Ritschl's powerful contemporary Joachim Pecci, Pope Leo XIII, as a Christian of the synthetic school. During his epoch-making pontificate he drew the Roman Catholic church out of its isolationism and its tendency to think of true Christianity as an alien society in a strange world. In his social encyclicals on "Christian Marriage," "The Christian Constitution of States," "Human Liberty," "On the Chief Duties of Christians as Citizens," and "The Condition of the Working Classes," he showed his concern for wise Christian participation in the common life, and his sense of responsibility for the maintenance or reformation of the great institutions. He was active in promoting education and encouraged the study of philosophy, for "the natural helps with which the grace of the divine wisdom, strongly and sweetly disposing all things, has supplied the human race are neither to be despised nor neglected, chief among which is evidently the right use of philosophy."[25] At the same time and without any sense of tension he proclaimed the Lordship of Christ, because he is "the origin and source of all good and just as mankind could not be freed from slavery but by the sacrifice of Christ, so neither can it be preserved but by his power."[26]

Yet Leo XIII and all who followed him in calling for a new synthesis on a Thomistic basis are not synthesists. The synthesis of Christ and culture is doubtless their goal, but they do not synthesize Christ with present culture, present philosophy, present institutions as Thomas did. When they address themselves to the "Gentiles" they do not take common ground with them,

[25] "The Study of Scholastic Philosophy," in Wynne, J. D., *The Great Encyclicals of Pope Leo XIII*, p. 36.

[26] "Christ our Redeemer," in Wynne, p. 463. Cf. also "On the Consecration of Mankind to the Sacred Heart of Jesus," Wynne, p. 454 ff.

arguing on the basis of a common philosophy, but recommend
to them the philosophy of Thomas' day. Leo XIII discourses on
"Christian Democracy" as Thomas wrote on "The Governance
of Rulers," but Leo writes in the patriarchal spirit of a feudal
society, not as one who participates in the modern political
movement as Thomas shared in the medieval.[27] What is sought
here is not the synthesis of Christ with present culture, but the
re-establishment of the philosophy and the institutions of another culture. Instead of belonging to the synthetic type, this
Christianity is of the cultural sort; its fundamental allegiance
seems to be to a kind of culture of which, to be sure, Jesus Christ
and especially his church are an important part. But the reign
and the Lordship of Jesus have been so identified with the
dogmas, organization, and mores of a cultural religious institution that the dynamic counterpoises characteristic of Thomas'
synthesis have disappeared, save in the accepted theory itself,
that is, in a kind of reflection and refraction. "By the law of
Christ," wrote Leo XIII, "we mean not merely the natural precepts of morality, or what supernatural knowledge the ancient
world acquired, all which Jesus Christ perfected and raised to
the highest plane by his explanation, interpretation, and ratifi-
cation; but we mean, besides, all the doctrine and in particular
the institutions he has left us. Of these the Church is the chief.
Indeed, what institution is there that she does not fully embrace
and include? By the ministry of the Church, so gloriously
founded by him, he willed to perpetuate the office assigned to
him by the Father, and having on the one hand conferred upon
her all effectual aids for human salvation, he ordained with the
utmost emphasis on the other that men should be subject to
her as to himself and zealously follow her guidance in every de-

[27] See Leo XIII, "Christian Democracy," Wynne, p. 479 ff.

partment of life."[28] Such a position is an exact counterpart in the Roman Catholic sphere of the cultural Christianity of the social gospel in Protestantism, for which Jesus Christ is the founder and perfecter of democratic society and of free religion and the ethics of freedom. What quarrel there is between such Roman Catholics and such Protestants is a family contention; both are primarily concerned with culture; only their ideas about the organization of society and the values to be realized by human achievement differ. Hence also their debate is carried on in the cultural society rather than in the church; these Catholics and Protestants contend with each other about the organization of states, the management and content of education, the control of trade unions, and the choice of true philosophy, not about participation or nonparticipation in the secular tasks of the world or about law and grace or the radical nature of sin. Yet we do well to remember that Leo XIII is not Catholicism and Ritschl is not Protestantism.

A better example of the synthesis of Christ and culture might be found in the Anglican bishop Joseph Butler, who in his *Analogy of Religion* and in his sermons on ethical subjects sought to relate science, philosophy, and revelation, the cultural ethics of rational self-love—so eighteenth-century English—and the ethics of Christian conscience, of the love of God and the neighbor. Alongside of Thomas Aquinas his thought seems prosaic and thin, more like a well-built village church than a cathedral; there are no vaulting arches here nor flying buttresses; the altar is not very high. In America Roger Williams ried to give an answer to the question of Christ and culture, especially with respect to political institutions, which would do justice to the distinctions of the claims of reason in society and

---

[28] "Christ Our Redeemer," in Wynne, pp. 469 f. The most objective description of Leo XIII's life and work I have found is in Schmidlin, Josef, *Papstgeschichte der Neuzeit,* Vol. II, 1934.

of Christ in the gospel. But though he distinguished he could not reunite, and left himself and his followers with a parallelism of claims rather than with a synthesis. The parallelism often resulted in a bifurcation of the spiritual and the temporal life, or of individual Christian and social rational morality, that could be resolved only by the acceptance in practice of cultural Christianity or of the solution proposed by those who follow Luther.

Whether the synthetic answer is absent from modern Christianity on account of the nature of our culture, or because of the understanding of Christ that prevails, we shall not attempt to analyze. There are many yearnings after such an answer; one hears demands that it be furnished. But none is in sight, either as the product of a great thinker or, what is more important, as an active, social life, a climate of opinion, and a living, all-permeating faith.

III. SYNTHESIS IN QUESTION

The attractiveness of the synthesist type of answer to the Christ-and-culture problem is doubtless felt by all Christians, whether or not they are drawn to the acceptance of the Thomistic system. Man's search for unity is unconquerable, and the Christian has a special reason for seeking integrity because of his fundamental faith in the God who is One. When he has realized, in consequence of experience and reflection, that he cannot be at one with himself if he denies nature and culture in the effort to be obedient to Christ, or that such denial itself involves a kind of disobedience to the commandments of love, since the social institutions are instruments of that love, then he must seek some sort of reconciliation between Christ and culture without denial of either. The drive toward moral unity in the self is mated with the urgent quest of reason to discover the unity of its principles and the unified principle of the realities toward which it is directed. In the synthesis of reason and revelation, in which the philosopher's inquiry and the prophet's proclamation are combined without confusion, reason seems to be promised the satisfaction of its hunger. With the drives toward moral and intellectual integrity the social demand for the unity of society is inseparably connected. Society itself is an expression of the desire of the many for oneness; its ills are al⁻ forms of dissension; peace is another name for social health The union of church and state, of state with state and class with class, and the union of all these with the supernatural Lord and Companion is the ineluctable desire of the believer. Synthesis seems required above all by the demand of God, not only as He operates in human nature, reason, and society by His unifying spirit, but as He reveals himself through His words and His Word. To the New Testament as well as to the Old Testament church the great proclamation is made, "Hear, O Israel, the Lord our God is one Lord." Because the synthetic type of answer seems to meet these needs and demands, therefore it will always be attractive to Christians. Even when they must reject the form in which it is offered they will see it as a symbol of the ultimate answer.

Apart perhaps from some radical and exclusive believers, all Christians find themselves in agreement with the synthesists' affirmation of the importance of the civil virtues and of just social institutions. Augustinians and Lutherans, as we shall note, regard these virtues and institutions in a different light, but join in acknowledgment of their importance for the follower of Christ and for every citizen of the commonwealth of God. What distinguishes the synthesist of Thomas' sort is his concern to discover the bases of right in the given, created nature of man and his world. His insistence that the "ought" is founded on the "is," though this in turn be founded on the "ought" in God's mind, appeals with its realism to all who are aware of the dangers of wishful thinking—not of its dangers to social life only, but of the perils to faith it involves. For the concentration on the future kingdom of God can easily lead to the denial that God reigns now; the desire for what is not present may easily bring with it the affirmation that what is presented comes from a devil rather than from God. There is an appealing greatness in the synthesist's resolute proclamation that the God who is to rule now rules and has ruled, that His rule is established in the nature of things, and that man must build on the established foundations. He expresses in this way a principle that no other Christian group seems to assert so well but which all need to share; namely, the principle that the Creator and the Savior are one, or that whatever salvation means beyond creation it does not mean the destruction of the created. Practically stated, he affirms most clearly that the conduct of life among the redeemed cannot fall short of life under law, however high it must rise beyond it; and that law is never merely a human invention, but contains the will of God. With these recognitions the synthesist offers to Christians an intelligible basis for the work they must do in co-operation with nonbelievers. Though a Tertullian says to the non-Christians, "We sail with you and fight with you, and till the ground with you; and . . . unite with you in your traffickings," he does not indicate on what ground the Christian can join such a united front, or give directions how and within what limits he can co-operate. The cultural Christian, on the other hand, makes common cause with the nonbeliever to an extent which deprives him of distinctively Christian principles. The synthesist alone seems to provide for willing and intelligent co-operation of Christians with nonbelievers in carrying on the work of the world, while yet maintaining the distinctiveness of Christian faith and life.

Alongside of this achievement of the synthetic answer stands the other—its unswerving witness to the fact that the gospel promises and requires more than the rational knowledge of the Creator's plan for the creature and willing obedience to the law of nature demand and assure. Radical critics too often forget how exalted a view of the law and the goal of love is presented by Clement and Thomas. To the synthesists the Christian life is like that of the servants to whom Jesus compared his disciples. They can never fulfill their duties, working in the fields, waiting on the tables, keeping the house in order. Yet these unworthy servants have an invitation to a royal feast at the end of the day, and so carry on a double preparation; all their menial labor is transformed for them by the inner glow of expectancy—not of their pay envelope but of an unpurchasable and unmeritable joy. There is always the *more* and the *other*; there is always "all this and heaven too"; and for the true synthesist the *more* is not an afterthought, as it so often seems to be with the cultural Christian.

Not only church but culture also is immensely indebted to the synthesists for these and other contributions. In the history of Western civilization the work of Clement, Thomas, and their followers or companions has been immeasurably influential. The arts and sciences, philosophy, law, government, education, and economic institutions have been profoundly affected by it. The men of this group have been mediators of Greek wisdom and Roman law to modern culture. They have molded and directed the most influential single religious institution in our civilization, the Roman Catholic Church; and have also helped to shape less widely effective religious organizations and movements.

When we reflect on the value to faith and to society of this way of dealing with the Christ-culture problem, it is difficult to avoid the judgment that it is a necessary approach to the question, and that the answer is a necessary affirmation of a truth or truths. That it is the whole truth and nothing but the truth is less evident. Apart from specific objections to specific formulations of the synthesis, Christians of other groups will point out that the enterprise in and of itself must lead into an error. The effort to bring Christ and culture, God's work and man's, the temporal and the eternal, law and grace, into one system of thought and practice tends, perhaps inevitably, to the absolutizing of what is relative, the reduction of the infinite to a finite form, and the materialization of the dynamic. It is one thing to assert that there is a law of God inscribed in the very structure of the creature, who must seek to know this law by the use of his reason and govern himself accordingly; it is another thing to formulate the law in the language and concepts of a reason that is always culturally conditioned. Perhaps a synthesis is possible in which the relative character of all creaturely formulations of the Creator's law will be fully recognized. But no synthesist answer so far given in Christian history has avoided the equation of a cultural view of God's law in creation with that law itself. Clement's understanding of what is natural to man is often pathetically provincial. The hierarchical view of natural order in Thomas Aquinas is historical and medieval. Provincial and historical truths may be true in the sense of corresponding to reality, but are nevertheless fragmentary, and become untrue when overemphasized. No synthesis—since it consists of fragmentary, historical, and hence of relative formulations of the law of creation, with acknowledgedly fragmentary previsions of the law of redemption—can be otherwise than provisional and symbolic. But when the synthesist recognizes this he is on the way to accepting another than the synthetic answer; he is saying then in effect that all culture is subject to continuous and infinite conversion; and that his own formulation of the elements of the synthesis, like its social achievement in the structure of church and society, is only provisional and uncertain.

It has often been remarked that Thomas, along with his whole period, lacked historical understanding. The modern recognition that reason is involved with all of culture in the continual movement of history, and that social institutions, despite the presence in them of recognizably stable elements, are everlastingly changing, coincides with the Christian reflection that all human achievement is temporal and passing. A synthesist who makes the evanescent in any sense fundamental to his theory of the Christian life will be required to turn to the defense of that temporal foundation for the sake of the superstructure it carries when changes in culture threaten it. It is logical that when a synthetic answer has been given to the problem of Christ and culture, those who accept it should become more concerned about the defense of the culture synthesized with the gospel than about the gospel itself. The two things then seem to be so interconnected that the perennial gospel seems involved in the withering of the annual culture. Whether medieval or modern, feudal or democratic, agrarian or urban civilization has been united with the gospel, whether the synthesist is Roman or Anglican or Protestant, he tends to devote himself to the restoration or conservation of a culture and thus becomes a cultural Christian. The tendency toward cultural conservatism seems endemic in the school.

On the other hand, it appears that the effort to synthesize leads to the institutionalization of Christ and the gospel. It may be that a synthesis is possible in which the law of Christ is not identified with the law of the church, in which his grace is not effectively confined to the ministry of the social religious institution, in which his Lordship is not equated with the rule of those who claim to be his successors. It may be that a synthetic answer is possible in which it is recognized that the social religious institution that calls itself the church is as much a part of the temporal order and as much a human achievement as are state, school, and economic institutions. But it is hard to see how this could be; for if Christ's grace, law, and reign are not institutionalized every synthesis must again be provisional and open, subject to radical attack, to conversion and replacement by the action of a free Lord and of men subject to his commandment rather than to the religious institution.

These objections all meet in the one point: that integrity and peace are the eternal hope and goal of the Christian, and that the temporal embodiment of this unity in a man-devised form represents a usurpation in which time seeks to exercise the power of eternity and man the power of God. As a purely symbolic action, as a humble, acknowledgedly fallible attempt, as the human side of an action that cannot be completed without the deed of the God who also initiated it, synthesis is one thing; as an authoritative statement about the way things fit together in the kingdom of God, it is another. But if it is the former it is not really synthesis.

There are other criticisms that dualists, conversionists, and radicals urge against the Thomists. One to which we shall only allude is that the effort to combine culture with Christ has involved a tendency to distinguish grades of Christian perfection; with all the mischief that results from the division of Christians into those who obey lower and higher laws, who are "psychics" or "Gnostics," secular or religious. Doubtless there are stages in the Christian life; but no succesion of finite stages brings man nearer the infinite, and no institutionalized

orders, methods of education, types of worship, or standards
of judgement can be correlated with the stages. Pastoral care
which adjusts its demands and its expectations to the immaturity or maturity of its charges is one thing; the judgment that
the contemplative life is more Christlike than the practical, or
that the monk fulfills the law of Christ more perfectly than the
economic or political man, is a different matter altogether.
Such judgments are beyond the range of men and sinners. Synthesists, however, do not seem able to combine life in the
world with life in Christ save with the aid of the idea of stages.

The major objection to the synthesists' answers which all
but the cultural Christians raise is the protest that however
much they profess that they share the presupposition of human
sinfulness, and therefore of the necessity and greatness of
Christ's salvation, they do not in fact face up to the radical
evil present in all human work. Since this objection is most
effectively raised by the dualists, we shall defer our development of the theme to the next chapter.

CHAPTER 5

※

Christ and Culture in Paradox

I. The Theology of the Dualists

Efforts to synthesize Christ and culture have been subject to sharp attacks throughout Christian history. Radicals have protested that these attempts are disguised versions of cultural accommodation of the rigorous gospel, and that they broaden the narrow way of life into an easy highway. Cultural Christians have objected that synthesists retain as evangelical truth vestigial remnants of old, immature ways of thought. The strongest opposition, however, has been voiced by neither left- nor right-wing parties but by another central group, that is to say, by one which also seeks to answer the Christ and culture question with a "both-and." This is the group which, for want of a better name, we have called *dualist*, though it is by no means dualistic in the sense that it divides the world in Manichaean fashion into realms of light and darkness, of kingdoms of God and Satan. Though the members of this group dissent from the synthesists' definitions and combinations of Christ and culture they also seek to do justice to the need for holding together as well as for distinguishing between loyalty to Christ and responsibility for culture.

If we would understand the dualists, we must note the place where they stand and take up our position with them as they

deal with our problem. For them the fundamental issue in
life is not the one which radical Christians face as they draw
the line between Christian community and pagan world.
Neither is it the issue which cultural Christianity discerns as
it sees man everywhere in conflict with nature and locates Christ
on the side of the spiritual forces of culture. Yet, like both of
these and unlike the synthesist in his more irenic and developing world, the dualist lives in conflict, and in the presence of
one great issue. That conflict is between God and man, or
better—since the dualist is an existential thinker—between
God and us; the issue lies between the righteousness of God and
the righteousness of self. On the one side are we with all of
our activities, our states and our churches, our pagan and our
Christian works; on the other side is God in Christ and Christ
in God. The question about Christ and culture in this situation
is not one which man puts to himself, but one that God asks
him; it is not a question about Christians and pagans, but a
question about God and man.

No matter what the dualist's psychological history may have
been, his logical starting point in dealing with the cultural
problem is the great act of reconciliation and forgiveness that
has occurred in the divine-human battle—the act we call Jesus
Christ. From this beginning the fact that there was and is a
conflict, the facts of God's grace and human sin are understood.
No dualist has found it easy to arrive at this starting point. Each
is quick to point out that he was on the wrong road until he
was stopped and turned round in his tracks by another will
than his own. The knowledge of the grace of God was not given
him, and he does not believe it is given to any, as a self-evident
truth of reason—as certain cultural Christians, the Deists for
instance, believe. What these regard as the sin to be forgiven and
as the grace that forgives are far removed from the depths and

heights of wickedness and goodness revealed in the cross of Christ. The faith in grace and the correlate knowledge of sin that come through the cross are of another order from that easy acceptance of kindliness in the deity and of moral error in mankind of which those speak who have never faced up to the horror of a world in which men blaspheme and try to destroy the very image of Truth and Goodness, God himself. The miracle with which the dualist begins is the miracle of God's grace, which forgives these men without any merit on their part, receives them as children of the Father, gives them repentance, hope, and assurance of salvation from the dark powers that rule in their lives, especially death, and makes them companions of the one they willed to kill. Though His demands on them are so high that they daily deny them and Him, still He remains their savior, lifting them up after every fall and setting them on the road to life.

The fact that the new beginning has been made with the revelation of God's grace does not change the fundamental situation as far as grace and sin are concerned. Grace is in God, and sin is in man. The grace of God is not a substance, a *mana*-like power, which is mediated to men through human acts. Grace is always in God's action; it is God's attribute. It is the action of reconciliation that reaches out across the no-man's land of the historic war of men against God. If something of the graciousness of Christ is reflected in the thankful responses of a Paul or a Luther to the gracious action of Christ, they themselves cannot be aware of it; and those who behold it cannot but see that it is only reflection. As soon as man tries to locate it in himself it disappears, as gratitude disappears in the moment when I turn from my benefactor to the contemplation of this beneficial virtue in me. The faith also with which man acknowledges and turns in trust to the gracious Lord is nothing that he can bring forth out of his native capacities. It is the reflection of the faithfulness of God. We trust because he is faithful. Therefore in the divine-human encounter, in the situation in which man is after as well as before he hears the word of reconciliation, grace is all on God's side. And Jesus Christ is the grace of God and the God of grace.

But sin is in man and man is in sin. In the presence of the crucified Lord of glory, men see that all their works and their work are not only pitifully inadequate, measured by that standard of goodness, but sordid and depraved. The dualist Christians differ considerably from the synthesists in their understanding of both the extent and the thoroughness of human depravity. As to extent: Clement, Thomas, and their associates note that man's reason may be darkened, but is not in its nature misdirected; for them the cure of bad reasoning lies in better reasoning, and in the aid of the divine teacher. Moreover, they regard man's religious culture in its Christian form—the institutions and doctrines of the holy church—as beyond the range of sinful corruption, however many minor evils calling for reform may now and again appear in the sacred precincts. But the dualist of Luther's type discerns corruption and degradation in all man's work. *Before the holiness of God* as disclosed in the grace of Jesus Christ there is no distinction between the wisdom of the philosopher and the folly of the simpleton, between the crime of the murderer and his chastisement by the magistrate, between the profaning of sanctuaries by blasphemers and their hallowing by priests, between the carnal sins and the spiritual aspirations of men. The dualist does not say that there are no differences between these things, but that before the holiness of God there are no significant differences; as one might say that comparisons between the highest skyscrapers and the meanest hovels are meaningless in the presence of Betelgeuse. Human culture is corrupt; and it includes all human work, not simply the achievements of men outside the church but also those in it, not only philosophy so far as it is human achievement but theology also, not only Jewish defence of Jewish law but also Christian defence of Christian precept. If we would understand the dualist here we must keep two things in mind. He is not passing judgment on other men—save as in the sinfulness to which he is subject he abandons his position before God—but testifies rather to the judgment that is being passed on him and on the whole of mankind, with which he is inseparably united not only by nature but in culture. When he speaks of the sinfulness of the law-abiding man he does so as a Paul who has been zealous in observance of the law, and as a Luther who has rigorously sought to keep the letter and the spirit of the monastic vows. When he speaks about the corruption of reason, he does so as a reasoner who has tried ardently to ascend to the knowledge of truth. What is said about the depravity of man is said therefore from the standpoint and in the situation of cultured, sinful man confronting the holiness of divine grace. The other thing that must be kept in mind is that for these believers the attitude of man before God is not an attitude man takes in addition to other positions, after he has confronted nature, or his fellow men, or the concepts of reason. It is the fundamental and ever-present situation; though man is forever trying to ignore the fact that he is up against God, or that what he is up against when he is "up against it" is God.

The dualist differs from the synthesist also in his conception of the nature of corruption in culture. Perhaps the two schools share that religious sense of sin that can never be translated into moral or intellectual terms, and the dualist only feels more profoundly the sordidness of everything that is creaturely,

human, and earthly when it is in the presence of the holy.[1]
Having contended like Job for his own goodness, he also joins
in the confession: "I had heard of thee by the hearing of the ear;
but now mine eye seeth thee: wherefore I abhor myself and
repent in dust and ashes." Yet the holiness of God as presented
in the grace of Jesus Christ has too precise a character to permit definition of its negative counterpart, human sin, in the
vague terms of primitive feeling. The sense of sordidness, of
shame, dirtiness, and pollution is the affective accompaniment
of an objective moral judgment on the nature of the self and
its society. Here is man before God, deriving his life from God,
being sustained and forgiven by God, being loved and being
lived; and this man is engaged in an attack on the One who is
his life and his being. He is denying what he must assert in the
very act of denial; he is rebelling against the One without
whose loyalty he could not even rebel. All human action, all
culture, is infected with godlessness, which is the essence of
sin. Godlessness appears as the will to live without God, to
ignore Him, to be one's own source and beginning, to live without being indebted and forgiven, to be independent and secure
in one's self, to be godlike in oneself. It has a thousand forms
and expresses itself in the most devious ways. It appears in the
complacency of self-righteously moral and of self-authenti-
catedly rational men, but also in the despair of those for whom
all is vanity. It manifests itself in irreligion, in atheism and
antitheism; but also in the piety of those who consciously carry
God around with them wherever they go. It issues in desperate
acts of passion, by which men assert themselves against the
social law with its claims to divine sanction; but also in the
zealous obedience of the law-abiding, who desperately need the

[1] Cf. Otto, Rudolf, *The Idea of the Holy*, 1924, pp. 9 ff.; also Taylor, A. E.,
The Faith of a Moralist, 1930, Vol. I, pp. 163 ff.

assurance that they are superior to the lesser breeds without the law. Thwarted in its efforts to found divine, enduring empires, the desire to be independent of God's grace expresses itself in attempts to establish godlike churches that have stored up all necessary truth and grace in doctrines and sacraments. Unable to impose its will on others through the morality of masters, the will to be god tries the methods of slave morality. When man cannot any longer assure himself that he is the master of his physical fate, he turns to the things he believes are really under his control, such things as sincerity and integrity, and tries to shelter himself under his honesty; in this domain, at least, he thinks he can get along without grace, an independent good man, needing nothing he cannot himself supply. The dualist likes to point out that the will to live as gods, hence without God, appears in man's noblest endeavors, that is, those that are noblest according to human standards. Men whose business it is to reason exalt reason to the position of judge and ruler of all things; they call it the divine element in man. Those who have the vocation of maintaining order in society deify law—and partly themselves. The independent, democratic citizen has a little god inside himself in an authoritative conscience that is not under authority. As Christians we want to be the forgivers of sins, the lovers of men, new incarnations of Christ, saviors rather than saved; secure in our own possession of the true religion, rather than dependent on a Lord who possesses us, chooses us, forgives us. If we do not try to have God under our control, then at least we try to give ourselves the assurance that we are on His side facing the rest of the world; not with that world facing Him in infinite dependence, with no security save in Him.

Thus in the dualist's view the whole edifice of culture is cracked and madly askew; the work of self-contradicting builders, erecting towers that aspire to heaven on a fault in the earth's crust. Where the synthesist rejoices in the rational content of law and social institutions, the dualist, with the skepticism of the Sophist and positivist, calls attention to the lust for power and the will of the strong which rationalizes itself in all these social arrangements. In monarchies, aristocracies, and democracies, in middle-class and proletarian rules, in episcopal, presbyterian, and congregational polities, the hand of power is never wholly disguised by its soft glove of reason. In the work of science itself reason is confounded; as on the one hand it humbly surrenders itself to the given in disinterested questioning, and on the other hand seeks knowledge for power. In all the synthesists' defences of rational elements in culture the dualist sees this fatal flaw, that reason in human affairs is never separable from its egoistic, godless, perversion. The institution of property, he points out, not only guards against theft but also sanctions the great seizures of alien possessions, as when it protects the settler in his rights over lands taken by force or deceit from Indians. The reasonable institution rests on a great irrationality. Institutions of celibacy and marriage prevent and also cover a multitude of sins. Hence the dualist joins the radical Christian in pronouncing the whole world of human culture to be godless and sick unto death. But there is this difference between them: the dualist knows that he belongs to that culture and cannot get out of it, that God indeed sustains him in it and by it; for if God in His grace did not sustain the world in its sin it would not exist for a moment.

In this situation the dualist cannot speak otherwise than in what sound like paradoxes; for he is standing on the side of man in the encounter with God, yet seeks to interpret the Word of God which he has heard coming from the other side. In this tension he must speak of revelation and reason, of law and grace, of the Creator and Redeemer. Not only his speech is paradoxical under these circumstances, but his conduct also. He is under law, and yet not under law but grace; he is sinner, and yet righteous; he believes, as a doubter; he has assurance of salvation, yet walks along the knife-edge of insecurity. In Christ all things have become new, and yet everything remains as it was from the beginning. God has revealed Himself in Christ, but hidden Himself in His revelation; the believer knows the One in whom he has believed, yet walks by faith, not sight.

Among these paradoxes two are of particular importance in the dualists' answer to the Christ-culture problem: those of law and grace, and of divine wrath and mercy. The dualist joins the radical Christian in maintaining the authority of the law of Christ over all men, and in stating it in its plain literal sense, objecting to the attenuations of the gospel precepts by cultural or synthetic Christians. The law of Christ is not, in his understanding, an addition to the law of man's nature but its true statement, a code for the average, normal man, and not a special rule for spiritual supermen. Yet he also insists that no human self-culture, in obedience to that law or any other, can avail to extricate man out of his sinful dilemma. Nor are institutions that claim this law as their basis—monastic orders or pacifist customs or communistic communities—less subject to the sin of godlessness and self-love than are the cruder forms of custom and society. The law of God in the hands of men is an instrument of sin. Yet as coming from God and heard from His lips it is a means of grace. But, again, it is a kind of negative means, driving man to despair of himself and so preparing him to turn away from himself to God. When, however, the sinner throws himself on the divine mercy and lives by that mercy alone, the law is reinstated in a new form, as something written on the heart—a law of nature, not an external commandment. Still, it is the law of God which the forgiven receives as the will of the Other rather than as his own. Thus the dialogue about law proceeds. It sounds paradoxical, because the effort is being made to state in a monologue a meaning that is clear only in the dramatic encounters and re-encounters of God and the souls of men. In his shorthand synopsis of the great action, the dualist seems to be saying that the law of life is not law but grace; that grace is not grace but law, an infinite demand made on man; that love is an impossible possibility and hope of salvation an improbable assurance. These are the abstractions; the reality is the continuing dialogue and struggle of man with God, with its questions and answers, its divine victories that look like defeats, its human defeats that turn into victories.

The situation the dualist is attempting to describe in his paradoxical language is further complicated by the fact that man encountering God does not meet a simple unity. The dualist is always a Trinitarian, or at least a binitarian, for whom the relations of the Son and the Father are dynamic. But besides this he notes in God as revealed in nature and Christ and the Scriptures the duality of mercy and wrath. In nature man meets not only reason, order, and life-giving goodness, but also force, conflict, and destruction; in the Scriptures he hears the word of the prophet, "Shall evil befall a city and the Lord hath not done it?" On the cross he sees a Son of God who is not only the victim of human wickedness but is also one delivered to death by the power that presides over all things. Yet from this cross there comes the knowledge of a Mercy which freely gives itself and its best-beloved for the redemption of men. What seemed to be wrath is now seen to have been love, which chastised for the sake of correction. But this love is also a demand, and appears as wrath against the despisers and violators of love. Wrath and mercy remain to the end intermingled. The temptation of the dualist is to separate the two principles; and to posit two gods, or a division in the Godhead. The true dualist resists the temptation, but continues to live in the tension between mercy and wrath. When he deals with the problems of culture, he cannot forget that the dark sides of human social life, such things as vices, crimes, wars, and punishments, are weapons in the hands of a wrathful God of mercy, as well as assertions of human wrath and man's godlessness.

II. The Dualistic Motif in Paul and Marcion

In the case of dualism even more than in that of the previous answers to the Christ and culture question we ought to speak of a *motif* in Christian thinking rather than of a school of thought. It is more difficult to find relatively clear-cut, consistent examples of this approach than of the others; and the *motif* often appears in some isolation, confined to special areas of the cultural problem. It may be used in dealing with reason and revelation by a thinker who does not employ it when he considers political questions. It may appear in discussions about Christian participation in government and war, by believers whose solution of the reason-revelation problem sounds more like that of the synthesists. Important in the thought of many Christians, it is so strongly emphasized a *motif* in the writings of some, such as Luther, that it may be permissible to speak also of a group or a school, relatively distinct from the others.

Whether or not Paul may be counted a member of such a group, it is evident that its later representatives are his spiritual descendants, and that the *motif* is more pronouncedly present in his thought than are synthetic or radical, not to speak of cultural, tendencies. The issue of life, as Paul sees it, lies between the righteousness of God and the righteousness of man, or between the goodness with which God is good and desires to make men good on the one hand, and on the other the kind of independent goodness man seeks to have in himself. Christ defines the issue, and solves the problem of life by his continuous action of revelation, reconciliation, and inspiration. There is no question about the centrality of Jesus Christ in the life and thought of the man for whom Christ was "the power of God and the wisdom of God," the mediator of divine judgment, the offering for sin, the reconciler of men to God, the giver of peace and eternal life, the spirit, the interceder for men, the head of the church and progenitor of a new humanity, the image of the invisible God, the "one Lord, through whom are all things and through whom we exist." On his cross Paul had died to the world and the world had died to him; henceforth to live meant to be with Christ and for Christ and under Christ, knowing nothing and desiring nothing save him. This Christ of the apostle was Jesus. The time is past when the identity of Paul's Lord with the Rabbi of Nazareth could be questioned. The one he had seen, who dwelt in his mind and possessed him body and soul, was most evidently that friend of sinners and judge of the self-sufficiently righteous, that prophet and lawgiver of the Sermon on the Mount, and that healer of diseases who had been condemned by Paul's fellow Jews, crucified by his fellow Romans, and seen in resurrected as in mortal existence by his fellow apostles.[2]

In a double sense the encounter with God in Christ had relativized for Paul all cultural institutions and distinctions, all the works of man. They were all included under sin; in all of them men were open to the divine ingression of the grace of the Lord. Whether men were by culture Jews or pagans, bar-

[2] Cf. especially Porter, F. C., *The Mind of Christ in Paul*, 1930.

barians or Greeks, they stood on the same level of a sinful humanity before the wrath of God, "revealed from heaven against all ungodliness and unrighteousness." Whether law was known by reason or made known through past revelation it condemned men equally, was equally ineffective in saving them from lawlessness and self-seeking, and was equally instrument of divine wrath and mercy. God by the revelation of His glory and grace in Jesus Christ had convicted all religion of faithlessness, whether it was the worship of images resembling men, birds, beasts, and reptiles, or trust in the Torah, whether it stressed ritual observances or the keeping of ethical laws. Both the knowledge that found its basis in reason, and the one that looked to revelation for its foundation, were equally remote from the knowledge of the glory of God in the face of Jesus Christ. Christ destroyed the wisdom of the wise and the righteousness of the good, which had rejected him in different ways but to the same degree. But he did not sanction the folly of the unwise or the iniquity of transgressors; these also were included under sin, the evident subjects of its rule. If human spiritual attainments fell short of the glorious achievement of Christ and appeared corrupted when illuminated by his cross, the total inadequacy and depravity of physical values was also evident. Had Paul spoken in this connection more explicitly than he did of the institutions of culture—family, school, state, and religious community—he would, it seems clear, have had to deal with them in the same fashion. Christ had brought to light the unrighteousness of every human work.

Yet in every position in culture and in every culture, in all the activities and stations of men in civilized life, they were also equally subject to his redemptive work. Through his cross and resurrection he redeemed them from their prison of self-centeredness, the fear of death, hopelessness and godlessness.

The word of the cross came to married and unmarried, to moral and immoral, to slaves and freemen, to the obedient and disobedient, the wise and the righteous, the fools and the unrighteous. By the redemption they were born anew, given a new beginning which was not in themselves but in God, a new spirit which proceeded from Christ, a love to God and neighbors which constrained them to do without constraint what law had never been able to accomplish. In freedom from sin and freedom from law they were empowered by love to rejoice in the right, to bear all things, to be patient and kind. Out of the inner fountains of the spirit of Christ there would flow forth love, joy, peace, patience, kindness, goodness, faithfulness, gentleness, self-control. Not as lawgiver of a new Christian culture but as the mediator of a new principle of life—a life of peace with God—Christ did and does this mighty work in the creation of a new kind of humanity.

It would be false to interpret all this in eschatological terms, as if Paul looked upon human culture from the point of view of a time when it would be judged at a final assize, and a new era of life would be inaugurated. In the cross of Christ man's work was now judged; by his resurrection the new life had now been introduced into history. Whoever had had his eyes opened to the goodness with which God is good and to His wrath upon all godlessness saw clearly that human culture had been judged and condemned; if long-suffering patience kept such men and their works alive a little longer, if the final assize was delayed, that was not an invalidation but a further demonstration of the Pauline gospel. The new life, moreover, was not simply a promise and a hope but a present reality, evident in the ability of men to call upon God as their Father and to bring forth fruits of the spirit of Christ within them and their community.

The great revolution in human existence was not past; neither was it still to come: it was now going on.

With this understanding of the work of Christ and the works of man, Paul could not take the way of the radical Christian with his new Christian law by attempting to remove himself and other disciples out of the cultural world into an isolated community of the saved. He warns, as a matter of course, against participation in actions and customs that are flagrant exhibitions of human faithlessness, lovelessness, hopelessness, and godlessness. "The works of the flesh are plain: immorality, impurity, licentiousness, idolatry, sorcery, enmity, strife, jealousy, anger, selfishness, dissension, party spirit, envy, drunkenness, carousing and the like. . . . Those who do such things shall not inherit the kingdom of God."[3] But he is far from suggesting that those who refrain from such conduct will therefore inherit the kingdom, or that training in good moral habits is a step in preparation for the gift of the spirit. His experience with Galatian and Corinthian, with Judaizing and spiritualizing Christians had taught him—if after his years of wrestling with Christ and the gospel he needed to be taught—that the anti-Christian spirit could not be evaded by any measures of isolation from pagan culture, by any substitution of new laws for old ones, or by supplanting the pride of Hellenistic philosophy with the pride of a Christian *gnosis*. The pervasive reign of sin could manifest itself in the actions and customs of Christians, in their lovelessness at love feasts, their speaking in tongues, their pride in spiritual attainments, their almsgivings, and their martyrdoms. Since the battle was not with flesh and blood but against spiritual principles in the minds and hearts of men, there was no hiding place from their attacks in a new, Christian culture. The Christians' citizenship was in heaven, their hiding

3 Gal. 5:19-21.

place was with the risen Christ. As far as this world was concerned it was their task to work out their salvation, and their gift to live in the spirit of Christ in whatever community or station in life they had been apprehended by the Lord. It was not possible to come closer to the reign of Christ by changing cultural customs, as in matters of food and drink or the keeping of holy days, by abandoning family life in favor of celibacy, by seeking release from chattel slavery, or by escaping from the rule of political authorities.

And yet Paul added to his proclamation of the gospel of a new life in Christ a cultural Christian ethics; for the new life in faith, hope, and love remained weak, and subject to struggle with Satan, sin, and death. It had to be lived, moreover, in the midst of societies evidently subject to the dark powers. This ethics was in part an ethics of Christian culture, in part an ethics for intercultural relations. For Christian culture it provided injunctions against sexual immorality, theft, idleness, drunkenness, and other common vices. It regulated marriage and divorce, the relations of husbands and wives, of parents and children; it dealt with the adjustment of quarrels among Christians, sought to prevent factions and heresies, gave directions for the conduct of religious meetings, and provided for the financial support of needy Christian communities. In so far as this ethics concerned itself with the relations of Christians and their churches to non-Christian social institutions, its provisions were various. Political authorities were recognized as divinely instituted, and obedience to their laws was required as a Christian duty; yet believers were not to make use of the law courts in pressing claims against each other. Economic institutions, including slavery, were regarded with a certain indifference or taken for granted. Only the religious institutions and customs of non-Christian society were completely rejected.

This ethics of Christian culture and of Christian life in culture had various sources. Little effort was made to derive it directly from the teachings of Jesus, though in a number of instances his words were of basic importance. For the rest it was based on common notions of what was right and fitting, on the Ten Commandments, on Christian tradition, and on Paul's own common sense. Direct inspiration, apart from such use of tradition and reason, is not referred to as source of the laws and the counsels.

Thus Paul seems to move in the direction of a synthetic answer to the Christ-and-culture problem; and yet the manner in which he relates the ethics of Christian culture to the ethics of the spirit of Christ is markedly different from the way in which a Clement and a Thomas proceed from the one to the other. For one thing, the order is different; since the synthesists move from culture to Christ, or from Christ the instructor to Christ the redeemer, whereas Paul moves from Christ the judge of culture and the redeemer to Christian culture. This variation in order is connected with something more significant. The synthesist regards the cultural life as having a certain positive value of its own, with its own possibilities for the achievement of an imperfect but real happiness. It is directed toward the attainment of positive values. But for Paul it has a kind of negative function. The institutions of Christian society and the laws for that society, as well as the institutions of pagan culture in so far as they are to be recognized, seem more designed, in his view, to prevent sin from becoming as destructive as it might otherwise be, rather than to further the attainment of positive good. "Because of the temptation to immorality, each man should have his own wife and each woman her own husband." The governing authorities are servants of God "to execute his wrath on the wrong-doer."[4] The function of law is to restrain and expose sin rather than to guide men to divine righteousness. Instead of two ethics for two stages on life's way or for two kinds of Christians, the immature and the mature, Paul's two ethics refer to contradictory tendencies in life. The one is the ethics of regeneration and eternal life, the other is the ethics for the prevention of degeneration. In its Christian form it is not exactly an ethics of death, but it is an ethics for the dying. Hence there is no recognition here of two sorts of virtues, the moral and the theological. There is no virtue save the love that is in Christ, inextricably combined with faith and hope. From this all other excellence flows. The ethics of Christian culture, and of the culture in which Christians live, is as such without virtue; at its best it is the ethics of nonviciousness —though there are no neutral points in a life always subject to sin and to grace.

In this sense Paul is a dualist. His two ethics are not contradictory, but neither do they form parts of one closely knit system. They cannot do so, because they refer to contradictory ends, life and death, and represent strategies on two different fronts—the front of the divine-human encounter, and the front of the struggle with sin and the powers of darkness. The one is the ethics of Christians as they yield to the overwhelming mercy of God; the other has in view His inclusive wrath against all unrighteousness. Paul's dualism is connected not only with this view of Christian life as being lived in the time of the final struggle and of the new birth, but also with his belief that the whole cultural life together with its natural foundations is so subject to sin and to wrath that the triumph of Christ must involve the temporal end of the whole temporal creation as well as of temporal culture. "Flesh" in his thought represents not

[4] I Cor. 7:2; Rom. 13:4.

only an ethical principle, the corrupt element in human spiritual life, but also something physical from which man must be redeemed. Life in grace is not only life coming from God, but life outside the human body. "While we are still in this tent, we sigh with anxiety; . . . while we are at home in the body we are away from the Lord."[5] Dying to self and rising with Christ are spiritual events, yet remain incomplete without the death of the terrestrial body and its renewal in celestial form. As long as man remains in the body he has need then, it seems, of a culture and of the institutions of culture not because they advance him toward life with Christ but because they restrain wickedness in a sinful and temporal world. The two elements in Paul are by no means of equal importance. His heart and mind are all devoted to the ethics of the kingdom and eternal life. Only the necessities of the moment, while the new life remains hidden and disorder reappears in the churches themselves, wring from him the laws, admonitions, and counsels of a Christian cultural ethics.

In the second century the dualistic answer to the Christ-and-culture question was confusedly and erratically offered by Paul's strange follower Marcion. He is often counted with the Gnostics, for he was almost violent in his efforts to wrest Christian faith free from its associations with Jewish culture, particularly in his attempt to exclude the Old Testament and all elements derived from it from the Christian Scriptures. At the same time he used Gnostic ideas in his theology. On the other hand we must associate him with the radical Christians, for he founded a sect separated from the church and marked by rigorous asceticism. He is often thought to have gone beyond this and to have become a kind of Manichaean, who distinguished two principles in reality and divided the world between God and the power

---

[5] II Cor. 5:4, 6. See below, ch. VI. note 2.

of evil. But as Harnack and others have made clear, Marcion was first of all a Paulinist, for whom the gospel of divine grace and mercy was the wonder of wonders, arousing astonishment and ecstasy, something which could not be compared with anything else.[6] He did not begin with the law of Christ, but with the revelation of divine goodness and mercy. But there were two things he could not rhyme with that gospel. One of these was the Old Testament presentation of God as the wrathful guardian of justice, and the other was the actual life of man in this physical world with the demands, the indignities and the horrors to be faced in it. Had only the Old Testament bothered him he might have dismissed it, and developed a theology of a kind Father Creator and an ethics of love bound to be successful in a world fashioned for grace. But the actual world as Marcion saw it was "stupid and bad, crawling with vermin, a miserable hole, an object of scorn." How was it possible to think that the God of all grace, the Father of mercies, had made it, and was responsible among other things for "the disgusting paraphernalia of reproduction and for all the nauseating defilements of the human flesh from birth to final putrescence"?[7] In such a world, family, state, economic institutions, and harsh justice doubtless had their place; but the whole arrangement was evidently a botched piece of work, the product of poor workmanship and vile material. The life in Christ and his spirit, the blessedness of mercy responding to mercy, belonged to a wholly different sphere.

With this understanding of Christ, and of a culture founded on nature, Marcion sought for his solution. He found his answer in the belief that men were dealing with two gods: the just but bungling and limited deity who had created the world

---

[6] Harnack, A. v., *Marcion, Das Evangelium vom Fremden Gott*, chaps. iii and vi; cf. Lietzmann, H., *The Beginnings of the Christian Church*, pp. 333 ff.

[7] So Harnack describes Marcion's view; *op. cit.*, pp. 144, 145; cf. pp. 94, 97.

out of evil matter; and the good God, the Father, who through Christ rescued men from their desperate plight in the mixed world of justice and matter. He recognized two moralities, the ethics of justice and the ethics of love; but the former was inextricably bound up with corruption, and Christ lived, preached, and communicated only the latter.[8] Hence Marcion sought to draw Christians out of the physical as well as the cultural world as much as possible, and formed communities in which the sex life was sternly suppressed—even marriage being prohibited to believers—in which fasting was more than religious rite, but in which also relations of mercy and love between men were to be realized in accordance with the gospel.[9] Even so, while men remained physically alive they could only live in hope of and in preparation for their salvation by the good God.

Marcion's answer, then, in effect was not truly dualistic but more like that of an exclusive Christian. The true dualist lives in tension between two magnetic poles; Marcion broke the poles apart. Justice and love, wrath and mercy, creation and redemption, culture and Christ, were sundered; and the Marcionite Christian endeavored to live not only outside the world of sin but as far as possible, outside the world of nature, with which sin and justice were inextricably united. Under these circumstances the gospel of mercy became for him a new law, and the community of the redeemed a new cultural society.

The dualistic motif is strong in Augustine; but since the conversionist note seems more characteristic of his thought we defer consideration of his views to a later connection. In medieval Christianity the dualistic solution appears in special areas, as when Scotists and Occamists abandon the synthetic way of dealing with revelation and reason yet seek to maintain the

[8] Harnack, *op. cit.*, p. 150.
[9] *Ibid.*, pp. 186 ff.

validity of each. It is offered also in connection with the problem of church and state, as in Wycliffe's reply to that question.

III. Dualism in Luther and Modern Times

Martin Luther is most representative of the type, though he like Paul is too complex to permit neat identification of an historic individual with a stylized pattern. The strongly dualistic note in his answer to the Christ-culture problem is apparent when we place alongside each other his two most widely known (though by no means best) works, the *Treatise on Christian Liberty* and the call to resistance *Against the Robbing and Murdering Hordes of Peasants*. They differ from each other somewhat as Paul's hymn on the love which is not irritable or resentful differs from his attack on the Judaizers, with its wish that those who unsettle the new Christians with their talk about circumcision would mutilate themselves.[10] But the distance between these writings of Luther is far greater than anything of the sort to be found in Paul. Doubtless personal temperament plays its role here; but another factor must also be considered. Luther had a responsibility for a total national society in a time of turmoil which Paul could have shared only if he had been Cicero or Marcus Aurelius and Paul in one person. Yet, be that as it may, it is a far cry from Luther's celebration of the faith that works by love, suffering all things in serving the neighbor, to his injunction to the rulers to "stab, smite, slay, whoever can." In *Christian Liberty* he writes, "From faith flow forth love and joy in the Lord, and from love a joyful, willing and free mind that serves one's neighbor willingly and takes no account of gratitude or ingratitude, of praise or blame, of gain or loss. . . . For as his Father does, distributing all things

[10] Gal. 5:12.

to all men richly and freely, causing His sun to shine upon the
good and upon the evil, so also the son does all things and suffers
all things with that freely bestowing joy which is his delight
when through Christ he sees it in God, the dispenser of such
great benefits."[11] But in the pamphlet against the peasants we
read that "a prince or lord must remember in this case that he
is God's minister and the servant of his wrath to whom the
sword is committed for use upon such fellows. . . . Here there
is no time for sleeping; no place for patience or mercy. It is the
time of the sword, not the day of grace."[12] The duality which
is so evident in the juxtaposition of these statements appears at
many other points in Luther, though it is not usually quite so
sharp. He seems to have a double attitude toward reason and
philosophy, toward business and trade, toward religious organizations and rites, as well as toward state and politics. These
antinomies and paradoxes have often led to the suggestion that
Luther divided life into compartments, or taught that the Christian right hand should not know what a man's worldly left hand
was doing. His utterances sometimes seem to support this view.
He makes sharp distinctions between the temporal and spiritual
life, or between what is external and internal, between body
and soul, between the reign of Christ and the world of human
works or culture. It is very important for him that there should
be no confusion of these distinctions. Accordingly in defending
his pamphlet against the peasants he writes, "There are two
kingdoms, one the kingdom of God, the other the kingdom of
the world. . . . God's kingdom is a kingdom of grace and mercy
. . . but the kingdom of the world is a kingdom of wrath and
severity. . . . Now he who would confuse these two kingdoms
—as our false fanatics do—would put wrath into God's kingdom

[11] *Works of Martin Luther*, Philadelphia, 1915-1932, Vol. II, p. 338.
[12] *Ibid.*, Vol. IV, pp. 251 f.

and mercy into the world's kingdom; and that is the same as putting the devil in heaven and God in hell."[13]

Luther does not, however, divide what he distinguishes. The life in Christ and the life in culture, in the kingdom of God and the kingdom of the world, are closely related. The Christian must affirm both in a single act of obedience to the one God of mercy and wrath, not as a divided soul with a double allegiance and duty. Luther rejected the synthesist solution of the Christian problem, but was at least equally firm in maintaining the unity of God and the unity of the Christian life in culture. He rejected it for a number of reasons: it tended to make the radical commandments of Christ relevant only to the few more perfect Christians, or to a future life, rather than to accept them as they stood—unconditional demands on all souls in every present moment; it tended both to disquiet and to comfort the consciences of men in ways hard to reconcile with the gospel; it passed over too easily the sin of godlessness which infects both the efforts to live an ordinary, virtuous life and the striving after saintliness; it did not adequately present the singular majesty of Christ both as lawgiver and as savior, associating him too much with other masters and redeemers. The basis for Luther's thought and for his career as a reformer of Christian morals was laid when he came under the conviction that what was demanded of man in the gospel was absolutely required by an absolute Lord.[14]

[13] *Works,* Vol. IV, pp. 265, 266.

[14] An excellent description of Luther's development as Christian ethical thinker and reformer is given in Prof. Karl Holl's article "Der Neubau der Sittlichkeit" in his *Gesammelte Aufsaetze zur Kirchengeschichte,* Vol. I, 6th ed., pp. 155 ff. Holl's treatment unfortunately is marked by an anti-Catholic bias, corresponding to the anti-Lutheran animus of such writers as Grisar, and by a desire to show how original Luther was even in comparison with Augustine The article, however, is superior to the widely used treatment of Luther's ethics by Ernst Troeltsch in his *Social Teachings of the Christian Churches,* Vol. II. Holl's interpretation of Luther's attitude toward culture makes him more of a conversionist than the present writer finds tenable.

If this realization seemed to direct him to take the exclusive Christian position and to reject life in culture as
incompatible with the gospel, he was prevented from making
that choice by the realization that the law of Christ was more
demanding than radical Christianity believed; that it required
complete, spontaneous, wholly self-forgetful love of God and
neighbor, without side glances toward one's temporal or eternal
profit. The second step in Luther's moral and religious development came, then, when he thoroughly understood that the
gospel as law and as promise was not directly concerned with
the overt actions of men but with the springs of conduct; that
it was the measure by which God recreated the souls of men so
that they might really perform good works. As lawgiver Christ
puts all men under the conviction of their sinfulness, their lovelessness and faithlessness. He shows them that an evil tree cannot bring forth good fruit, and that they are evil trees; that they
cannot become righteous by acting righteously, but can act righteously only if first of all they are righteous; and that they are
unrighteous.[15] But as savior he creates in those in whom he
destroyed self-confidence that trust in God out of which can
flow love of neighbor. As long as man mistrusts his Creator he
will in his anxiety for himself and his goods be unable to do
anything in all his service of others but serve himself. He is
involved in the vicious circle of self-love, which leads him to
look for credit for every apparently altruistic action, and which
makes even his service of God a work for which he expects the
reward of approval. Christ by his law and by his deed of
redemption breaks this circle of self-love, and creates trust in
God and reliance on Him as the only one who can and does
make men righteous—not within themselves but in the response
to Him of their humbled and grateful hearts. Luther under-

[15] Cf. "Treatise on Good Works," *Works*, Vol. I, "Treatise on Christian
Liberty," *Works*, Vol. II; cf. Holl, *op. cit.*, pp. 217 ff., 290 f.

stood that the self could not conquer self-love, but that it was conquered when the self found its security in God, was delivered from anxiety and thus set free to serve the neighbor self-forget-fully.

This is the basis of Luther's dualism. Christ deals with the fundamental problems of the moral life; he cleanses the springs of action; he creates and recreates the ultimate community in which all action takes place. But by the same token he does not directly govern the external actions or construct the immediate community in which man carries on his work. On the contrary, he sets men free from the inner necessity of finding special voca-tions and founding special communities in which to attempt to acquire self-respect, and human and divine approval. He releases them from monasteries and the conventicles of the pious for service of their actual neighbors in the world through all the ordinary vocations of men.

More than any great Christian leader before him, Luther affirmed the life in culture as the sphere in which Christ could and ought to be followed; and more than any other he dis-cerned that the rules to be followed in the cultural life were independent of Christian or church law. Though philosophy offered no road to faith, yet the faithful man could take the philosophic road to such goals as were attainable by that way. In a person "regenerate and enlightened by the Holy Spirit through the Word" the natural wisdom of man "is a fair and glorious instrument and work of God."[16] The education of youth in languages, arts, and history as well as in piety offered great opportunities to the free Christian man; but cultural education was also a duty to be undertaken.[17] "Music," said

[16] Kerr, H. T., *A Compend of Luther's Theology*, pp. 4-5; cf. Holl's remarks on the effect of the Reformation on philosophy, *op. cit.*, 529 ff.

[17] Cf. "To the Councilmen of All Cities in Germany That They Establish and Maintain Christian Schools," *Works*, Vol. IV, pp. 103 ff.

Luther, "is a noble gift of God, next to theology. I would not change my little knowledge of music for a great deal."[18] Commerce was also open to the Christian for "buying and selling are necessary. They cannot be dispensed with and can be practiced in a Christian manner."[19] Political activities, and even the career of the soldier, were even more necessary to the common life, and were therefore spheres in which the neighbor could be served and God be obeyed.[20] A few vocations were ruled out, of course, since they were evidently irreconcilable with faith in God and love of neighbor. Among these Luther eventually included the monastic life. In all these vocations, in all this cultural work in the service of others, the technical rules of that particular work needed to be followed. A Christian was not only free to work in culture but free to choose those methods which were called for, in order that the objective good with which he was concerned in his work might be achieved. As he cannot derive the laws of medical procedure from the gospel when he deals with a case of typhus, so he cannot deduce from the commandment of love the specific laws to be enacted in a commonwealth containing criminals. Luther had great admiration for the geniuses among men, who in their various spheres hit upon novel procedures rather than followed the traditional processes.

We may say, then, that the dualism in Luther's solution of the Christ-and-culture problem was the dualism of the "How" and the "What" of conduct. From Christ we receive the knowledge and the freedom to do faithfully and lovingly what culture teaches or requires us to do. The psychological premise of Luther's ethics is the conviction that man is a dynamic being,

18 Kerr, *op. cit.*, p. 147.
19 "On Trading and Usury," *Works*, Vol. IV, p. 13.
20 "Secular Authority: To What Extent It Should be Obeyed," *Works*, Vol. III, pp. 230 ff.; "Whether Soldiers, Too, Can Be Saved," *Works*, Vol. V, pp. 34 ff.

forever active. "The being and nature of man cannot for an instant be without doing or not doing something, enduring or running away from something, for life never rests."[21] The drive to action, it seems, comes from our God-given nature; its direction and spirit is a function of faith; its content comes from reason and culture. Hunger drives us to eat; our faith or lack of it determine whether we eat as good neighbors, with concern for others and to the glory of God, or anxiously, immoderately, and selfishly; our knowledge of dietetics and the dietary customs of our society—not Hebraic legislation about clean and unclean or church laws about fasting—determine what and when to eat. Or, our curiosity makes us seek knowledge; our religious attitude determines how we seek it, whether with anxiety for reputation or for the sake of service, whether for the sake of power or for God's glory; reason and culture show us by what methods and in what areas knowledge may be gained. As there is no way of deriving knowledge from the gospel about what to do as physician, builder, carpenter, or statesman, so there is no way of gaining the right spirit of service, of confidence and hopefulness, of humility and readiness to accept correction, from any amount of technical or cultural knowledge. No increase of scientific and technical knowledge can renew the spirit within us; but the right spirit will impel us to seek knowledge and skill in our special vocations in the world in order that we may render service. It is important for Luther that these things be kept distinct despite their interrelations, for to confuse them leads to the corruption of both. If we look to the revelation of God for knowledge of geology, we miss the revelation; but if we look to geology for faith in God, we miss both Him and the rocks. If we make a rule for civil government out of the structure of the early Christian community, we

---

[21] "Treatise on Good Works," *Works,* Vol. I, pp. 198 f.

substitute for the spirit of that community, with its dependence on Christ and his giving of all good gifts, a self-righteous independence of our own; if we regard our political structures as kingdoms of God, and expect through papacies and kingdoms to come closer to Him, we cannot hear His word or see His Christ; neither can we conduct our political affairs in the right spirit.

Great tensions remain, for technique and spirit interpenetrate, and are not easily distinguished and recombined in a single act of obedience to God. Technique is directed toward temporal things; but spirit is a function of the Christian's relations to the eternal. The spirit is something highly personal; it is the deepest thing in man; technique is a habit, a skill, a function of the office or vocation he has in society. The Christian spirit of faith is oriented toward the divine mercy; the techniques of men are often designed to prevent the evils that arise from the flouting of divine justice. The Christian is dealing every moment, as a citizen of the eternal kingdom and over-arching empire of God, with the immediate transitory values of physical men, his own but above all his neighbors'. The sort of conflict a statesman must feel when he causes crops of cereal to be plowed under for the sake of the long-range prosperity of a nation is here immensely increased. Temporally we employ our best knowledge to gain our daily bread; as citizens of eternity we are (or ought to be) without anxiety. This tension is made the more acute by the fact that it is combined with the polarity of person and society. For himself, as an individual infinitely dependent on God and trusting in Him, a person feels the demand and perhaps the possibility of doing his work without hope of earthly reward; but he is also father and breadwinner, an instrument by which God supplies daily food to children. As such he cannot in obedience to God forgo his claims to his wages. The tension becomes still more acute when what is required of man in his service of others is the use of instruments of wrath for the sake of protecting them against the wrathful. Luther is quite clear on this point. So far as a person is responsible only for himself and his goods, faith makes possible what the law of Christ demands, that he do not defend himself against thieves or borrowers, against tyrants or foes. But where he has been entrusted with the care of others, as father or governor, there in obedience to God he must use force to defend his neighbors against force. The greater sin here is to want to be holy or to exercise mercy where mercy is destructive.[22] As God does a "strange" work—that is, a work not apparently merciful but wrathful—in natural and historical calamities, so He requires the obedient Christian to do "strange" work that hides the mercy of which it is the instrument.

Living between time and eternity, between wrath and mercy, between culture and Christ, the true Lutheran finds life both tragic and joyful. There is no solution of the dilemma this side of death. Christians along with other men have received the common gift of hope that the present evil state of affairs in the world will come to an end and a good time will come. And yet there is no two-fold happiness for them, since as long as life lasts there is sin. The hope of a better culture "is not their chief concern, but rather this, that their own particular blessing should increase, which is the truth as it is in Christ. . . . But besides this they have . . . the two greatest future blessings in their death. The first, in that through death the whole tragedy of this world's ills is brought to a close. . . . The other blessing of death is this, that it not only concludes the pains and evils

<hr/>

[22] Cf. especially "Secular Authority," *Works*, Vol. III, pp. 236 ff. Cf. Kerr, *op. cit.*, pp. 213 ff., for other relevant passages.

of this life, but (which is more excellent) makes an end of sins and vices. . . . For this our life is so full of perils—sin, like a serpent, besetting us on every side—and it is impossible for us to live without sinning; but fairest death delivers us from these perils, and cuts our sin clean away from us."[23]

Luther's answer to the Christ-and-culture question was that of a dynamic, dialectical thinker. Its reproductions by many who called themselves his followers were static and undialectical. They substituted two parallel moralities for his closely related ethics. As faith became a matter of belief rather than the fundamental, trustful orientation of the person in every moment toward God, so the freedom of the Christian man became autonomy in all the special spheres of culture. It is a great error to confuse the parallelistic dualism of separated spiritual and temporal life with the interactionism of Luther's gospel of faith in Christ working by love in the world of culture.

The dualistic *motif* has appeared in post-Lutheran Christianity in nonparallelistic forms also. But most of its expressions when compared with Luther's seem thin and abstract. In paradoxical sayings and ambivalent writings Søren Kierkegaard sets forth the dual character of the Christian life. He is himself an essayist, an aesthetic writer, who wants to be understood as a man of his culture, yet not as aesthetic writer and man of culture but as a religious author.[24] He seeks to argue philosophically the impossibility of stating philosophically the truth that is "truth for me." The Christian life has for him the double aspect of an intense inward relation to the eternal, and a wholly nonspectacular external relation to other men and to things. In these respects he appears to represent rather than to argue for the dual ethics of Luther; he is a man in his office, using

[23] "The Fourteen of Consolation," *Works*, Vol. I, pp. 148 f.
[24] Cf. *The Point of View for My Work as an Author*, Part I.

the instruments of his office in the spirit of faith. In consciousness of sin, in utter humility, and in reliance on grace, Kierkegaard, a cultured man in his culture, goes about his work as *litterateur* and aspirant to the ministry (another duality in him). But this is not his essential problem, that as a Christian he should do the dubious work of an aesthetic writer and the possibly more dubious work of writing edifying discourses. The dualism with which he wrestles is that of the finite and the infinite; and because this characterizes all his writings he skirts but never comes to grips with the problem of Christ and culture. The debate in which he is engaged is a lonely debate with himself. Sometimes it seems that he doesn't want so much to become a Christian as a kind of Christ; one in whom the infinite and the finite are united, and one who suffers for the sins of the world rather than one for whom first of all the eternal victim has suffered. In his isolation as "the individual" he beautifully analyzes the character of true Christian love, but is more concerned with the virtue than with the beings to be loved. So far as he deals with the Christ and culture problem, it is much more in the spirit of exclusive Christianity than as synthesist or dualist; even so, it is the exclusive Christianity of the hermit rather than of the cenobite. "The spiritual man," he writes, "differs from us men in being able to endure isolation, his rank as a spiritual man is proportionate to his strength for enduring isolation, whereas we men are constantly in need of 'the others,' the herd. . . . But the Christianity of the New Testament is precisely reckoned upon and related to this isolation of the spiritual man. Christianity in the New Testament consists in loving God, in hatred to man, in hatred of oneself, and thereby of other men, hating father, mother, one's own child, wife, etc., the strongest expression for the most agonizing isolation."[25] So

[25] *Attack upon "Christendom,"* p. 163.

extreme an expression, which deals so abstractly with the New Testament, can of course be balanced by other Kierkegaardian dicta. But the theme of isolated individuality is dominant; there is no genuine sense of the fact that persons exist only in "I-Thou" relations, and the feeling for the "We" is almost completely absent. Hence cultural societies do not concern Kierkegaard. In state, family, and church he sees only the defections from Christ. He assumes that he alone in Denmark is struggling hard to become a Christian; he seems to think that social religion, the state church, should be able to express more easily than his literary productions do what it means to be contemporaneous with Christ.[26]

Kierkegaard in effect is protesting as a Christian in nineteenth century culture against the cultural Christianity or Christianized culture of his day, which in Central Europe had used Luther's dualism as a way of domesticating the gospel and easing all tensions. More truly dualistic answers were offered by others, who could not in obedience to Christ avoid the claims of culture yet also understood how much Christ was entangled with culture. Ernst Troeltsch experienced the problem as a double dilemma. On the one hand he wrestled with the question of the absoluteness of a Christianity that was the cultural religion of the West; on the other hand he was concerned with the conflict between the morality of conscience and the social morality directed toward the attainment and conservation of the values represented by state and nation, science and art, economics and technology. Was not Christianity itself a cultural tradition, with no greater claims than any of the other parts of a historical and transitory civilization? Troeltsch could not give this question the answer of the cultural Christian; Christianity

[26] The best introductions to Kierkegaard are Bretall, Robert (ed.), *A Kierkegaard Anthology;* Dru, A. (ed.), *The Journals of Søren Kierkegaard;* Swenson, David, *Something about Kierkegaard.*

indeed was relative, but through it there came to men an absolute claim; even if that claim came only to Western men, it was still an absolute one in the midst of relativity.[27] The claim of Jesus was identified by Troeltsch with the ethics of conscience. However historical the growth of conscience may be, still it confronts historical men with the demand to attain and defend free personalities, independent from mere fate, internally unified and clarified; and at the same time to honor free personality in all men and to unite them in the moral bonds of humanity. The morality of conscience will no doubt always be engaged in a struggle with nature. "The kingdom of God, just because it transcends history, cannot limit and shape history. Earthly history remains the foundation and the presupposition of the final personal decision and sanctification; but in itself it goes on its way as a mixture of reason and natural instinct, and it can never be bound in any bonds except in a relative degree and for a temporary space."[28] This struggle with nature, however, is not the only one man must endure. There is in his ethical consciousness another morality besides that of conscience. He is directed toward the attainment of the cultural values, the objective and obligatory goods which his institutions represent—justice, peace, truth, welfare, etc. Though conscience and the morality of cultural values are closely related, the "two spheres meet only to diverge." Conscience is transhistorical; it scorns death, for "no evil can befall a good man in life or in death"; but the morality of cultural values is historical, and concerned with the maintenance of perishable things. No synthesis is possible save in individual acts of achievement. At the end we are justified only by faith.[29] Troeltsch himself experi-

[27] *Glaubenslehre,* pp. 100 ff.; also *Christian Thought,* 1923, pp. 22 ff.
[28] *Ibid.,* Section II, Pt. I, "The Morality of the Person and of Conscience," pp. 39 ff.
[29] *Ibid.,* Pt. II, "The Ethics of Cultural Values," pp. 71 ff.

enced these tensions in acute fashion as he undertook to carry on political tasks in the Weimar Republic. It is clear that his version of the claims of Christ was more akin to the cultural Christian interpretation of the New Testament prevalent in his day than to a more literal and radical reading of the gospels. Even so, a tension between Christ and culture remained, and could not be solved save in a life of continuous struggle.

In our time many versions of the dualistic solution are current.[30] It is often maintained, for instance, that faith and science can be neither in conflict with each other nor in positive relation, since they represent incommensurable truths. Man is a great amphibian who lives in two realms, and must avoid using in one the ideas and methods appropriate to the other.[31] Dualism appears in practical measures and theoretic justifications for the separation of church and state. Roger Williams has become the symbol and example of such dualism in America. He rejected the synthetic and conversionists attempts of Anglicanism and Puritanism to unite politics and the gospel, both because the union corrupted the gospel by associating spiritual force with physical coercion, and because it corrupted politics by introducing into it elements foreign to its nature. He dismissed also the Quaker effort to found a commonwealth on the foundations of Christian spirituality, because it was politically as inadequate as it was Christianly perverse.[32] The problem of combining loyalty to Christ with the acceptance of social reli-

[30] Among these dualisms that eschew parallelism or the compartmentalization of the moral life may be mentioned Reinhold Niebuhr's *Moral Man and Immoral Society,* 1932, and A. D. Lindsay's *The Two Moralities: Our Duty to God and to Society,* 1940.

[31] For a typical statement of this position see J. Needham, *The Great Amphibium,* 1931.

[32] Cf. *The Bloudy Tenent of Persecution, George Fox Digg'd Out of His Burrowes, Experiments in Spiritual Life and Health,* and *Letters.* All these, except the *Experiments,* are most readily available in the *Publications of the Narragansett Club.*

gion was even more difficult for him than that of Christ and Caesar. The attitude of Seeker which he took after leaving Anglican, Puritan, and Baptist churches represented a *modus vivendi* rather than a solution of the problem. In both instances, the political and the ecclesiastical, Williams remains representative of a common dualism in Protestantism.

The dualistic answer has also been accepted in theory and practice by exponents of culture. Political defenders of the separation of church and state, economists who contend for the autonomy of the economic life, philosophers who reject the combinations of reason and faith proposed by synthesists and cultural Christians, are often far removed from an anti-Christian attitude. A Nikolai Hartmann, for instance, having set up the antitheses between Christian faith and cultural ethics, allows the antinomies to stand without suggesting that they must be resolved in favor of culture. Even positivists who cannot find a basis for faith in the life of reason may be unwilling to dismiss it; it belongs to a different order of human existence.[33]

Often such solutions, whether offered by churchmen or others, lack moral seriousness as well as rational depth. Dualism may be the refuge of worldly-minded persons who wish to make a slight obeisance in the direction of Christ, or of pious spiritualists who feel that they owe some reverence to culture. Politicians who wish to keep the influence of the gospel out of the realm of "Real-Politik," and economic men who desire profit above all things without being reminded that the poor shall inherit the kingdom, may profess dualism as a convenient rationalization. But such abuses are no more characteristic of the position itself than are the abuses associated with each of the other attitudes. Radical Christianity has produced its wild

[33] See Ayer, A. J., *Language, Truth and Logic*, 1936. Religion and ethics are here described as meaningless in the strict sense; they express emotion only.

monks, its immoral cloisters, and its moral exhibitionists. Cultural Christianity and synthesis have allowed men to justify the
lust for power and the retention of old idolatries. Moral integrity and sincerity does not follow the adoption of one or the
other of these positions; though each of them, including dualism especially, has been taken by men in consequence of sincere
and earnest striving for integrity under Christ.

IV. The Virtues and Vices of Dualism

There is vitality and strength in the dualistic *motif* as this is
set forth by its great exponents. It mirrors the actual struggles
of the Christian who lives "between the times," and who in the
midst of his conflict in the time of grace cannot presume to live
by the ethics of that time of glory for which he ardently hopes.
It is a report of experience rather than a plan of campaign. If
on the one hand it reports the power of Christ and his spirit,
on the other it does not balk at the recognition of the strength
and prevalence of sin in all human existence. There is an im-
pressive honesty in Paul's description of the inner conflict and
in Luther's "Pecca fortiter" that is too often lacking in the
stories of the saints. Their recognition of the sin that is not only
in believers but also in their community is more in accord with
what the Christian knows about himself and about his churches
than are the descriptions of holy commonwealths and perfect
societies set forth by radicals and synthesists. Whether or not
the dualistic accounts are intelligible from the viewpoint of
their inner consistency, they are intelligible and persuasive as
corresponding to experience.

The dualists, however, are not only reporters of Christian
experience. Far more than any of the preceding groups with
which we have dealt they take into account the dynamic character of God, man, grace, and sin. There is something static about

the radical Christians' idea of faith; it is for him a new law and a new teaching. To a great extent this is true of the synthesists also, except as in the higher reaches of the Christian life a dynamic element is recognized. The dualist, however, is setting forth the ethics of action, of God's action, man's and the wicked powers'. Such an ethics cannot consist of laws and virtues nicely arranged in opposition to vices, but must be suggested and adumbrated; for living action can only be suggested and indicated. It is an ethics of freedom not in the sense of liberty from law, but in the sense of creative action in response to action upon man. With their understanding of the dynamic nature of existence, the dualists have made great and unique contributions both to Christian knowledge and to Christian action. They have directed attention to the profundity and the power of the work of Christ, how it penetrates to the depths of the human heart and mind, cleansing the fountains of life. They have put aside all the superficial analyses of human viciousness, and have tried to bring into view the deep roots of man's depravity. Accompanying these insights and partly in consequence of them, they have been reinvigorators of both Christianity and culture. To Christianity they have mediated new apprehensions of the greatness of God's grace in Christ, new resolution for militant living, and emancipation from the customs and organizations that have been substituted for the living Lord. To culture they have brought the spirit of a disinterestedness that does not ask what cultural or gospel law requires directly, or what profit for the self may be gained; but rather what the service of the neighbor in the given conditions demands, and what these given conditions really are.

It is evident, of course, that dualism has been beset by the vices that accompany its virtues; and to these other groups in Christianity continue to call attention. We may leave out of account those abuses of the position to which reference has been made, and deal only with the two most frequently voiced charges: that dualism tends to lead Christians into antinomianism and into cultural conservatism. Something is to be said for both of these indictments. The relativization of all the laws of society, of reason and all other works of men—through the doctrine that all are comprehended under sin no matter how high or low they stand when measured by human standards— has doubtless given occasion to the light-minded or the despairing to cast aside the rules of civilized living. They have claimed Luther or Paul as authority for the contention that it makes no difference whether men are sinfully obedient or sinfully disobedient to law, whether they are obedient or disobedient to sinful law, whether they sinfully seek truth or live as sinful skeptics, whether they are self-righteously moral or self-indulgently amoral. It is evidently far from the dualists' intention to encourage sublegal and subcultural behavior, because he knows of a superlegal life and discerns the sin in culture. Yet he must accept responsibility for putting, if not temptation, at least forms of rationalization for refusing to resist temptation, in the way of the wayward and the weak. The fact that this is so by no means invalidates what he has to say about the prevalence of sin and the difference between grace and all human work. It does indicate that he cannot say everything that needs to be said; and that cultural and synthetic Christians need to stand at his side with their injunctions to obedience to cultural law— though they in turn cannot say what dualism must preach about the sinfulness that attaches to obedience. The church chose more wisely than Marcion did when it associated with the epistles of Paul the Gospel of Matthew and the Letter of James.

Both Paul and Luther have been characterized as cultural conservatives. Much can be said for the ultimate effect of their work in promoting cultural reform; yet it seems to be true that they were deeply concerned to bring change into only one of the great cultural institutions and sets of habits of their times— the religious. For the rest they seemed to be content to let state and economic life—with slavery in the one case and social stratification in the other—continue relatively unchanged. They desired and required improvement in the conduct of princes, citizens, consumers, tradesmen, slaves, masters, etc.; but these were to be improvements within an essentially un- changed context of social habit. Even the family, in their view, retained its dominantly patriarchal character, despite their counsels to husbands, wives, parents, and children to love each other in Christ.

Such conservatism seems indeed to be directly connected with the dualist position. If it has nevertheless contributed to social change, this has resulted largely without its intention, and not without the assistance of other groups. Conservatism is a logical consequence of the tendency to think of law, state, and other institutions as restraining forces, dykes against sin, preventers of anarchy, rather than as positive agencies through which men in social union render positive service to neighbors advancing toward true life. Moreover, for the dualists such institutions belong wholly to the temporal and dying world. A question arises in connection with this point. There seems to be a tendency in dualism, as represented by both Paul and Luther, to relate temporality or finiteness to sin in such a de- gree as to move creation and fall into very close proximity, and in that connection to do less than justice to the creative work of God. The idea which in Marcion and Kierkegaard is set forth in heretical fashion is at least suggested by their great prede- cessors. In Paul the idea of creation is used significantly only for the sake of reinforcing his first principle of the condemnation of all men because of sin; while his ambiguous use of the term "flesh" indicates a fundamental uncertainty about the goodness of the created body. For Luther the wrath of God is manifested not only against sin, but against the whole temporal world. Hence there is in these men not only a yearning for the new life in Christ through the death of the self to itself, but also a desire for the death of the body and for the passing of the temporal order. Dying to self and rising with Christ to life in God are doubtless more important; but self-centeredness and finiteness belong so closely together that spiritual transformation cannot be expected this side of death. These thoughts lead to the idea that in all temporal work in culture men are dealing only with the transitory and the dying. Hence, however important cultural duties are for Christians their life is not in them; it is hidden with Christ in God. It is at this point that the conversionist *motif*, otherwise very similar to the dualist, emerges in distinction from it.

CHAPTER 6

Christ The Transformer of Culture

I. THEOLOGICAL CONVICTIONS

The conversionists' understanding of the relations of Christ and culture is most closely akin to dualism, but it also has affinities with the other great Christian attitudes. That it represents a distinct *motif*, however, becomes apparent when one moves from the Gospel of Matthew and the Letter of James through Paul's epistles to the Fourth Gospel, or proceeds from Tertullian, the Gnostics, and Clement to Augustine, or from Tolstoy, Ritschl, and Kierkegaard to F. D. Maurice. The men who offer what we are calling the conversionist answer to the problem of Christ and culture evidently belong to the great central tradition of the church. Though they hold fast to the radical distinction between God's work in Christ and man's work in culture, they do not take the road of exclusive Christianity into isolation from civilization, or reject its institutions with Tolstoyan bitterness. Though they accept their station in society with its duties in obedience to their Lord, they do not seek to modify Jesus Christ's sharp judgment of the world and all its ways. In their Christology they are like synthesists and dualists; they refer to the Redeemer more than to the giver of a new law, and to the God whom men encounter more than to the representative of the best spiritual resources in humanity. They understand that his work is concerned not with the specious, external aspects of human behavior in the first place, but that he tries the hearts and judges the subconscious life; that he deals with what is deepest and most fundamental in man. He heals the most stubborn and virulent human disease, the phthisis of the spirit, the sickness unto death; he forgives the most hidden and proliferous sin, the distrust, lovelessness, and hopelessness of man in his relation to God. And this he does not simply by offering ideas, counsel, and laws; but by living with men in great humility, enduring death for their sakes, and rising again from the grave in a demonstration of God's grace rather than an argument about it. In their understanding of sin the conversionists are more like dualists than synthesists. They note that it is deeply rooted in the human soul, that it pervades all man's work, and that there are no gradations of corruption, however various its symptoms. Hence they also discern how all cultural work in which men promote their own glory, whether individualistically or socially, whether as members of the nation or of humanity, lies under the judgment of God—who does not seek His own profit. They see the self-destructiveness in its self-contradictoriness. Yet they believe also that such culture is under God's sovereign rule, and that the Christian must carry on cultural work in obedience to the Lord.

What distinguishes conversionists from dualists is their more positive and hopeful attitude toward culture. Their more affirmative stand seems to be closely connected with three theological convictions. The first of these relates to creation. The dualist tends so to concentrate on redemption through Christ's cross and resurrection that creation becomes for him a kind of prologue to the one mighty deed of atonement. Though with Paul he affirms that in Christ "all things were created, in heaven and on earth, visible and invisible, whether thrones or domin-

ions or principalities or authorities—all things were created
through him and for him,"[1] yet this is a relatively unemphasized
idea, used mostly to introduce the great theme of reconciliation.
For the conversionist, however, the creative activity of God
and of Christ-in-God is a major theme, neither overpowered by
nor overpowering the idea of atonement. Hence man the creature, working in a created world, lives, as the conversionist sees
it, under the rule of Christ and by the creative power and ordering of the divine Word, even though in his unredeemed mind
he may believe that he lives among vain things under divine
wrath. To be sure, the dualist often also says something like
this; but he tends to qualify it so much by references to God's
anger as peculiarly manifest in the physical world that the
beneficence of the Ruler of nature becomes somewhat doubtful.
The effect of the conversionist's theory of culture on his positive
thought about creation is considerable. He finds room for affirmative and ordered response on the part of created man to the
creative, ordering work of God; even though the creature may
go about his work unwillingly as he tills the ground, cultivates
his mind, and organizes his society, and though he may admin-
ister perversely the order given him with his existence. In connection with this interest in creation, the conversionist tends
to develop a phase of Christology neglected by the dualist. On
the one hand he emphasizes the participation of the Word, the
Son of God, in creation, not as this took place once upon a time
but as it occurs in the immediate origin, the logical and
momentary beginning of everything, in the mind and power
of God. On the other hand he is concerned with the redemptive
work of God in the incarnation of the Son, and not merely with
redemption in his death, resurrection, and return in power. Not
that the conversionist turns from the historical Jesus to the

[1] Col. 1:16.

Logos that was in the beginning, or that he denies the wonder of the cross in marvelling at the birth in a barn; he seeks to hold together in one movement the various themes of creation and redemption, of incarnation and atonement. The effect of this understanding of the work of Christ in incarnation as well as creation on conversionist thought about culture is unmistakable. The Word that became flesh and dwelt among us, the Son who does the work of the Father in the world of creation, has entered into a human culture that has never been without his ordering action.

The second theological conviction that modifies the conversionist view of human work and custom is its understanding of the nature of man's fall from his created goodness. As we have noted, dualism often brings creation and fall into such close proximity that it is tempted to speak in almost Gnostic terms, as if creation of finite selfhood or matter involved fall. To be in the body is to be away from Christ; nothing good dwells in the flesh; to be carnal is to be sold under sin. All this is true for a Paul and a Luther not only because the spirit of man that dwells in his body is sinful but because the body offers unconquerable temptation to sin.[2] Hence such Christians tend to think of the institutions of culture as having largely a negative function in a temporal and corrupt world. They are orders for corruption, preventatives of anarchy, directives for the

[2] On this much disputed point cf. Lietzmann, Hans, *An die Roemer* (*Handbuch zum Neuen Testament*, Vol. VIII), pp. 75 ff. Commenting on Romans vii, 14-25, Lietzmann says: "The view that the sinful actions of man have their origin in an 'evil drive' working within him is also to be found in contemporary Jewish theology; but what is foreign to the latter is the idea, which is here of decisive importance, that this drive is connected with the flesh. . . . One may make one's choice, whether to regard Paul as an independent originator of this doctrine, or to take cognizance of the fact that a contemporary of the Apostle's (Philo), who was also a Hellenistic Jew, presents the same long-current teaching. If the latter choice seems by standards of historical method to be more correct, then one may say that Paul like Philo derived it from the Hellenistic atmosphere which surrounded him."

physical life, concerned wholly with temporal matters. The conversionist agrees with the dualist in asserting a doctrine of a radical fall of man. But he distinguishes the fall very sharply from creation, and from the conditions of life in the body. It is a kind of reversal of creation for him, and in no sense its continuation. It is entirely the action of man, and in no way an action of God's. It is moral and personal, not physical and metaphysical, though it does have physical consequences. The results of man's defection from God, moreover, all occur on man's side and not on God's. The word that must be used here to designate the consequences of the fall is "corruption." Man's good nature has become corrupted; it is not bad, as something that ought not to exist, but warped, twisted, and misdirected. He loves with the love that is given him in his creation, but loves beings wrongly, in the wrong order; he desires good with the desire given him by his Maker, but aims at goods that are not good for him and misses his true good; he produces fruit, but it is misshapen and bitter; he organizes society with the aid of his practical reason, but works against the grain of things in self-willed forcing of his reason into irrational paths, and thus disorganizes things in his very acts of organization. Hence his culture is all corrupted order rather than order for corruption, as it is for dualists. It is perverted good, not evil; or it is evil as perversion, and not as badness of being. The problem of culture is therefore the problem of its conversion, not of its replacement by a new creation; though the conversion is so radical that it amounts to a kind of rebirth.

With these convictions about creation and fall the conversionists combine a third: a view of history that holds that to God all things are possible in a history that is fundamentally not a course of merely human events but always a dramatic interaction between God and men. For the exclusive Christian, history is the story of a rising church or Christian culture and a dying pagan civilization; for the cultural Christian, it is the story of the spirit's encounter with nature; for the synthesist, it is a period of preparation under law, reason, gospel, and church for an ultimate communion of the soul with God; for the dualist, history is the time of struggle between faith and unbelief, a period between the giving of the promise of life and its fulfillment. For the conversionist, history is the story of God's mighty deeds and of man's responses to them. He lives somewhat less "between the times" and somewhat more in the divine "Now" than do his brother Christians. The eschatological future has become for him an eschatological present. Eternity means for him less the action of God before time and less the life with God after time, and more the presence of God in time. Eternal life is a quality of existence in the here and now. Hence the conversionist is less concerned with conservation of what has been given in creation, less with preparation for what will be given in a final redemption, than with the divine possibility of a present renewal. Such differences of orientation in time are not to be defined with nice precision. There is a strain toward the future in every Christian life, as well as a reliance upon the God of Abraham, Isaac, and Jacob and the recognition that this is the day of salvation. But there is a difference between Paul's expectation of the time when the last enemy, death, will have been destroyed by Christ, and John's understanding of Christ's last words upon the cross, "It is finished." The conversionist, with his view of history as the present encounter with God in Christ, does not live so much in expectation of a final ending of the world of creation and culture as in awareness of the power of the Lord to transform all things by lifting them up to himself. His imagery is spatial and not temporal; and the movement of life he finds to be issuing from Jesus Christ is an upward movement, the rising of men's souls and deeds and thoughts in a mighty surge of adoration and glorification of the One who draws them to himself. <u>This is what human culture can be—a transformed human life in and to the glory of God.</u> For man it is impossible, but all things are possible to God, who has created man, body and soul, for Himself, and sent his Son into the world that the world through him might be saved.

II. THE CONVERSION MOTIF IN THE FOURTH GOSPEL

These ideas and the conversionist *motif* are presented on many pages of the New Testament. They are suggested in the First Letter of John; but are accompanied there by so many references to the darkness, transitoriness, and lovelessness of the world on the one hand, and to the distinction of the new community from the old on the other, that the tendency of this document seems to be toward exclusive Christianity. The theme of conversionism is prepared for by Paul, but overshadowed in the end by his thoughts about flesh and death and the restraint of evil. Perhaps it is most clearly indicated in the Gospel of John; though, as the close relation of this work to the First Letter of John at once suggests, it is accompanied there also by a separatist note. What has been said about the "Janus-like reality" of the Fourth Gospel, about its "union of opposites" and its seeming contradictions, applies to it also with respect to its attitudes toward the world of culture.[3] The basic ideas of conversionist thought are, however, all present in it; and the work itself is a partial demonstration of cultural conversion, for it undertakes not only to translate the gospel of Jesus Christ into the concepts of its Hellenistic readers, but also lifts these

[3] Cf. MacGregor, G. H. C., *The Gospel of John* (*The Moffatt New Testament Commentary*), 1928, p. ix, where the views of a number of critics about the antitheses in the Gospel are summarized; also Scott, E. F., *The Fourth Gospel*, 1908, pp. 11 ff., 27.

ideas about Logos and knowledge, truth and eternity, to new levels of meaning by interpreting them through Christ.

In what was said above about the conversionist's faith in the Creator, allusion has already been made to the Fourth Gospel. It begins where in a sense Paul ends, with the genesis of the Word and the origin of all things through him. Without him nothing has been created; the world made through him is his home. John could not say more forcefully that whatever is is good. There is no longer any suggestion here that the physical or material as such is subject to a special wrath of God, or that man, being carnal, is sold under sin. Flesh and spirit are carefully distinguished by John: "That which is born of the flesh is flesh, and that which is born of the Spirit is spirit." But the physical, material, and temporal are never regarded as participating in evil in any peculiar way because they are not spiritual and eternal. On the contrary, natural birth, eating, drinking, wind, water, and bread and wine are for this evangelist not only symbols to be employed in dealing with the realities of the life of the spirit but are pregnant with spiritual meaning. Spiritual and natural events "are interlocking and analogous." "It is not required of men that they should remove themselves or be removed into some esoteric and aloof spirituality."[4] In his convictions about creation through the Word and about the incarnation of the Word, John expresses his faith in God's wholly affirmative relation to the whole world, material and spiritual. Creation means what redemption does, that "God so loved the world that he gave his only Son, that whoever believes in him should not perish but have eternal life. For God sent the Son into the world, not to condemn the world, but that the world might be saved through him."[5]

[4] Hoskyns, Edwyn Clement, *The Fourth Gospel*, 1940, Vol. I, p. 217; cf. pp. 231, 317 ff.
[5] John 3:16 f.

One of the apparent paradoxes of the Fourth Gospel is that the word "world," so used for the totality of creation and especially of humanity as the object of God's love, is also used to designate mankind in so far as it rejects Christ, lives in darkness, does evil works, is ignorant of the Father, rejoices over the death of the Son.[6] The ruler of the world is not the Logos but the devil.[7] Its principle is not truth but the lie; it is the realm of murder and of death, rather than of life. Yet it is evident that John is not writing of two distinct realities, an uncreated realm of matter in opposition to a created world of spirit, or a demonically formed cosmos separated from the world as created by the divine Word. The idea of the fall, of the perversion of the created good, is implicit in the whole Gospel. The creation, which is fundamentally good as it comes from God through his Word, becomes self-contradictory and God-contradictory in its response to God. God loves the world in His creating and redeeming action; the world responds to that love with denial of its actuality and with hatred of the Word. This is a simple situation; and yet in the infinite interactions of Father and Son, God, Word, and world it issues in great complexities, which no other Christian writing has undertaken to describe, or at least to suggest, so well as this Fourth Gospel does. The nature of the world's perversion is indicated by the constant comparison of the response of Jesus Christ to the Father with that of the world of men to its Creator. The Son obeys the Father's will and does His works; the world obeys the will not of the One from whom it derives its existence but of its "father," the devil, that is, the will to do its own will. The Son honors and glorifies the Father, who has made him glorious and will make him glorious; the world, created glorious by God, answers the

[6] Cf. John 7:7; 8:23; 14:17; 15:18 ff.; 17:25, *et passim.*
[7] John 8:44; 12:31; 14:30; 16:11.

Creator's deed by glorifying itself rather than Him. The Son loves the Father, who has loved him and will love him; the world, loved by God, responds perversely, with self-love. The Son bears witness to a Father who has borne and will bear witness to him; the world calls attention to itself. Jesus Christ draws his life from the Father, and offers his life to the One who gives life; the world loves its life in itself.[8] Christ in his relations to the Father thus makes apparent the nature of human sinfulness. But it is not only by comparison of Christ and this perverted world of men with their works that the Gospel sets forth its doctrine of the fall. The corruptness of the world appears in its relation to the Son of the Father, and not only in its attitude toward the Father of the Son. Christ, the lover of God, loves the world; it responds to his love with rejection and hatred. He comes to lay down his life for it; instead of laying down its life for its friend it says, "It is expedient that one man should die for the people, and not that the whole nation should perish." He comes to give life; men give him death. He comes to tell men the truth about themselves; they lie about him. He comes to testify about God; the world answers, not with its corroborative testimony about its maker and redeemer, but with references to its lawgivers, its holy days and its culture. "He came unto his own and his own received him not."

Though John does not formulate his doctrine of sin and the fall in abstract terms, but illustrates rather than defines it, it seems fair to say that for him sin is the denial of the principle of life itself; it is the lie that cannot exist except on the basis of an accepted truth; the murder that destroys life in the act

[8] These themes, which run through the whole gospel, are particularly illustrated in chapter xv, in which the symbol of vine-dresser, vine, and branches is used to show the reciprocal and comparative relations of Father, Son, and world.

of affirming it, and affirms life in the act of destroying it; the hatred that presupposes love. Sin exists because life, truth, glory, light, and love exist only in communication and community; and because in such community it is possible for men who live by the deeds of another to refuse to respond in kind. It is present therefore at all levels of life; but its root is in the contradictory relations of man to God and the Word, to the Father and the Son. Sir Edward Hoskyns has well said that "the biblical, Johannine analysis of human behaviour is . . . a theological distinction between those actions which, regarded as complete in themselves, leave no room for the righteousness of God, and those actions—they may be visibly identical with actions judged to be evil—which make room for the righteousness of God. The latter demand faith, for they are in themselves incomplete, the former exclude it, for they are self-sufficient."[9] The Johannine analysis of human behavior, however, extends backward as well as forward. It distinguishes between those actions that take the love of God so for granted as something due to the self that they reply to His love with self-love, and those that answer love with love—not in simple reciprocal fashion, but with outpouring devotion to all who are beloved by the Father and the Son.

With these convictions about the goodness of God and the perversity of man in the community of Father, Son, and the world, John unites a view of history in which temporal dimensions—the past and the future—are largely subordinated to the eternity-time relation. The creation of which he speaks in his prologue is not an event in the past, but the origin and foundation of all that is—the eternal beginning and principle of being. The fall is not an event connected with the life of a first man in the sequence of historical generations; it is a present falling away from the Word. The judgment of the world is *now*; it is

[9] *Op. cit.,* p. 237.

given with the advent of the Word and with the present coming of the Spirit.[10] The Fourth Gospel's historical view is characterized by its substitution of the phrase "eternal life" for "kingdom of God." As practically all students of the Gospel have pointed out, that phrase means a quality, a relation of life, a present community through the Spirit with the Father and the Son, a present spiritual worship, love, and integrity. Some tension toward the future doubtless remains; and it may be questioned whether in any case it is possible for any Christian to banish this completely. But the great point of the Gospel is that the new beginning, the new birth, the new life, is not an event that depends on a change in temporal history or in the life of the flesh. It is the beginning with God, from above, from heaven, in the spirit; it is citizenship in a kingdom that "is not of this world" yet is not a kingdom of the future. John has largely substituted for the doctrine of the return of Christ the teaching about the coming of the Paraclete; for the idea of leaving this body in order to be with Christ he has substituted the thought of a present life with Christ in the spirit. "The flesh is of no avail," either positively by its birth or negatively by its death. This new beginning is God's possibility and God's action in Jesus Christ and in the sending of the Spirit; not at history's end, but in each living, existential moment.[11] Yet this possibility is not realized in a mystical, nonhistorical human life; it is realized through the concrete events of Jesus' life and the concrete responses to him of men in the church. "The theme of the Fourth Gospel is the nonhistorical that makes sense of history, the infinite that makes sense of time, God who makes sense of men and is therefore their Saviour."[12] Hence the complex inter-

[10] John 9:39; 12:31; 16:7-11; cf. Scott, *op. cit.*, chap. X.
[11] Cf. Hoskyns, *op. cit.*, pp. 229; Scott, op. cit., pp. 247 ff., 317 ff.
[12] Hoskyns, *op. cit.*, p. 120.

weaving of historical record and spiritual interpretation in this enigmatic and enlightening book.

The conversionist theme that appears in this attitude toward history is implicitly and sometimes explicitly presented in what John has to say about human culture and its institutions. His apparently ambivalent attitude toward Judaism, Gnosticism, and the sacraments of early Christianity is partly explicable if we think of him as conversionist. On the one hand he presents Judaism as anti-Christian; on the other he emphasizes that "salvation is from the Jews," and that their Scriptures bear witness to Christ. The dualism in this attitude may be explained by reference to the conflicts of the second century, and to the church's claim to be the true Israel;[13] but it may also be maintained that such an attitude is consonant in all times and places with the view that Christ—not the Christian church as a cultural institution—is the hope, the true meaning, the new beginning of a Judaism that accepts his transformation of itself not into a Gentile religion but into a nondefensive worship of the Father. Similarly, John's relations to Gnosticism are ambiguous. On the one hand he seems to take the exclusive attitude of the First Letter of John toward the accommodation of the gospel to this brand of popular wisdom; on the other hand he appears to be very much like the Christian Gnostics in his interest in knowledge and his concern with spirit.[14] Historically explicable in part, this dual attitude is more intelligible in conversionist terms as a Christian transformation of cultural religious thought. John is a conversionist, too, in his attitude toward the church of the second century, its doctrine, sacraments, and organization. He seems to be a defender of this cultural religion against Judaism. Yet he is far removed from those exclusive

[13] Scott, *op. cit.*, pp. 70-77.
[14] *Ibid.*, pp. 86-103.

Christians who find the distinctively Christian element in the external forms of fasting, praying, and observing the sacraments.

He seems to understand and interpret Christian faith and practice with the aid of terms derived from mystery cults, though nothing can be more alien to his spirit than the idea of making Christ a cult-hero.[15] He is concerned throughout his book with the transformation by the spirit of Christ of the spirit that expresses itself in external acts of religion. He is concerned that each symbolic act should have the true source and the true direction toward its true object. Perhaps John does not record the words of the Lord's Prayer because he takes for granted that his readers know them; but other writers of the time repeated them, and it is evident that this man distinguishes between spirit and letter even when the letter is Christian. His interpretation of the sacraments of the Lord's Supper and baptism stresses the same note of participation in Christ and his spirit, without denying and without emphasizing the importance of physical bread and wine and water.[16] As far, then, as the religious culture and institutions of men are concerned, it seems clear that the Fourth Gospel thinks of Christ as the converter and transformer of human actions. The man who wrote, "The hour is coming and now is, when the true worshippers will worship the Father in spirit and in truth, for such the Father seeks to worship him," doubtless had Christians in mind as well as Jews and Samaritans; and was far from supposing that the substitution of Christian forms for others in religion issued in integrity and true adoration.

One would need to force matters were one to read a conversionist attitude into John's brief references to other phases

15 Cf. Strachan, R. H., *The Fourth Gospel*, 1917, pp. 46-53.
16 Hoskyns, *op. cit.*, pp. 335 ff.; Scott, *op. cit.*, pp. 122 ff.

of culture. The special treatment he accords to Pilate, who would have had no power over Christ if it had not been given him from above, and whose sense of justice was defeated with some difficulty, may be variously explained; as may the reference to the kingdom of this world whose servants fight. It can only be said that in general John's interest is directed toward the spiritual transformation of man's life in the world, not toward the substitution of a wholly spiritual existence for a temporal one, nor toward the replacement of the present physical environment and bodies of men by new physical and metaphysical creations, nor toward the gradual ascent from the temporal to the eternal.

We are prevented from interpreting the Fourth Gospel as a wholly conversionist document, not only by its silence on many subjects but also by the fact that its universalistic note is accompanied by a particularist tendency. The Christian life consists, indeed, in the transformation of all actions by Christ, so that they are acts of love to God and man, glorify the Father and the Son, and are obedient to the commandment to love one another. It is a life of work, in which the Christian does what he sees the Son doing as the Son does the works of the Father. But this life seems to be possible only to the few. To be sure, Christ is the lamb of God who takes away the sins of the world, and it was God's love of the world that caused Him to send His Son into it; and when Christ is lifted up he will draw all men to himself.[17] Yet such universalistic statements, which seem to look forward to the complete transformation of human life and work, are balanced in the Gospel by sayings that voice the sense of the world's opposition to Christ and of his concern for the few. "I have manifested thy name," Jesus says in his high-priestly prayer, "to the men thou gavest me out

[17] John 1:29; 3:16 ff.; 12:32, 47.

of the world. . . . I am praying for them; I am not praying for the world. . . . They are not of the world, even as I am not of the world."[18] Hence Prof. Scott comments: "The Fourth Gospel, which gives the grandest expression to the universalism of the Christian religion, is . . . at the same time the most exclusive of the New Testament writings. It draws a sharp division between the Church of Christ and the outlying world, which is regarded as merely foreign or hostile."[19] The antinomy can be partly explained by the reflection that while John is mostly concerned with the conversion of the church from a separatist, legalist society into a free, spiritual, dynamic community, which draws its life from the living Christ, he is also on his guard against the confusion of faith with the speciously universal spiritualism of contemporary secular culture. Hence for him the Christian life is cultural life converted by the regeneration of man's spirit; but the rebirth of the spirit of all men and the transformation of all cultural existence by the incarnate Word, the risen Lord, and the inspiring Paraclete does not enter into his vision. He has combined the conversionist *motif* with the separatism of the Christ-against-culture school of thought.

A similar combination of conversionism with separatism is suggested in the second-century Letter to Diognetus. Christians, it says, "are distinguished from other men neither by country, nor language, nor the customs which they observe. For they neither inhabit cities of their own, nor employ a peculiar form of speech, nor lead a life which is marked by any singularity. . . . Inhabiting Greek as well as barbarian cities, according as the lot of each of them has determined, and following the customs of the natives in respect to clothing, food and the rest of their ordinary conduct, they display to us their wonderful

[18] John, 17:6, 9, 16.
[19] Scott, *op. cit.*, p. 115; cf. pp. 138 ff.

and confessedly striking mode of life."[20] What makes this mode of life striking is the scorn of death, the love, meekness, and humility which have been infused into it by God through His redeeming as well as creative Word. Yet the suggestion that Christian life is a transformed mode of cultural existence, and the statement that "what the soul is in the body, that are Christians in the world" are not connected by the author of this document with a hope for the conversion of the whole of humanity in all its cultural life.

III. AUGUSTINE AND THE CONVERSION OF CULTURE

The expectation of universal regeneration through Christ emerges somewhat more clearly in the great Christian leaders of the fourth century. Even then, however, the universalist note does not come to as full an expression as the idea of conversion, since, as in the case of the Fourth Gospel, the conversionists need to contend on two fronts—against the anti-culturalism of exclusive Christianity, and against the accommodationism of culture-Christians. Both these tendencies had been given a powerful impetus by the acceptance of the new faith as the religion of the state. Charles Norris Cochrane has brilliantly described the various movements of the time in his study of classical culture from Augustan reconstruction through Constantinian renovation to Augustinian regeneration.[21] According to his interpretation, the regeneration of human society through the replacement of pagan by Trinitarian principles is the theme of that Christian movement which Athanasius and Ambrose began and which Augustine brought to a great climax in his *City of God*.[22] These men achieved the sound theory for

[20] *Ante-Nicene Fathers*, Vol. I, p. 26.

[21] *Christianity and Classical Culture, A Study of Thought and Action from Augustus to Augustine*, 1940.

[22] *Ibid.*, esp. pp. 359 ff., 510 ff.

the renewal of human cultural existence that Roman Caesars and thinkers had essayed in vain because their first principles were fatally self-contradictory. To interpret Augustine in this fashion is to make him fit neatly into our scheme of Christian ethical types—a little too neatly. The conversionist or transformation *motif* is the great thing in this theologian, who, in the words he applied to John, "was one of those mountains concerning which it is written: 'Let the mountains receive peace for thy people.' "[23] Yet it is not to be forgotten that this *motif* is accompanied in his thought by other ideas about the relations of Christ and culture. His interest in monasticism allies him with the radical school of Christians; as does his antithesis of heavenly and earthly cities, as far as this contrast applies to the opposition between organized Christian religion and the organized political communities. His Neo-Platonist philosophy connects him with cultural Christianity, and makes possible, if not plausible, the argument that his conversion was more a turning to Plato than to the Christ of the New Testament. Thomas and Thomists claim him as their own, calling attention to his concern for the right ordering of values and to his hierarchical view of the relations of body, reason, and soul, as well as of social authorities and of earthly to heavenly peace.[24] When Augustine speaks of slavery and war, he thinks in dualistic terms of obedience to orders that are relative to sin and simply prevent greater corruption.[25] Moreover, for him as for other dualists, despite his doctrine of creation, the animal body by its corruption often seems to weigh down the spirit more than the corrupted spirit weighs down the body. Finally, it is questionable whether Augustine's "fresh vision of society based on

[23] *Tractates on the Gospel According to St. John*, I, 2.
[24] Cf. for instance Bourke, V. J., *Augustine's Quest of Wisdom*, 1945, pp. 225 f., 266, 277.
[25] *City of God*, XIX, 7, 15.

the unity of faith and the bond of concord' " was truly "universal in a sense undreamed of even by the so-called universal empire, . . . potentially . . . as broad and inclusive as the human race itself."[26] His doctrines of predestination and of eternal punishment, both individualistically conceived, stand in such contrast to his views about human solidarity in sin and salvation that it is difficult to credit him with the idea of universal regeneration. Once more, then, we deal with a man who is much more than representative of a type.

Nevertheless, the interpretation of Augustine as the theologian of cultural transformation by Christ is in accord with his fundamental theory of creation, fall, and regeneration, with his own career as pagan and Christian, and with the kind of influence he has exercised on Christianity. The potential universalism of his theory also cannot be gainsaid. Augustine not only describes, but illustrates in his own person, the work of Christ as converter of culture. The Roman rhetorician becomes a Christian preacher, who not only puts into the service of Christ the training in language and literature given him by his society, but, by virtue of the freedom and illumination received from the gospel, uses that language with a new brilliance and brings a new liberty into that literary tradition. The Neo-Platonist not only adds to his wisdom about spiritual reality the knowledge of the incarnation which no philosopher had taught him, but this wisdom is humanized, given new depth and direction, made productive of new insights, by the realization that the Word has become flesh and has borne the sins of the spirit. The Ciceronian moralist does not add to the classical virtues the new virtues of the gospel, nor substitute new law for natural and Roman legislation, but transvalues and redirects in consequence of the experience of grace the morality

[26] Cochrane, *op. cit.*, p. 511.

in which he had been trained and which he taught. In addition to this, Augustine becomes one of the leaders of that great historical movement whereby the society of the Roman empire is converted from a Caesar-centered community into medieval Christendom. Therefore he is himself an example of what conversion of culture means; in contrast to its rejection by radicals, to its idealization by culturalists, to the synthesis that proceeds largely by means of adding Christ to good civilization, and to the dualism that seeks to live by the gospel in an inconquerably immoral society.[27] Yet even Tertullian, the Roman lawyer, and Tolstoy, the Russian artist, Thomas, the Aristotelian monk, Paul, the Jewish Pharisee, and Luther, the nominalist, illustrate the conversionist theme. What is distinctive about Augustine is that his theory largely duplicates his demonstration.

Christ is the transformer of culture for Augustine in the sense that he redirects, reinvigorates, and regenerates that life of man, expressed in all human works, which in present actuality is the perverted and corrupted exercise of a fundamentally good nature; which, moreover, in its depravity lies under the curse of transiency and death, not because an external punishment has been visited upon it, but because it is intrinsically self-contradictory. His vision of human actuality and divine possibility did not begin with the idea of a good creation; but the description of the theory may well begin there. How Augustine, after many false starts in speculative and practical reasoning, was enabled to begin with God, Father, Son, and Holy Spirit, and to proceed thence to the understanding of the self and the creature, is the story of his *Confessions*. After he made this beginning—or after his life was so rebegun—he saw that all creation was good, first as good for God, the source and center

27 *Ibid.,* p. 510.

of all being and value, and secondly as good in its order, with the goodness of beauty and of the mutual service of the creatures. His *Confessions* end with an ecstatic expression of the idea which is repeated in more abstract formulations in many other works: "Thou, O God, sawest everything that thou hadst made, and, behold, it was very good. Yea we also see the same, and behold, all things are very good. . . . Seven times have I counted it to be written, that thou sawest that that which thou madest was good: and this is the eighth, that thou sawest everything that thou hadst made and, behold, it was not only good, but also very good, as being now altogether. For severally, they were only good; but altogether both good and very good. All beautiful bodies express the same; by reason that a body consisting of members all beautiful, is far more beautiful than the same members by themselves are, by whose well-ordered blending the whole is perfected. . . . It is one thing then for a man to think that to be ill which is good . . . ; another, that that which is good, a man should see that it is good, (as thy creatures be pleasing unto many, because they be good, whom yet thou pleasest not in them, when they prefer to enjoy them to thee;) and another, that when a man sees a thing that it is good, God should in him see that it is good, so namely that he should be loved in that which he made, who cannot be loved but by the Holy Ghost which he hath given . . . , by whom we see that whatsoever in any degree is, is good. For from him it is who himself is not in degree, but what he is, is. . . . Let thy works praise thee that we may love thee, and let us love thee that thy works may praise thee."[28]

Though whatever is is good, Augustine is very far from saying in eighteenth-century fashion either that whatever is is right, or that only the social institutions are wrong and that by a

[28] *Confessions*, XIII, xxvii, 43; xxxi, 46; xxxiii, 48.

return to primitive conditions man can return to felicity. The good nature of man has been corrupted and his culture has become perverse in such fashion that corrupt nature produces perverse culture and perverse culture corrupts nature. The spiritual, psychological, biological, and social depravity of man does not mean that he has become a bad being, for Augustine insists that there "cannot be a nature in which there is no good. Hence not even the nature of the devil himself is evil, in so far as it is nature, but it was made evil by being perverted."[29] The moral sickness of man, which could not exist unless there were some order of health in his nature, is as complex as his nature; but it has a single origin in man's self-contradictory self-assertion. Man is by his created nature made to obey, to worship, to glorify, and depend on the Goodness which made him and made him good; on God, who is his chief good. As his primary goodness consists in adhering to God, so his primal sin lies in turning away from God to himself or to some inferior value. "When the will abandons what is above itself, and turns to what is lower, it becomes evil—not because that is evil to which it turns, but because the turning itself is wicked."[30] This primal sin, which is more significantly named the first sin of man than the sin of the first man, may be variously described as falling away from the word of God, as disobedience to God, as vice, i.e., as that which is contrary to nature, as living according to man and as pride, for "what is pride but the craving for an undue self-exaltation?" It always has this double aspect: that it is a departure from the One from whom man draws his life, and a clinging to a created good, as though it were the chief value. From this root sin arise other disorders in human life. One of these is the confusion that enters

[29] *City of God*, XIX, 13.
[30] *Ibid.*, XII, 6.

into the ordered pattern of man's rational and emotional psychophysical nature. "What but disobedience was the punishment of disobedience in that [first] sin? For what else is man's misery but his own disobedience to himself, so that in consequence of his not being willing to do what he could do, he now wills to do what he cannot? . . . For who can count how many things he wishes which he cannot do, so long as he is disobedient to himself, that is so long as his mind and his flesh do not obey his will?"[31] The disorder in the emotional and rational life of man is acutely felt in the great disturbance of his existence by sexual passion; but it appears also in all the other expressions of his libido. The disordered soul is corrupt in all its parts, not because a part has been disordered but because the fundamental relation of the soul to God has been disordered.

A second consequence of the root sin is the social sinfulness of mankind. "There is nothing," says Augustine, "so social by nature, so unsocial by its corruption, as this race." "The society of mortals . . . although bound together by a certain fellowship of our common nature, is yet for the most part divided against itself, and the strongest oppress the others, because all follow after their own interests and lusts."[32] Friendship is corrupted by treachery; the home, "natural refuge from the ills of life," is itself not safe; the political order in city and empire is not only confused by wars and oppressions, but the very administration of justice becomes a perverse business in which ignorance seeking to check vice commits new injustice.[33] Disorder extends to every phase of culture; diversity of language and efforts to impose a common language, just wars as well as unjust, efforts to achieve peace and to establish dominion, the injustice of slavery and the requirement that men act justly as masters and

[31] *Ibid.*, XIV, 15; cf. the following chapters.
[32] *Ibid.*, XII, 27; XVIII, 2.
[33] *Ibid.*, XIX, 5.

slaves in the midst of this injustice—all these and many other aspects of social existence are symptoms of man's corruption and misery. The very virtues themselves, in which men are trained in society, are perverse; since courage, prudence, and temperance used for egoistic or idolatrous ends become "splendid vices." Yet all this social sinfulness is dependent on the presence of a fundamentally good, created order. "Even what is perverted must of necessity be in harmony with, and in dependence on, and in some part of the order of things, for otherwise it would have no existence at all. . . . There may be peace without war, but there cannot be war without some kind of peace, because war presupposes the existence of some natures to wage it, and these natures cannot exist without peace of one kind or another."[34] Moreover, God rules and overrules men in their corrupt personal and social existence. "As he is the supremely good Creator of good natures so he is of evil wills the most just Ruler, so that while they make an ill use of good natures, he makes a good use even of evil wills." By the ill will of rulers he checks and chastises the perversity of their subjects, and by giving earthly kingdoms both to good and to bad, "according to the order of things and times . . . himself rules as Lord."[35]

To mankind with this perverted nature and corrupted culture Jesus Christ has come to heal and renew what sin has infected with the sickness unto death. By his life and his death he makes plain to man the greatness of God's love and the depth of human sin; by revelation and instruction he reattaches the soul to God, the source of its being and goodness, and restores to it the right order of love, causing it to love whatever it loves in God and not in the context of selfishness or of idolatrous devotion to the creature. "This is the mediation whereby a hand is

---

[34] *Ibid.*, XIX, 12, 13.
[35] *Ibid.*, XI, 17; I, 1, 8, 9; IV, 33.

stretched out to the lapsed and the fallen." Since man, moving in his vicious circle of godlessness, could not save himself from himself, "the truth itself, God, God's Son, assuming humanity without destroying his divinity, established and founded this faith, that there might be a way from man to man's God through a God-man. For this is the Mediator between God and men, the man Christ Jesus," who as God is our end and as man is our way.[36] By humbling human pride and detaching man from himself on the one hand, by revealing God's love and attaching man to his one good, Christ restores what has been corrupted and redirects what has been perverted. He transforms the emotions of men, not by substituting reason for emotion, but by attaching fear, desire, grief, and joy to their right object. "The citizens of the holy city of God, who live according to God in the pilgrimage of this life, both fear and desire, and grieve and rejoice. And because their love is rightly placed, all these affections of theirs are right."[37] The moral virtues men develop in their perverse cultures are not supplanted by new graces, but are converted by love. "Temperance is love keeping itself entire and incorrupt for God; fortitude is love bearing everything readily for the sake of God; justice is love, serving God only, and therefore ruling well all else, as subject to man; prudence is love making a right distinction between what helps it towards God and what might hinder it."[38] The life of reason above all, that wisdom of man which the wisdom of God reveals to be full of folly, is reoriented and redirected by being given a new first principle. Instead of beginning with faith in itself and with love of its own order, the reasoning of redeemed man begins with faith in God and love of the order which He has put into all His creation; therefore

[36] *Ibid.*, X, 24; XI, 2; cf. VII, 31; IX, 15.
[37] *Ibid.*, XIV, 9.
[38] *On the Morals of the Catholic Church*, XV.

it is free to trace out His designs and humbly to follow His ways.[39] There is room within the Augustinian theory for the thought that mathematics, logic, and natural science, the fine arts and technology, may all become both the beneficiaries of the conversion of man's love and the instruments of that new love of God that rejoices in His whole creation and serves all His creatures. The Christian life can and must make use not only of these cultural activities but of "the convenient and necessary arrangements of men with men"—conventions regarding dress and rank, weights and measures, coinage, and the like.[40] Everything, and not least the political life, is subject to the great conversion that ensues when God makes a new beginning for man by causing man to begin with God. Were one to pursue Augustine's conversionist ideas only, one might represent him as a Christian who set before men the vision of universal concord and peace in a culture in which all human actions had been reordered by the gracious action of God in drawing all men to Himself, and in which all men were active in works directed toward and thus reflecting the love and glory of God.[41]

Augustine, however, did not develop his thought in this direction. He did not actually look forward with hope to the realization of the great eschatological possibility, demonstrated and promised in the incarnate Christ—the redemption of the created and corrupted human world and the transformation of mankind in all its cultural activity. The possibility of the re-direction of all man's work among temporal things into an activity glorifying God by rejoicing in and cultivating the

[39] For the Augustinian interpretation of philosophy and science cf. Cochrane, *op. cit.*, chap. XI, where the subject is dealt with extensively.

[40] Cf. *On Christian Doctrine*, II, 25, 26.

[41] The statement about peace of body and soul, of men with men and God, at the beginning of chap. 13, Bk. XIX, of the *City of God* is sometimes presented as if it were an Augustinian prophecy, which it is not.

beauty in His creation, by rendering mutual service in the spirit of self-forgetful love, by scorning death and the fear of it in the conviction of divine power over death, by tracing out in disinterested reasoning the order and design of the creation and by using all temporal goods with sacramental reverence as incarnations and symbols of eternal words—this possibility rises to view in Augustinian thought only to be dismissed. What is offered instead is the eschatological vision of a spiritual society, consisting of some elect human individuals together with angels, living in eternal parallelism with the company of the damned. The elect are not the remnant from which a new humanity arises; they are a saved but not a saving remnant. Why the theologian whose fundamental convictions laid the groundwork for a thoroughly conversionist view of humanity's nature and culture did not draw the consequences of these convictions is a difficult question. It may be argued that he sought to be faithful to the Scriptures with its parables of the last judgment and the separatist ideas in it. But there is also a universal note in the Scriptures; and faithfulness to the book does not explain why one who otherwise was always more interested in the spiritual sense than in the letter, not only followed the letter in this instance but exaggerated the literal sense. The clue to the problem seems to lie in Augustine's defensiveness. From his confession of his sin and of divine grace he turns to the defense of the justice of a God who having chosen Christians through the revelation of His goodness does not appear to have chosen the non-Christians. From the confession of sin and grace as a member of the Catholic church, he turns to the justification of the church in the face of charges brought against it by pagans. From the hope of the conversion of culture he turns to the defense of Christian culture, that is, of the institutions and habits of the Christian society. He defends also the endangered though unregenerate morality of man by threats of hell and promises of heaven. In consequence of (or as cause of) this turn to self-justification, his Christology remains weak and undeveloped when compared with Paul's or Luther's. He often tends to substitute the Christian religion—a cultural achievement—for Christ; and frequently deals with the Lord more as the founder of an authoritative cultural institution, the church, than as savior of the world through the direct exercise of his kingship. Hence also, faith in Augustine tends to be reduced to obedient assent to the church's teachings, which is doubtless very important in Christian culture but nevertheless is no substitute for immediate confidence in God. In his predestinarian form of the doctrine of election, Augustine, again with a large trace of defensiveness, changes his fundamental insight that God chooses man to love Him before man can love God, into the proposition that God chooses some men and rejects others. So the glorious vision of the City of God turns into a vision of two cities, composed of different individuals, forever separate. Here is a dualism more radical than that of Paul and Luther.

Calvin is very much like Augustine. The conversionist idea is prominent in his thought and practice. More than Luther he looks for the present permeation of all life by the gospel. His more dynamic conception of the vocations of men as activities in which they may express their faith and love and may glorify God in their calling, his closer association of church and state, and his insistence that the state is God's minister not only in a negative fashion as restrainer of evil but positively in the promotion of welfare, his more humanistic views of the splendor of human nature still evident in the ruins of the fall, his concern for the doctrine of the resurrection of the flesh, above all his emphasis on the actuality of God's sovereignty—all these lead to the thought that what the gospel promises and makes possible, as divine (not human) possibility, is the transformation of mankind in all its nature and culture into a kingdom of God in which the laws of the kingdom have been written upon the inward parts. But in this case also the eschatological hope of Christ's transformation of mankind's ruined life is turned into the eschatology of physical death, and the redemption of some men to a life in glory separated not only by its spirit but also by its physical conditions from life in the world. The eschatological hope of a new heaven and a new earth brought into being by the coming of Christ is modified by the belief that Christ cannot come to this heaven and earth but must await the death of the old and rising of a new creation. To the eternal over-againstness of God and man, Calvin adds the dualism of temporal and eternal existence, and the other dualism of an eternal heaven and an eternal hell. Though Calvinism has been marked by the influence of the eschatological hope of transformation by Christ and by its consequent pressing toward the realization of the promise, this element in it has always been accompanied by a separatist and repressive note, even more markedly than in Lutheranism.

IV. The Views of F. D. Maurice

How important the idea of Christ's transformation of culture can be, in distinction from the other main motifs of Christian ethics, the tenacity and vitality of the idea of perfection in church history helps to make clear. Wesley is the great Protestant exponent of this perfectionism. His thought upon the subject is often confused with that of exclusive Christians, but he differs from them profoundly, because he shares with Paul, John, Luther, Augustine, and Calvin the understanding that Christ is no new lawgiver who separates a new people from the old by giving them the constitution for a new kind of culture.

Christ is for Wesley the transformer of life; he justifies men by giving them faith; he deals with the sources of human action; he makes no distinctions between the moral and the immoral citizens of human commonwealths, in convicting all of self-love and in opening to all the life of freedom in response to God's forgiving love. But Wesley insists on the possibility—again as God's possibility, not man's—of a present fulfilment of that promise of freedom. By the power of Christ believers may be cleansed from all sin, may be like their Master, may be delivered "in this world." The New Testament does not say "the blood of Christ will cleanse at the hour of death, or in the day of judgment, but it 'cleanseth,' at the time present, 'us,' living Christians, 'from all sin.' "[42] For man this possibility meant an intensity of expectation and of striving toward a goal that could easily be perverted again into self-centered and self-empowered activity, into religious and moral self-culture in which holiness was sought as possession and God became instrument toward the attainment of self-respect. But what Wesley, amid all the inadequacies of his doctrine of sin,[43] and what his followers, amid all their relapses into pride, were concerned about was the Johannine idea of the present possibility of the transformation of temporal man into a child of God, living from and toward God's love in freedom from self.[44] In his individualism Wesley did not bring prominently to mind the promise of Christ to mankind rather than to separate men, but there are suggestions of that idea also and later followers of his have developed them, though often with a greater leaning toward cultural Christianity than was characteristic of the initiator of the Methodist movement.

Jonathan Edwards, with his sensitive and profound views of

---

[42] From the sermon "On Christian Perfection."
[43] Cf. Flew, R. Newton, *The Idea of Perfection*, 1934, pp. 332 ff.
[44] Cf. esp. Lindstroem. Harald. *Wesley and Sanctification*, 1946.

creation, sin, and justification, with his understanding of the
way of conversion and his millennial hopes, became in America
the founder of a movement of thought about Christ as the
regenerator of man in his culture. It has never wholly lost
momentum, though it was often perverted into banal, Pelagian
theurgisms in which men were concerned with the symptoms
of sin, not its roots, and thought it possible to channel the
grace and power of God into the canals they engineered. Thus
the conversionism of Edwards was used to justify the psychological mechanics of a shabby revivalism, with its mass produc-
tion of renovated souls, and the sociological science of that part
of the social gospel which expected to change prodigal mankind
by improving the quality of the husks served in the pigsty.

In the nineteenth century, in the generations represented by
Tolstoy, Ritschl, Kierkegaard and Leo XIII, the conversionist
idea had many exponents. Notable among them is F. D. Maurice, the English theologian whose work is so variously assessed
that judgments about its profundity and comprehensiveness are
always balanced by references to its mistiness, confusion, and
fragmentariness.[45] Yet Maurice's influence is pervasive and per-
meative. He is above all a Johannine thinker, who begins with
the fact that the Christ who comes into the world comes into
his own, and that it is Christ himself who exercises his kingship
over men, not a vicegerent—whether pope, Scriptures, Christian religion, church, or inner light—separate from the incarnate Word. Early in life the conviction had been forced upon
him that Christ is Lord of mankind whether men believe it or
not. So in a letter to his mother he wrote, "God tells us, 'in

---

[45] Cf. Vidler, Alec R., *The Theology of F. D. Maurice*, 1948, pp. 7 ff. This
book, published in America under the title *Witness to the Light*, is an excellent
introduction to Maurice's thought. Indispensable for the understanding of
Maurice is *The Life of Frederick Denison Maurice Chiefly Told in His Letters*,
edited by his son Frederick Maurice; 2 vols., 1884.

Him,' that is, in Christ, 'I have created all things whether they be in heaven or on earth. Christ is the head of every man.' Some men believe this; some men disbelieve it. Those men who disbelieve it 'walk after the flesh.' . . . They do not believe this, and therefore they do not act upon this belief. . . . But though tens of hundreds of thousands of men live after the flesh, yea, though every man in the world were so living, we are forbidden by Christian truth and the Catholic church to call this the real state of man. . . . The truth is that every man is in Christ . . . ; except he were joined to Christ he could not think, breathe, live a single hour."[46] Men, Maurice understood, were social by nature; they had no existence save as sons, brothers, members of community. This conviction united him with the socialists. But the community in which men were created was not merely human; it could not be truly human if it were not more—the community of men with Father, Son, and Holy Spirit. In Maurice's understanding of the "spiritual constitution" of mankind, all the intricate interrelations of love in the Godhead, of the Father's love of men and of Christ's, of the human and divine natures of the Son, of the Creating and Redeeming Word, of man's love of neighbor in God and of God in the neighbor, of family, nation, and church, have their place.[47] But the center is Christ. In him all things were created to live in union with God and each other; he reveals the true nature of life and the law of the created society as well as the sin and rebellion of its members; he redeems men in and for community with one another in God. "The essence and the meaning of the whole history" recorded in the Scriptures is contained in Christ's "amazing prayer, 'That they may all be one, as thou,

[46] *Life*, Vol. I, p. 155.
[47] Cf. especially *The Kingdom of Christ*, Vol. I, Part II, chaps. II and III; cf. Vidler, *op. cit.*, chap. II.

Father, art in me, and I in thee, that they may be one in us.' "[48]
Hence Maurice found himself in conflict not only with "unsocial Christians" but also with "unchristian socialists"; the
former based man's relation to Christ on external rites, substituted religion for Christ, and took no responsibility for
human social life; the latter were inclined to base society on
man's animal nature, and to make common self-interest the
ground for social action. Men are "not animals plus a soul,"
Maurice contends, "but they are spirits with an animal nature;
. . . the bond of their union is not a commercial one, not submission to a common tyrant, not brutal rage against him; but
. . . it does rest and has always rested on spiritual ground; . . .
the sin of the Church—the horrible apostasy of the Church—
has consisted in denying its own function, which is to proclaim
to men their spiritual condition, the eternal foundation on
which it rests, the manifestation which has been made of it by
the birth, death, resurrection and ascension of the Son of God,
and the gift of the Spirit."[49]

The deep disease of man, the self-contradiction in which he
is involved as individual and member of human societies, is his
denial of the law of his being. He seeks to possess within or by
himself, whether in the form of physical or spiritual goods, what
he can have only in the community of receiving and giving.
Maurice is so deeply aware of the sin of self-love and of the
tragedy of human divisiveness, the exploitation of man by
man, the self-glorification of nations and churches, that he needs
to say little in an explicit way about fall and corruption; it is
the undercurrent of all his thinking. "When I began to seek
God for myself," he wrote, "the feeling that I needed a deliverer
from an overwhelming weight of selfishness was the predomi-

[48] *The Kingdom of Christ*, Vol. I, p. 292.
[49] *Life*, Vol. II, p. 272.

nant one in my mind."[50] Both the weight and the ethereal pervasiveness of that selfishness continued to oppress him. He found selfishness in the commercial system, against which he protested as a leader of the Christian Socialist movement, and then discovered how it appeared among the protesters; it manifested itself in the individualism of religious people, who confessed that they belonged to a guilty race but hoped for a separate pardon; in a man's effort to justify himself by faith held as possession and by a righteousness of his own; in the cries of the parties and sects in the church, each pointing to themselves or their principles as the way to salvation. Man's sin is that he tries to be God to himself. "It is the effect of our sin to make us look upon ourselves as the centres of the universe; and then to look upon the perverse and miserable accidents of our condition as determining what we ourselves are."[51] In view of the pervasiveness and destructiveness of sin, the petition, "Deliver us from evil," could seem almost dishonest. "How hard when evil is above, beneath, within, when it faces you in the world, and scares you in the closet, when you hear it saying in your own heart, and saying in every one else, 'Our name is Legion,'. . . when all schemes of redress seem to make the evil under which the earth is groaning more malignant, when our own history, and the history of mankind, seems to be mocking at every effort for life, and to be bidding us rest contented in death; O, it is hard, most hard to think that such a prayer as this is not another of the cheats of self-delusion, in which we have worn out existence."[52] The prevalence of corruption and self-contradiction in human life was especially oppressive and disheartening because it appeared in the church, in Christian culture itself. So Maurice wrote, "I consider your sects—one

[50] *Ibid.*, p. 15; cf. Vidler, op. cit., pp. 42 ff.
[51] *The Lord's Prayer*, pp. 63 f.
[52] *Ibid.*, pp. 144 f. Cf. also *The Gospel of John*, pp. 91 f.

and all of them—as an outrage on the Christian principle, as a denial of it. . . . You do not really mean to unite us in Christ, as being members of his body; you mean us to unite in holding certain notions about Christ."[53] "Yes! Religion against God. This is the heresy of our age . . . and this is leading to the last, most terrific form of infidelity."[54]

What made Maurice the most consistent of conversionists, however, was the fact that he held fast to the principle that Christ was king, and that men were therefore required to take account of him only and not of their sin; for to concentrate on sin as though it were actually the ruling principle of existence was to be enmeshed in still further self-contradiction. Hence he took issue with the Evangelicals in Germany and England, for they "seem to make sin the ground of all theology, whereas it seems to me that the living and the holy God is the ground of it, and sin the departure from the state of union with him, into which he has brought us. I cannot believe that the devil is in any sense king of this universe. I believe Christ is its king in all senses, and that the devil is tempting us every day and every hour to deny Him, and think of himself as king. It is with me a question of life and death which of these doctrines is true; I would that I might live and die to maintain that which has been revealed to me."[55] For this reason Maurice rejected every dualistic tendency to turn from positive to negative action, from co-operation to attack on nonco-operation, from the practice of unity in Christ to conflict with dividers of the church, from forgiveness of sinners to their exclusion from the church. Every effort of this sort involves a recognition of the power of evil—as though it exists otherwise than as a spirit of self-seeking, self-willing, and self-glorification; as though it can be located some-

[53] *Life*, Vol. I, p. 259.
[54] *Ibid.*, p. 518.
[55] *Ibid.*, p. 450.

where outside ourselves. Hence it invokes Satan to cast out Satan, as when socialism in seeking to destroy the oppression of class by class appeals to class solidarity and class interest; or when Catholic movements in the church point to themselves and their principles as the ground of Christian concord. So Christianity is substituted for Christ, and the defense of Christian culture takes the place of obedience to its Lord. This is not compromising with evil, but accepting evil as our good; for between good and evil there can be no compromise, however much good and evil may be mixed in persons and actions. Maurice was well aware that he himself fell into negation at times, and into separation from his fellows in church and world; but he did not find his fall excusable. He knew that his own thought would be used defensively by some new party. But to all the inveterate tendency of men to turn their true insights into self-assertions and so to deny what they were affirming, there could be no other answer than renewed witnessing to Christ, the only center of life, the only power able to overcome self-will.[56]

The conversion of mankind from self-centeredness to Christ-centeredness was for Maurice the universal and present divine possibility. It was universal in the sense that it included all men; since all were members of the kingdom of Christ by their creation in the Word, by the actual spiritual constitution under which they lived. It was universal also in the sense that the church needed to direct all its interest toward the realization of the divine possibility of universal, willing acceptance of the actual rule. The inclusion in Christian witness to Christ of doctrines of double predestination—the election of men not only to life with God but also to separation from Him—and of

[56] For Maurice's views on socialism cf. *Life*, Vol. II, chaps. i-iii; on the High Church party, *ibid.*, Vol. I, pp. 160 ff., 205 f.

eternal punishment, were to Maurice aberrations of the sort that result from negative Christianity. "I ask no one to pronounce," he wrote, "for I dare not pronounce myself, what are the possibilities of resistance in a human will to the loving will of God. There are times when they seem to me—thinking of myself more than of others—almost infinite. But I know that there is something which must be infinite. I am obliged to believe in an abyss of love which is deeper than the abyss of death: I dare not lose faith in that love. I sink into death, eternal death if I do. I must feel that this love is compassing the universe. More about it I cannot know."[57] "I cannot believe that He will fail with any at last; if the work was in other hands it might be wasted; but His will must surely be done, however long it may be resisted."[58]

Universal salvation meant more than the turning of individual selves to their true center. By creation through the Word men are social; they are fathers and brothers and wives and husbands, members of nations, spiritual, voluntary participants in political, religious, and economic societies. The full realization of the kingdom of Christ did not, then, mean the substitution of a new universal society for all the separate organizations of men, but rather the participation of all these in the one universal kingdom of which Christ is the head. It meant transformation through humiliation and exaltation: through the humiliation which comes when members of the body willingly accept the fact that they are not the head, and through the exaltation which results from the knowledge that they have been given their own particular, necessary work in service to the head of the body and to all its other members. Maurice was keenly aware of the values in the varieties of national cultures, and was

[57] *Theological Essays,* 2d ed., p. 360.
[58] *Life,* Vol. II, p. 575.

no more interested in the eradication of nationality than of the self. The schools of philosophy, like the various groups and movements in the religious life, each had its particular value. Variety brought disorder in all these instances only because men mistook their partial contributions to truth for the whole truth; transformation occurred when humility and service supplanted self-assertion and self-glorification. In this sense Maurice dealt with all phases of culture; with social customs, political systems, languages, economic organizations. In his view of the kingdom of Christ, which is both actuality and possibility, the Protestant doctrines of vocation and Christian nationality Thomistic regard for philosophy and social morality, Catholic interest in unity and sectarian emphases on special truths—all were combined in a great positive affirmation that there is no phase of human culture over which Christ does not rule, and no human work which is not subject to his transforming power over self-will—as there is none, however holy, which is not subject to deformation.[59]

With universality Maurice mated the idea of eschatological immediacy. Eternity meant for him, as for John, the dimension of divine working, not the negation of time. As creation was the eternal, not the pretemporal, work of God, so redemption also meant what God-in-Christ does in that eternal working that ever stands over against man's temporal action. The eternal does not cancel man's past, present, and future; neither is it dependent on one of these: God was and is and is to come; He reigns and He will reign. The better order for which men hope is not dependent on the change of physical conditions which a new creation will bring. "Our Lord speaks of his kingdom or his Father's kingdom, not as if it were to set aside that constitu-

[59] Cf. especially *The Kingdom of Christ*, Pt. II, chaps, ii, iii, v; also Vidler, *op. cit.*, pp. 183 ff., and Raven, C. E., *Christian Socialism, 1848-1854*. p. 13 ff.

tion of the universe, of which men had seen the tokens in family and national institutions, of which they had dreamed when they thought of a higher and more general fellowship. . . . The lofty expressions of contempt for the littleness of mere earthly transactions and the vicissitudes of human government, which some divines affect, are not learnt in his school." Though he cherished and confirmed men's hope for the future, he did not encourage "anticipations incompatible with an entire recognition of the sacredness of our life here," or "Manichaean notions that the earth or the flesh is the devil's creature and property."[60] Yet Christ's kingdom is not of this world; it is not a rule over external conditions, but over the spirits of men. "When he cast out evil spirits, he bore witness that he was holding converse with the spirit of man; that with the pride, lust, hatred, the powers of spiritual wickedness in high places which have enslaved us, he was carrying on his great controversy. . . . Here in this inner region, in this root of man's being, he is still subduing his enemies, he is conducting his mysterious education."[61] The time of the conflict is now; the time of Christ's victory is now. We are not dealing with human progress in culture, but with the divine conversion of the spirit of man from which all culture rises. "The kingdom of God begins within, but it is to make itself manifest without . . . It is to penetrate the feelings, habits, thoughts, words, acts, of him who is the subject of it. At last it is to penetrate our whole social existence."[62] The kingdom of God is transformed culture, because it is first of all the conversion of the human spirit from faithlessness and self-service to the knowledge and service of God. This kingdom is real, for if God did not rule nothing would exist; and if He had not heard the prayer for the coming of the kingdom, the world

[60] *The Lord's Prayer,* pp. 41 f., 44.
[61] *Ibid.,* pp. 48 f.
[62] *Ibid.,* p. 49.

of mankind would long ago have become a den of robbers. Every moment and period is an eschatological present, for in every moment men are dealing with God.

In Maurice the conversionist idea is more clearly expressed than in any other modern Christian thinker and leader. His attitude toward culture is affirmative throughout, because he takes most seriously the conviction that nothing exists without the Word. It is thoroughly conversionist and never accommodating, because he is most sensitive to the perversion of human culture, as well in its religious as in its political and economic aspects. It is never dualistic; because he has cast off all ideas about the corruption of spirit through body, and about the separation of mankind into redeemed and condemned. Furthermore, he is consistent in rejecting negative action against sin; and always calls for positive, confessional, God-oriented practice in church and community. The question arises, of course, whether even his work would have been effective had he not been associated in the Christian Socialist movement, in education and religious work, with synthesists and dualists and radical Christians. This question he doubtless would have answered himself with the reflection that no Christian thought can encompass the thought of the Master, and that as the body is one but has many members so also the church.

※

CHAPTER 7

A "Concluding Unscientific Postscript"

I. CONCLUSION IN DECISION

Our examination of the typical answers Christians have given to their enduring problem is unconcluded and inconclusive. It could be indefinitely extended. The study could be brought more nearly up to date in a consideration of manifold essays on the theme which theologians, historians, poets, and philosophers have published in recent years for the enlightenment and sometimes to the confusion of their fellow citizens and fellow Christians.[1] Wider and deeper inquiry into the past would bring into view a host of Christian leaders, quite as significant

---

[1] Among such recent essays the following may be mentioned as illustrative of the interest in the problem and the scope of the discussion: Baillie, John, *What Is Christian Civilization?*; Barth, Karl, *Christengemeinde und Buergergemeinde*; *Church and State*; Berdyaev, Nicolas, *The Destiny of Man*; Brunner, Emil, *Justice and the Social Order*; *Christianity and Civilization*; Cochrane, Charles Norris, *Christianity and Classical Culture*; Dawson, Christopher, *Religion and Culture*; *Religion and the Rise of Western Culture*; Eliot, T. S., *The Idea of a Christian Society*; *Notes Towards a Definition of Culture*; Maritain, Jacques, *True Humanism*; Niebuhr, Reinhold, *The Nature and Destiny of Man*; *Faith and History*; Reckitt, M. B. (ed.), *Prospect for Christendom*; Tillich, Paul, *The Protestant Era*; Toynbee, Arnold, *Civilization on Trial*; *A Study of History*. Papal encyclicals since the time of Leo XIII and the ecumenical conferences of recent decades have been much concerned with various aspects of the problem; cf. Hughes, Philip, *The Popes' New Order*; Husslein, Joseph, *Social Wellsprings*; *The Churches Survey Their Task, The Report of the Conference at Oxford, July 1937, On Church, Community and State*; First Assembly of the World Council of Churches, *Findings and Decisions*; also the studies issued in preparation for these conferences: *The Oxford Series; Man's Disorder and God's Design.*

as those we have mentioned, who also wrestled with the problem and gave their answers both in words and in potent decisions. We might spread a wider net and seine out of the sea of history not only theological but also political, scientific, literary, and military examples of loyalty to Christ in conflict and adjustment to cultural duties. Constantine, Charlemagne, Thomas More, Oliver Cromwell and Gladstone, Pascal, Kepler, and Newton, Dante, Milton, Blake and Dostoievsky, Gustavus Adolphus, Robert E. Lee and "Chinese" Gordon—these and many more in all fields of cultural activity offer fascinating prospects for study to those who marvel at the interweaving strains/of faith in Christ and reasoning performance of duty in society, or are full of wonder at the tenacious hold Christ exercises on men in the midst of their temporal labors. The study could be interminably and fruitfully continued by multiplying types and subtypes, *motifs* and counter*motifs*, for the purpose of bringing conceptual patterns and historical realities into closer relations, or reducing the haze of uncertainty that surrounds every effort to analyze form in the manifold richness of historical life, of drawing sharper boundaries between the interfusing, interacting thoughts and deeds of separate men.

Yet it must be evident that neither extension nor refinement of study could bring us to the conclusive result that would enable us to say, "This is the Christian answer." Reader as well as writer is doubtless tempted to essay such a conclusion; for it will have become as evident to the one as to the other that the types are by no means wholly exclusive of each other, and that there are possibilities of reconciliation at many points among the various positions. It will perhaps have become clear also that in theology as in any other science the seeking of an inclusive theory is of great practical importance; and that a great work of construction in this sphere might enable one to see more unity in what is now divided, and to act in greater harmony with movements that seem to be at cross purposes. Yet one is stopped at one point or another from making the attempt to give a final answer, not only by the evident paucity of one's historical knowledge, as compared with other historical men, and the evident weakness of one's ability in conceptual construction, as compared with other thinkers, but by the conviction, the knowledge, that the giving of such an answer by any finite mind, to which any measure of limited and little faith has been granted, would be an act of usurpation of the Lordship of Christ which at the same time would involve doing violence to the liberty of Christian men and to the unconcluded history of the church in culture. If we should make such an attempt we should need to assume that our particular place in the church and history is so final that we can hear not only the word of God addressed to us but His whole word. We should need to assume that in exercising our freedom in reasoning interpretation of that word and in obedience to it we should not be exercising the freedom of a finite reason and will but acting as though our reason and will were universal. We should need to assume, if we tried to give *the* Christian answer, that we are representatives of the head of the church, not members of the body, that we represent its reason rather than being subject to it as hands or feet, ears or eyes, arthritic fingers or stiffened joints. Our incapacity to give *the* Christian answer is not merely a relative one; one man may indeed be more capable than another to state the answer of a majority of his fellow Christians, or to move toward a more enlightened and faithful answer. But whatever our capacities to state relatively inclusive and intelligible answers to the problem of Christ and culture, they all meet their limit in a moral imperative that commands, "Thus far shalt thou go and no further."

Yet in one sense we must go farther, and arrive at a con-clusion. This farther step cannot be taken on the plane of understanding, and this conclusion cannot be reached in the realm of theoretic insight and outlook. They are rather under-taken and attained in the movement from consideration to action, from insight to decision. Each believer reaches his own "final" conclusion, in resolutions that involve a leap from the chair in which he has read about ancient battles into the middle of a present conflict. No amount of speculative insight into the reasoning and believing of other men, and no continuation of consideration of the imperatives and values issuing from Christ and culture, can relieve the Christian individual or the respon-sible Christian community from the burden, the necessity, the guilt and glory, of arriving at such conclusions in present decisions and present obedience. The study of types of reflection and action represented by other men in other times offers no more of an escape from this burden of freedom than does any other study. After we have said that in our view of the situation we are Thomists or Lutherans, Tolstoyans or Augustinians, we still need to resolve a present issue in specific terms; and in that decision we shall determine, purely by the way, whether our reflections about ourselves were moderately correct. Doubtless in the nature of the case our decisions will show that we are always both more and less than members of a group.

If this is the conclusion of our study—that the problem of Christ and culture can and must come to an end only in a realm beyond all study in the free decisions of individual believers and responsible communities—it does not follow that it is not also our duty to attend to the ways in which other men have answered and answer the question, and to ask what reason-ing accompanied their free, relative, and individual choices. For to believe is to be united with both the one in whom we believe and with all those who believe in him. In faith, because we believe, we are made aware of our relativity and our relatedness; in faith our existential freedom is acknowledgedly as well as actually exercised in the context of our dependence. To decide in faith is to decide in awareness of this context. To understand that context as best he may is as much the duty of the believer as to do his duty *in* the context.

What is meant here may be made clearer by an examination of the character of the decisions we make in the freedom of faith. They are made, it appears, on the basis of relative insight and faith, but they are not relativistic. They are individual decisions, but not individualistic. They are made in freedom, but not in independence; they are made in the moment, but are not nonhistorical.

II. The Relativism of Faith

The conclusions at which we arrive individually in seeking to be Christians in our culture are relative in at least four ways. They depend on the partial, incomplete, fragmentary knowledge of the individual; they are relative to the measure of his faith and his unbelief; they are related to the historical position he occupies and to the duties of his station in society; they are concerned with the relative values of things. It is scarcely necessary to elaborate the first point. Though the evil that ignorant good men do is gleefully exposed in our times by men who think that science is a substitute for morals, it must also be continually exposed and repented of by those who know that morals are no substitute for science. The Christ who commended a good Samaritan for pouring oil and wine into wounds would scarcely likewise honor a man who, trained in contemporary methods of giving first aid, regarded the Biblical example as his absolute guide. In politics, economics, and every other sphere of culture, no less than in medicine, we do the best we can on the basis of what we know about the nature of things and the processes of nature; but that best is always relative to fragmentary social and more fragmentary personal knowledge. Not only our technical knowledge but also our philosophical understanding—the larger patterns by means of which we gain an orientation in our complex world—makes our decisions relative. Everyone has some kind of a philosophy, some general world view, which to men of other views will seem mythological. That philosophy or mythology affects our actions and makes them relative. They are not less relative when affected by the mythology of the twentieth century than when influenced by the mythology of the first. We do not dare to act on the basis of the latter, and deal with mental patients by exorcising demons; we shall endeavor to use our best understanding of the nature and relations of spirit and body, yet we shall know that what is relatively true for us also contains mythological elements.

Our solutions and decisions are relative, because they are related to the fragmentary and frail measure of our faith. We have not found and shall not find—until Christ comes again—a Christian in history whose faith so ruled his life that every thought was brought into subjection to it and every moment and place was for him in the kingdom of God. Each one has encountered the mountain he could not move, the demon he could not exorcise. And it is evidently so with us. Sometimes it is the recalcitrance of pagan culture as a whole that makes one say, "God's mercy and power cannot budge this thing." Sometimes it is the evil in the flesh which leads to the judgment that it is not possible for God to redeem man in the body and in the history which began with his creation. Sometimes the faith in His goodness and power stops short at the sight of evil-doers among men, animals, or other powers of nature. And wherever faith stops there decision in faith stops, as well as reasoning in faith; there decision and reasoning in unbelief begin. If I do not believe that the power that ultimately presides over human societies is merciful toward them but only toward individuals, then I will not only turn to the service of individuals but will direct my social actions by my underlying unbelief about the redeemability of society. If I have no confidence that the power that manifests itself in nature is God, I will accept nature's bounties without gratitude and its blows without repentance; though I be ever so God-conscious when I meet gracious or critical spirits in church or society. All our faith is fragmentary, though we do not all have the same fragments of faith. The littleness of second-century faith became apparent in its attitude toward the "world"; the littleness of medieval faith appeared in its relation to the heretics; the littleness of modern faith is manifest in our attitude to death. But faith is a far smaller and more fragmentary thing than its most evident failures indicate. When we reason and act in faith and so give our Christian answer, we act on the ground of partial, piecemeal faith, so that there is perhaps a little Christianity in our answer.

The historical and cultural relativity of our reasoning and our decisions is evident, not only when we consider the historical changes in knowledge but when we think of our duties in the historical process or in the social structure. A great and powerful church cannot responsibly do what a small and persecuted sect found to be required of it. Christians in an industrial culture cannot think and act as if they lived in feudal society. It is true that we are not farther away from Christ because we live 1950 years after Jesus' birth than were disciples who lived five hundred or a thousand years ago; we are doubtless much further removed from some of our alleged contemporaries who never have and never will come into our view.

But from this particular standpoint in social history we necessarily see Christ against a background and hear his words in a context somewhat different from the background and context of our predecessors' experience. Our historical situation with its views and duties is further complicated by the relativity of our situation in society as men and women, parents and children, governors and governed, teachers and learners, manual and intellectual workers, etc. We must make our decisions, carry on our reasoning, and gain our experience as particular men in particular times and with particular duties.

Finally, there is a relativity of values that we must take into account in all our choices. Everything with which we deal has many value relations; it has value for ourselves, for other men, for life, for reason, for the state, and so on. Though we start with the bold affirmation of faith that all men have sacred value, because all are related to God, and that they are therefore equal in value, yet we must also consider that all men are in relations to other finite beings, and that in these relations they do not have equal value. The one who offends "one of the little ones" is not equal in value for the "little one" with its benefactor. Priest, Levite, and Samaritan must be considered equal in value as objects of divine valuation; but they are not equal in value to the victim of the robbers, quite apart from anything he thinks about them. In Christ there is neither Jew nor Greek, bond nor free, male nor female; but in relation to other men a multitude of relative value considerations arise. Nothing, not even truth, has value in only one relation—not to speak of the notion of intrinsic worth. Though truth has eternal value, value for God, it also stands in value relations to human reason, to life, to society in its order, to the self. Our work in culture is concerned with all these relative values of men, ideas, natural objects and processes. In justice we deal with the relative values of criminals and honest men for their fellowmen; in economics we are concerned about the relative values of things and actions that are related to millions of beings in multiple relations to each other. In every work of culture we relative men, with our relative points of view and relative evaluations, deal with relative values; thus we make our decisions.

The recognition and acknowledgment of our relativity, however, does not mean that we are without an absolute. In the presence of their relativities men seem to have three possibilities: they can become nihilists and consistent skeptics who affirm that nothing can be relied upon; or they can flee to the authority of some relative position, affirming that a church, or a philosophy, or a value, like that of life for the self, is absolute; or they can accept their relativities with faith in the infinite Absolute to whom all their relative views, values and duties are subject. In the last case they can make their confessions and decisions both with confidence and with the humility which accepts completion and correction and even conflict from and with others who stand in the same relation to the Absolute. They will then in their fragmentary knowledge be able to state with conviction what they have seen and heard, the truth for them; but they will not contend that it is the whole truth and nothing but the truth, and they will not become dogmatists unwilling to seek out what other men have seen and heard of that same object they have fragmentarily known. Every man looking upon the same Jesus Christ in faith will make his statement of what Christ is to him; but he will not confound his relative statement with the absolute Christ. Maurice had a principle, gained from J. S. Mill, that commends itself to us. He affirmed that men were generally right in what they affirmed and wrong in what they denied. What we deny is generally something that lies outside our experience, and about which we can therefore say nothing. The materialist is to be heard as he affirms the importance of matter; but what is he doing when he denies the importance of spirit but saying that he knows nothing about it? It is doubtless true that culture is wicked; but when Tolstoy affirms that there is nothing good in it he assumes that he has transcended his relative standpoint and can judge with the judgment of God. Just because faith knows of an absolute standpoint it can therefore accept the relativity of the believer's situation and knowledge.

If we have no faith in the absolute faithfulness of God-in-Christ, it will doubtless be difficult for us to discern the relativity of our faith. Because that faith is weak, therefore we shall always endeavor to make our personal or our social faith into an absolute. But with the little faith we have in the faithfulness of God, we can make the decisions of little faith with some confidence, and with reliance on the forgiveness of the sin that is involved in our action. So also the performance of our relative duties in our particular times, places, and callings is far from being relativistic and self-assertive when it is carried out in obedience to the command of the Absolute. It does become relativistic and falsely absolute when I require that what is right for me be the whole right and nothing but the right; when I, in my relativity, demand that what I do in obedience be worthy of being regarded by myself, by other men and God, as right apart from all the complementary actions, the precedents and consequents in my own activity, the activity of my fellow men, and, above all, the activity of Christ. For faith in the Absolute, as known in and through Christ, makes evident that nothing I do or can do in my relative ignorance and knowledge, faithlessness and faith, time, place, and calling is right with the rightness of completed, finished action, right without the completion, correction, and forgiveness of an activity of grace working in all creation and in the redemption.

To deal as we must with the relative values of persons, things, and movements does not involve us in relativism, when we remember that all these realities which have many values in relation to each other also have a relation to God that must never be lost to view. It is true that if I consider only the value my neighbor has to God and ignore his value for other men, there will be no room for relative justice or for any kind of justice. But in that case I am not acting with piety but with impiety, for I am not exercising any faith in the actual God who has created neither me nor my neighbor as only-begotten sons but as brothers. If I consider my neighbor only in his value-relations to myself there is no room for justice either, but only for the reciprocity of eye for eye and helping hand for helping hand. But if I consider him in his value-relations to all his neighbors and also in his value-relation to God, then there is room not only for relative justice but for the formation and reformation of relative judgments by reference to the absolute relation. The relation to the Absolute will not come into consideration as an afterthought—as when a priest is sent to accompany a criminal on the way to the gallows—but as a forethought and a cothought that determines how everything is done that is done to him and for him. Provisions for fair trial, for the checking and balancing of partial, relative judgments, for the prohibition of certain kinds of punishment, for the physical, spiritual care of the offender, for his restoration to society—these may all reflect recognition of his value beyond all relative values. Relative justice becomes relativistic when some relative value is substituted for the truly absolute one; as when a man's worth for his state or his class or his biological race is accepted as his final value. There is a difference even in the treatment of beasts between the behavior of relativistic men and that of those who recognize a relation of the humblest creature to the Lord and Giver of life. In economics and in science, in art and technique, the decisions of faith in God differ from the decisions of faith in false absolutes, not because they ignore the relative values of things but because they are made in mindfulness of absolute value-relations.

Such a combination of relative insight and duty with faith in God does not involve compromise, for one cannot compromise among incommensurable interests and values; and an absolute standard cannot be compromised—it can only be broken. That we are forever forgetting the value to God of our neighbors and fellow creatures, that we are making our choices of relative values without reference to the absolute value-relation, that the choices we call Christian are made in unbelief—all this is too patently true. But we can not excuse ourselves by saying that we have made the best compromise possible. We shall try to recognize our faithlessness, and in faith rely on the grace that will change our minds while, at the cost of innocent suffering, it heals the wounds we have inflicted and cannot heal.

III. Social Existentialism

There is another term we can apply to the decisions we must make as Christians in the midst of cultural history. They are existential as well as relative decisions; that is to say, they are decisions that cannot be reached by speculative inquiry, but must be made in freedom by a responsible subject acting in the present moment on the basis of what is true for him. Kierkegaard, to whom belongs the honor of having underscored and ministered to this existential nature of the irreducible self more than any other modern thinker, can be something of a guide to us in our effort to understand how, in facing our enduring problem, we must and can arrive at our answer, rather than at *the* Christian answer. But he can easily become a fallacious guide if we accept his denials along with his affirmations.

In the *Concluding Unscientific Postscript* Kierkegaard has his alter ego, Johannes Climacus, present the problem of Christianity in this wise: "Without having understood Christianity . . . I have still understood enough to apprehend that it proposes to bestow an eternal happiness upon the individual man, thus presuming an infinite interest in his eternal happiness as *conditio sine qua non*; an interest by virtue of which an individual hates father and mother and thus doubtless also snaps his fingers at speculative systems and outlines of universal history."[2] With this as point of departure it is then argued that whatever may be true or untrue about the Scriptures or about eighteen centuries of Christian history, or whatever may be objectively true for the philosopher who has resolutely set aside self-interest for the sake of objectivity—all this is of no relevance to the individual who is passionately concerned with what is true for him. Such subjective truth—truth for me—is found only in faith and in decision. "The decision lies in the subject . . . The thing of being a Christian is not determined by the *what* of Christianity, but by the *how* of the Christian." This *how* is faith. A Christian is a Christian by faith; faith is something very different from all acceptance of doctrine and all inner experience. "*To believe* is specifically different from all other appropriation and inwardness. Faith is the objective uncertainty due to the repulsion of the absurd held fast by the passion of inwardness, which in this instance is intensified to the utmost degree. . . . Faith must not rest content with unintelligibility; for precisely the relation to or the repulsion from the unintelligible, the absurd, is the expression for the passion of faith."[3]

[2] *Op. cit.*, p. 19.
[3] *Ibid.*, p. 540.

Much of this seems to fit our situation as we confront our forced choices in the presence of Christ and our culture. We must decide; we must proceed from history and speculation to action; in deciding we must act on the basis of what is true for us, in individual responsibility; we must grasp what is true for us with the passion of faith; in our decision we need to go beyond what is intelligible and yet hold fast to it.

But there is also much in this doctrine of decision and faith that is not true for us. Our decisions are individual, that is true; they are not individualistic—as though we made them for ourselves and by ourselves as well as in ourselves. They are not individualistic in the Kierkegaardian sense, first of all, because what is at stake is not simply or primarily our own eternal happiness. We cannot read ourselves out of the picture, to be sure; but the Johannes Climacus who speaks for many a passionate believer—including if not the present writer then that self to whom he would commit himself—phrases his question in this wise: "Without having understood Christ, I have still understood enough to know that he proposes to bestow infinite happiness, eternal life, upon men and mankind and thus presumes, or creates in those to whom he comes, an infinite interest in the eternal happiness of their fellow-creatures as the *conditio sine qua non*; an interest by virtue of which they will hate whatever is merely private, their father and mother and their own life, and thus doubtless also snap their fingers at their subjective dialectics and their private histories." The existential problem, stated in despair or in faith, cannot be phrased simply in terms of the "I." *We* are involved, and every "I" confronts its destiny in *our* salvation or damnation. What will become of *us*? What is *our* whence and whither? What is the meaning—if meaning there is—in this whole march of mankind with which I am marching? Why have *we*, this human race, this unique historical reality, been thrown into existence? What is *our* guilt, *our* hope? What power confronts *us* in *our* birth and end? What must *we* do to be saved from villainy and vanity, emptiness and futility? How can *we* have a friendly God? We raise our existential questions individually, doubtless, and we do not forget our personal, individual selves. But the existentialist question is not individualistic; it arises in its most passionate form not in our solitariness but in our fellow-ship. It is the existential question of social men who have no selfhood apart from their relations to other human selves.

Kierkegaardian existentialism gives up the culture problem as irrelevant to faith, not because it is existentialist and prac-tical, but because it is individualistic and abstract; having ab-stracted the self from society as violently as any speculative philosopher ever abstracted the life of reason from his existence as a man. It abandons the social problem, not because it is in-sistent on the responsibility of the individual, but because it ignores the responsibility of the self to and for other selves. Its Joshuas can never say, "As for me and my house, we will serve the Lord," for they are homeless. Its "existing individuals" can-not even know the meaning of the capital "I" in Paul's pas-sionate statement, "I am speaking the truth in Christ, I am not lying; my conscience bears me witness in the Holy Spirit that I have great sorrow and unceasing anguish in my heart. For J could wish that I myself were accursed and cut off from Christ for the sake of my brethren, my kinsmen by race." These kins-men are not solitary individuals either; they are beings in a culture. "They are Israelites, and to them belong the sonship, the glory, the covenants, the giving of the law, the worship and the promises; to them belong the patriarchs, and of their race, according to the flesh, is Christ."[4]

[4] Romans 9:1-5.

Our individual Christian decisions are not individualistic, in the second place, because they cannot be made in solitariness on the basis of a truth that is "true for me." We do not confront an isolated Christ known to us apart from a company of witnesses who surround him, point to him, interpret this and that feature of his presence, explain to us the meaning of his words, direct our attention to his relations with the Father and the Spirit. Without direct confrontation there is no truth for me in all such testimony; but without companions, collaborators, teachers, corroborating witnesses, I am at the mercy of my imaginations. This is true of the most trivial instances of knowledge. Without companions and teachers we should not even know cats and dogs, their names and distinctive characters—though without meeting them in our experience we should not know them either. The more important our knowledge the more important is not only directness of meeting but also the companionship of fellow knowers. Though the voice of conscience is not the voice of society, it is not intelligible without the mediating aid of others who have heard it. It is not in lonely internal debate but in the living dialogue of the self with other selves that we can come to the point where we can make a decision and say, "Whatever may be the duty of other men, this is my duty," or, "Whatever others do, this is what I must do." Were it not for that first clause—"Whatever others think or do"—the second could not follow. So it is with the confrontations by Christ. If after the long dialogue with Mark, Matthew, John, and Paul, and Harnack, Schweitzer, Bultmann, and Dodd, I come to the conclusion that whatever Christ means to others and requires of others this is what he means to me and requires of me, I am in a wholly different position from the one in which I should be—if that were a possible position—were I confronted by him alone. The Christ who speaks to me without authorities and witnesses is not an actual Christ; he is no Jesus Christ of history. He may be nothing more than the projection of my wish or my compulsion; as, on the other hand, the Christ about whom I hear only through witnesses and never meet in my personal history is never Christ for me. We must make our individual decisions in our existential situation; but we do not make them individualistically in confrontation by a solitary Christ as solitary selves.

The existentialism that has emphasized the reality of decision and its free, individual character has also made us aware of the significance of the moment. The speculative, contemplative reason may live in past or future or in timelessness. It traces causal sequences and logical connections. As historical reason it journeys into the first, the fourth, or the thirteenth centuries, and looks at the world of Peter, of Augustine, of Thomas. It is an impersonal reason, which tries to forget the pressing individual concerns of the reasoner. But the thinker must return from his journeys, for he is a man. As a man he must make decisions; and the time of decision is neither past nor future, but the present. The speculative reason, which has asked about what has been done and why, or what will happen and why, must yield to the practical reasoner, who asks, "What ought I to do now?" In the moment of present decision the self becomes aware of itself; in awareness of selfhood we are aware of the present. The present moment is the time of decision; and the meaning of the present is that it is the time dimension of freedom and decision.

This insistence on the decisive character of the present moment, and on the discontinuity between it and the past or future or the timelessness with which we are concerned in reflection, is significant for us when we deal with the problem of Christ and culture. We arrive at the point where we must leave our studies of what Thomas and Luther thought and decided about the claims of reason and revelation, and take our own stand in the present in recognition and nonrecognition of their claims on us. And this decision must be repeated in every present moment. We can no more refer to a decision in our past as we deal with it, than pacifist or coercionist confronting a new war can rely on past decisions about the obedience to be rendered to the imperatives "Thou shalt not kill" and "Thou shalt love thy neighbor as thyself." Neither can we try to live in the future, referring to the time when the kingdom of God shall have come or we shall have been made perfect; for we must decide now, in the presence of the hidden kingdom and in our imperfection.

Yet, although this is true that the responsible self acting in the present moment must leave the past and future of speculation and reflection behind, it is not true that we decide in a nonhistorical present without connection with the past and future. Each present moment in which we decide is filled with memories and anticipations; and at each present moment there is present to us some other whom we have met before and expect to meet again. What makes the moment of crisis, the critical, decisive present, so pregnant with meaning is not the fact that the self is alone here with the responsibility of decision, but that there is someone compresent with it. And this one would not be important if he were not remembered and expected. A soldier at the zero hour of attack doubtless is highly aware of the critical present and of the freedom of obedience with which he meets the order to advance. Yet what is present to him is not his mere free self and the moment, but rather that self with its memories of past weakness and strength, and the enemy, remembered and anticipated, and his companions to whom he is bound in loyalty. Every "Now" is a historical

"Now," in which a historical self is compresent with a historical other and historical companions—that is to say, it is a present filled with memory and anticipation though these are focused in present decision.

For the Christian the critical present decision of loyalty and disloyalty to Christ in the midst of his cultural tasks is always such a historical decision. He confronts a compresent, a contemporaneous Christ; but this Christ has a history, he is remembered and he is expected. This Christian has a history of relations to Christ; he remembers his denials and mistaken interpretations of Christ's words. The Christian is a member of a company which has a history of relations to him and to Christ. To be contemporaneous with Christ is to be contemporaneous with one who was present to Augustine as well as to Paul, and is in the presence of the least of his brothers. Kierkegaard's abstract, individualistic existentialism is not only untrue to the social character of the self, but also to the historical nature of its present and the historical character of Christ. Says he: "What really occurred (the past) is not (except in a special sense, i.e., in contrast with poetry) the real. It lacks the determinant which is the determinant of truth (as inwardness) and of all religiousness, the *for thee*. The past is not reality—for me; only the contemporary is reality for me. What thou dost live contemporaneously with is reality—for thee. And thus every man can be contemporary only with the age in which he lives— and then with one thing more: with Christ's life on earth; for Christ's life on earth, sacred history, stands for itself alone outside history. . . . In relation to the absolute there is only one tense: the present. For him who is not contemporaneous with the absolute—for him it has no existence. And as Christ is the absolute, it is easy to see that with respect to Him there is only one situation: that of contemporaneousness. The five, the seven, the fifteen, the eighteen hundred years are neither here nor there; they do not change Him, neither do they in any wise reveal who He was, for who He is is revealed only to faith."[5] One is tempted to exclaim over this mixture of true affirmation and untrue denial, this confusion of the time of the self with the time of its body, and over the pitiful solitariness of a man without companions. We are contemporary with men who in their thoughts and actions represent the human race; we are contemporary with mankind in its history, to which the physically dead belong as truly as the biologically existent; we are contemporary with the sins of the fathers visited upon the children to the third and fourth generation, and with their loyal keeping of commandments for which we receive the reward; we are contemporary with the Church, the company of all Christ's contemporaries. And then we are contemporary with one thing more: with the absolute, the God of Abraham, Isaac, and Jacob, of the living rather than the dead, the one who in Christ binds all times together, God-in-Christ and Christ-in-God, whom we remember and expect even as we meet him in the least of our brothers and in the judgments which he executes through his unwilling servants. Our decisions must be made in the present moment—but in the presence of historical beings whose history has been made sacred by the historical, remembered actions of the one who inhabits eternity.

IV. FREEDOM IN DEPENDENCE

In our historical present we make our individual decisions with freedom and in faith; but we do not make them in independence and without reason.

We make them in freedom because we must choose. We are not free not to choose. Choice is involved in the resolution to

[5] *Training in Christianity*, pp. 67 f.

wait a while before we commit ourselves to a line of action; it is involved in the decision not to interfere in action but to be a spectator; it is present in our consent to accept an authority that will regulate all our lesser choices. Yet, though we choose in freedom, we are not independent; for we exercise our freedom in the midst of values and powers we have not chosen but to which we are bound. Before we choose to live we have been chosen into existence, and have been determined to love life as a value. We have not chosen human existence, but have been elected members of humanity. We did not choose to be rational rather than instinctive beings; we reason because we must. We have not chosen the time and place of our present, but have been selected to stand at this post at this hour of watch or of battle. We have not chosen to be social beings, immeasurably dependent on our fellows, nor have we chosen our culture; we have come to consciousness in a society and among established human works. Of these, life, humanity, reason, society, and culture are not only powers but also values, goods to which we have been attached by a necessary love. We are not able, it is true, to live with any of them in unfreedom. Even to live requires our consent; we continue to be human only by continued choices; we are not rational without espousing reason, social without commitment to our neighbors; we cannot be "all there" in the here and now without trying to be. But there has always been a choice prior to our own, and we live in dependence on it as we make our lesser choices among the things that are good for life, reason, and society.

We make our free decisions not only in such dependence on origins beyond our control, but also in dependence on consequences that are not in our power. The history of our culture illustrates in myriad ways this dependence of our freedom on consequences we do not choose. Columbus's decision to sail westward, Luther's decision to attack the traffic in indulgences, the resolve of the American Congress to declare the independence of the colonies—these were made without prevision or desire of their long-range consequences. It is doubtless so with the great social and the little personal choices of our present moment. What reactions and decisions on the part of others our actions will call forth, what interlacing of natural and moral processes will ensue on our choice to enter into loyal marriage, for instance, or to venture the defense of an invaded nation, we can neither know nor plan. We choose and are subject to many choices that are not our own.

Our ultimate question in this existential situation of dependent freedom is not whether we will choose in accordance with reason or by faith, but whether we will choose with reasoning faithlessness or reasoning faith. In faithlessness we shall make our choices as men whose existence is finally dependent on undependable chance. By chance, we shall think, we have been "thrown into existence," and by chance we in our individuality have come into this particular here and now with this particular constitution. By chance we are men and not beasts; by chance we are rational. When we reason about our decisions in this context, the element of chance begins to invade the very content of our choices; and a kind of arbitrary freedom of the moment asserts itself in our atheistic existentialism. Whether to throw away the life that has been thrown our way, whether to marry or not to marry, whether to be nonresistant or to fight— these are questions the free, atheistic existentialist self decides in the void merely by means of decision—that is, arbitrarily.

There is another possibility—that we shall choose and reason in faith. Though we speak of it as if it were possibility we choose, it seems clear when we attend to it that even more than life and reason it is a power and a value for which we have been chosen. It is a good we must consent to and receive and hold fast; it is not something that we originate and choose in independent freedom. What is this faith for which we have been chosen, and in which we are required to make our lesser choices?

When Kierkegaard dealt with faith he emphasized that it was a passion of inwardness, that it was objectively uncertain, and that it was a relation to the absurd. Following our previous method, we may attempt both to accept and to reject him by saying that it is an inward passion directed toward another, that it is subjectively as assured as it is objectively uncertain, and that it is relation to a surd that makes possible reasoning in existence. The passion of inwardness that we find in faith is the intensity of loyalty with which we cling not to ourselves but to that other without which our lives have no meaning. Wherever there is loyalty there is this passion, with its reflective significance for the self. The nationalist and the rationalist, everyone who has a cause, betrays the presence of this passion of inwardness when the principle to which he is attached is assailed. Faith in this sense is prior to all reasoning, for without a cause —let it be truth, or life, or reason itself—we do not reason. When we say that we live by faith and decide in faith, we may mean—at a minimum—that we live by inner attachment to an object of loyalty. Yet faith is not simply loyalty; it is assurance, too. It is confidence in the object toward which the inner passion is directed. It is the trust that the cause will not fail us, will not let us down. Such trust, to be sure, is mated with a kind of objective uncertainty; but it is not the uncertainty that makes it faith. To argue so is to be like a moralist who defines duty as that conduct that runs counter to inclination. I may not be aware of duty as duty unless I encounter the resistance of inclination; and I may not be aware of the extent of my trust save as it is exercised in the presence of objective uncertainty. But awareness of the fact that I trust may be in-versely proportionate to the actuality of my confidence. I shall be more conscious of the fact that I am acting on faith when I entrust my fortune to an unknown man than when I entrust it to an established bank. I am not trusting less in the latter in-stance, for I am still counting on something that is not objective —namely, on the loyalty, the trustworthiness of subjects, of men who have bound themselves by promises.

Here, then, are two strands of faith, loyalty, and trust. These stand in responsive relations. I trust the loyal other and am loyal to the trustworthy other. But it has still another character-istic. To act in faith means also to act in loyalty to all who are loyal to the same cause to which I am loyal and to which the cause is loyal. If truth is the name of my cause, then I am bound in loyalty to truth and to all who are loyal to the truth and to all to whom truth is loyal, whom truth will not let down. I am faithful to the truth only by being faithful in my truth-speaking to all men bound to the truth; but my confidence in the power of truth is not separable, either, from trust in all my compan-ions who are bound to its cause. Faith is a dual bond of loyalty and trust that is woven around the members of such a com-munity. It does not issue from a subject simply; it is called forth as trust by acts of loyalty on the part of others; it is infused as loyalty to a cause by others who are loyal to that cause and to me.[6] Faith exists only in a community of selves in the presence of a transcendent cause.

Without loyalty and trust in causes and communities, existen-tial selves do not live or exercise freedom or think. Righteous and unrighteous, we live by faith. But our faiths are broken and bizarre; our causes are many and in conflict with each other.

[6] Josiah Royce's *Philosophy of Loyalty* and *The Problem of Christianity* con-tain rich and fertile reflections on loyalty and community.

In the name of loyalty to one cause we betray another; and in our distrust of all, we seek our little unsatisfactory satisfactions and become faithless to our companions.

Here the great surd enters. What is the absurd thing that comes into our moral history as existential selves, but the conviction, mediated by a life, a death, and a miracle beyond understanding, that the source and ground and government and end of all things—the power we (in our distrust and disloyalty) call fate and chance—is faithful, utterly trustworthy, utterly loyal to all that issues from it? That it is not merely loyal to loyalty but loyal to the disloyal, not merely trustworthy by the loyal but also by the disloyal? To metaphysical thinking the irrational thing is the incarnation of the infinite, the temporalizing of the absolute. But this is not the absurdity to our existential, subjective, decision-making thought. What is irrational here is the creation of faith in the faithfulness of God by the crucifixion, the betrayal of Jesus Christ, who was utterly loyal to Him. We note not only that the faith of Jesus Christ in the faithfulness of the Creator runs counter to all our rational calculations based on the assumptions that we are being cheated in life, that its promises are not redeemed, that we must count not only on broken treaties among men but also on having everything taken from us that has been given us and that we hold most dear, that we have only chance to count on, and that our chances are small. This is a greater surd: that the man who reasoned otherwise, who counted on the faithfulness of God in keeping all the promises given to life, and who was loyal to all to whom he trusted God to be loyal, should come to his shameful end, like all the rest of us; and that, in consequence of this, faith in the God of his faith should be called forth in us. It is not a question of believing certain men or writings which assert that God raised him from the dead on the third day. We do not trust the God of faith because we believe that certain writings are trustworthy. Yet it is our conviction that God is faithful, that He kept faith with Jesus Christ who was loyal to Him and to his brothers; that Christ is risen from the dead; that as the Power is faithful so Christ's faithfulness is powerful; that we can say "Our Father" to that which has elected us to live, to die, and to inherit life beyond life.

This faith has been introduced into our history, into our culture, our church, our human community, through this person and this event. Now that it has been called forth in us through him we see that it was always there, that without it we should never have lived at all, that faithfulness is the moral reason in all things. Yet without the historical incarnation of that faith in Jesus Christ we should be lost in faithlessness. As the given historical reality in our human history, he is the cornerstone on which we build and the rock of offense. He is simply there with his faith and with his creation of faith.

On the basis of that faith we reason; and much that was un-intelligible on the ground of faithlessness or faith in the little gods who are not trustworthy is now illumined. Far beyond the limits of religious groups which seek to make the faith explicit in creeds, it forms the basis for our reasoning in culture; for our efforts to define a rational justice; for our endeavors after rational political order; for our attempts to interpret the beautiful and true. It does not form the only basis; for our faith, our loyalty, our confidence is small, and we forever lapse into faithlessness—even in those regions where it has won some victory over our thoughts. In that faith we seek to make decisions in our existential present, knowing that the measure of faith is so meager that we are always combining denials with our affirmations of it. Yet in faith in the faithfulness of God we count on being corrected, forgiven, complemented, by the company of the faithful and by many others to whom He is faithful though they reject Him.

To make our decisions in faith is to make them in view of the fact that no single man or group or historical time is the church; but that there is a church of faith in which we do our partial, relative work and on which we count. It is to make them in view of the fact that Christ is risen from the dead, and is not only the head of the church but the redeemer of the world. It is to make them in view of the fact that the world of culture—man's achievement—exists within the world of grace—God's Kingdom.

INDEX

257